Ian McNamara

ON THE ROAD WITH MACCA

Ian McNamara

ON THE ROAD WITH MACCA

◎

AUSTRALIA ALL OVER

ABC
Books

Published by ABC Books for the
Australian Broadcasting Corporation
GPO Box 9994 Sydney NSW 2001

First published October 2003

National Library of Australia
Cataloguing-in-Publication data
  McNamara, Ian
  On the road with Macca.
  ISBN 0 7333 1328 0.
  1. Popular music – Australia. 2. Australia – Social conditions. 3. Australia – Social life and customs.
  I. Australian Broadcasting Corporation. II. Title: Australia all over (Radio program).
  994

Cover, book design, illustrations
and typesetting by Helen Semmler
Editorial co-ordination by Neil Conning
Interview transcribing by Dawn Webb
Cover photograph taken in the Great Victoria Desert,
 South Australia by Kevin Killey
Project management by Richard Smart Publishing
Prepress files by PageSet, Victoria
Printed and bound by Shannon Books, Victoria

5 4 3 2 1

◎ FOR THE PEOPLE ◎

And to the memory of

Lorna Margaret McNamara

and

Coral Denise Reeves

◎ *Acknowledgements* ◎

Australia All Over is a team effort. I would especially like to thank my producer Lee Kelly without whom I couldn't do what I do; outside broadcast technical producers Eddie Coleman and Peter Scott; my good friends John Bamford and Dave Croxton for giving their time because they believe in the programme; Nerida Reeves for her tireless assistance; and the larger family of the ABC who help put programmes such as ours to air.

On the Road With Macca, too, involves a team. And once more I'd like to thank and acknowledge the flair and skill of Helen Semmler who has designed the covers and the insides of all my books, as well as producing the great drawings. Thanks again, too, to Dawn Webb for transcribing and editing the interviews and 'G'day' calls, and also to Neil Conning for co-ordinating the important editorial links. The front cover photograph, taken in South Australia's Great Victoria Desert, is a beauty—Kevin Killey take a bow!

And speaking of photographs, we receive many hundreds of excellent ones and that makes the task of selecting just a handful almost impossible. So a big 'thank you' not only to those whose photographs appear here* (we can't name you all because sometimes we don't know who sent them in!) but also to the rest of you 'happy snappers'. Keep sending them in. Thanks, too, to Alistair Nairn of Geo Science Australia and Michael Sherman of Blowup Pty Ltd for the map.

*Ron and Gladys Bone, Stewart Edwards, Libby Wood and Duncan Harcourt, Ken and Gidgee, Rowlie Mellor, Monica and Dave Taylor, Robin Tiffen, Dorothy Watt and Rob and Dot Woodheap.

◉ Contents ◉

◉ *Introduction* ◉

'GEE, YOU GET ABOUT A BIT MACCA,' people say to me when I turn up somewhere. And I suppose I do, but not nearly as much as many Australians who are on the road or, as we say on Sundays, 'on the wallaby'. I remember one lady getting her fauna mixed up when she called and said, 'G'day Macca, we're here on the kangaroo!' 'On the wallaby' is short for 'on the wallaby track', an old Australian saying meaning 'on the move', and I suspect it originates from the migrating habits of wallabies.

There are lots of places I haven't been to, and I'm reminded of this during the programme when I get calls from the Abrolhos, Thursday Island, Christmas Island, Emu Bottom, Goodnight, Happy Valley and Bulga, places I've never been to but where we can *all* travel via the programme thanks to the good people who ring in, write or email. The list now routinely includes far-flung places such as China, the Canary Islands, the Ivory Coast, Moscow, Greece, New York, Switzerland and Saudi Arabia, as Australians overseas call in to join the larger family at home on a Sunday morning.

I've spent the last few months going through six years' programme material (since the release of the last *Australia All Over* book in 1997) laughing to myself, gasping in recognition, remembering great letters, listening to phone calls that I'd forgotten all about. There's enough material for six books and it's a shame I've had to leave so many good things out of this one. It's been a real memory jogger, too. I'd forgotten all the little things that made us laugh, and sometimes groan. Remember the preamble? Trust an Aussie to put it into perspective – see the great poem in the 'Gross National Happiness' chapter!

Six years is a long time between books, and that hiatus coincided with the onset of my Mum's dementia around 1996, and her death at the end of 2001. My sister and I looked after Mum for the last six or seven years. It was a bit of a nightmare and, as anyone associated with dementia and Alzheimer's will attest, a sometimes very lonely and destructive time.

Lorna Probert, as she was born, was a remarkable, elegant woman, a wonderful mother in every sense of the word. She was my guide and inspiration and the most important person in my life. When I look back on our relationship I see how kind and caring she was, and how she helped me achieve anything and everything I've subsequently done. She was also a great Australian, and through her I came to realise what a wonderful community of Australians gathers together on Sunday mornings. She would always come up with ideas, or poetry she'd found, and even edit listeners' letters. You can imagine how much I miss this help.

When I think of my Mum I think of the words of the song:

'My memories of you are all soft and kind.
And you were never too far from my mind'.

Lorna often came on the road with me. To Perth to see a concert I did with the Western Australian Symphony Orchestra; to Kyogle, where she had spent a few years teaching as a young woman and recalled with fondness the people and the town; and Old Andado Station in the Simpson Desert. She always brought along a few bars of her sultana cake that, together with a cuppa, could keep you going when all else seemed lost.

I often left a pile of mail with Mum when I called in on the way home from work. 'Do you want some tea, "Neen"?' she'd ask. She always called me 'Neen'. She had pet names for everyone. She'd return the mail suitably edited, and once said to me, 'Gee, they're wonderful people.' And 'they' are, and she was, and that's one of the reasons I want to continue the programme. I believe in what I'm doing: offering Australians a forum to celebrate and discuss, laugh, smile and cry sometimes. And I hope that, like Lorna, and millions of other Australians, I'm contributing in some way.

I think some of my favourite programmes have been 'on the road' because I like being outside in the park, under the stars, in the early morning. In this book I want to bring readers some of that flavour so that they can come with us to places they may never get to, and meet people they'll probably otherwise never meet.

Whenever we go on an outside broadcast (OB) we spend the Saturday setting up a 'studio' in a park, on a rotunda, or under a beautiful ghost gum—at Fitzroy Crossing, in the main street of Leonora, under Brisbane's Story Bridge (or the 'carport' as the locals dubbed it), in Footscray Park, and so on. When I listen to tapes of past OBs I'm transported—I'm sailing the Horn with the Cape Horners who gathered at Port Victoria. I can still hear the sou-wester whistling through the great Norfolk Island pine in the main street there. And I can see Max and Jean Fatchen rugged up against the cold among a wonderfully happy crowd. Yes, I enjoy the freedom of being outside, away from the studio and in the company of friends.

Finally, I couldn't do this programme without contributions from you the listeners. I hope that through this book you will share some of the wonder I feel whenever I listen to tapes of past OBs. Maybe you were there? If not, next time we're in your neck of the woods come along and say G'day.

Talk to you Sunday

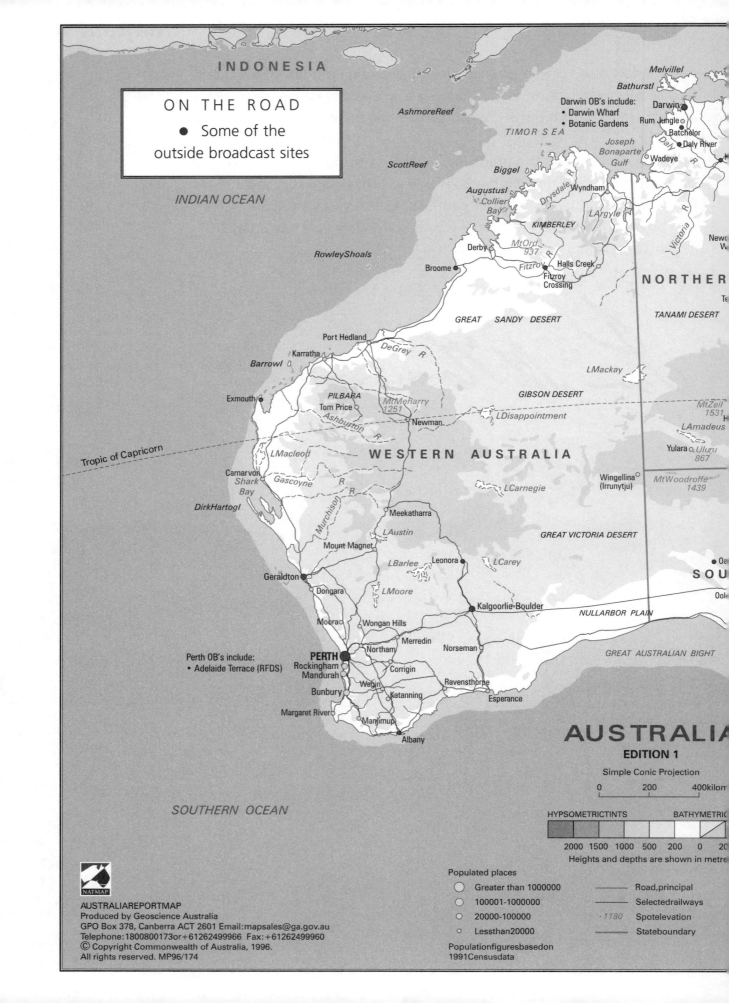

ON THE ROAD
● Some of the
outside broadcast sites

INDONESIA

AshmoreReef

TIMOR SEA

Darwin OB's include:
• Darwin Wharf
• Botanic Gardens

Melvillel

Bathurstl

Darwin

Rum Jungle

Batchelor

Daly River

Wadeye

INDIAN OCEAN

ScottReef

Biggel

Joseph
Bonaparte
Gulf

Daly R

RowleyShoals

Augustusl
Collier
Bay

Drysdale R

LArgyle

Victoria R

Newo
W

KIMBERLEY

Derby

MtOrd
937

Wyndham

NORTHER

Broome

Fitzroy

Halls Creek

Fitzroy
Crossing

GREAT SANDY DESERT

TANAMI DESERT

Te

Port Hedland

DeGrey R

LMackay

Karratha

BarrowI

GIBSON DESERT

MtZeil
1531

Exmouth

PILBARA
Tom Price

MtMeharry
1251

Ashburton R

Newman

LDisappointment

H

LAmadeus

Tropic of Capricorn

WESTERN AUSTRALIA

Yulara   Uluru
867

LMacleod

Wingellina
(Irrunytju)

MtWoodroffe
1439

Carnarvon
Shark
Bay

Gascoyne R

DirkHartogI

Murchison R

LCarnegie

GREAT VICTORIA DESERT

Meekatharra

LAustin

Mount Magnet

LBarlee

Leonora

LCarey

Oa

SOU

Geraldton

LMoore

Kalgoorlie-Boulder

Oole

Dongara

NULLARBOR PLAIN

Moora

Wongan Hills

Merredin

Northam

Norseman

GREAT AUSTRALIAN BIGHT

Perth OB's include:
• Adelaide Terrace (RFDS)

PERTH
Rockingham
Mandurah

Corrigin

Wegin

Ravensthorpe

Bunbury

Katanning

Esperance

Margaret River

Manjimup

AUSTRALIA

EDITION 1

Albany

Simple Conic Projection

0   200   400kilom

SOUTHERN OCEAN

HYPSOMETRICTINTS   BATHYMETRIC

2000 1500 1000 500 200 0   20
Heights and depths are shown in metre

Populated places

○ Greater than 1000000   —— Road,principal

○ 100001-1000000   —— Selectedrailways

○ 20000-100000   ·1180 Spotelevation

○ Lessthan20000   —— Stateboundary

NATMAP
AUSTRALIAREPORTMAP
Produced by Geoscience Australia
GPO Box 378, Canberra ACT 2601 Email:mapsales@ga.gov.au
Telephone:1800800173or+61262499966 Fax:+61262499960

Populationfiguresbasedon
1991Censusdata

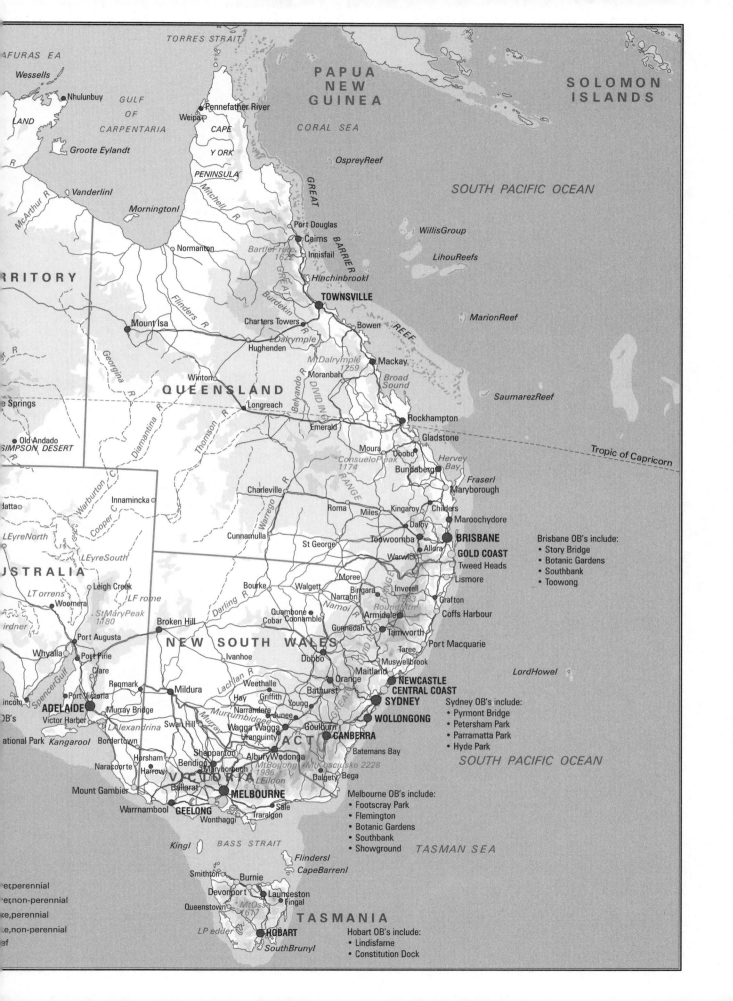

1

◎ On the Road... ◎

Take ten minutes to read this Ian, please. I spent a journey of four hours to post it, two hours on the wagon each way. The horse and I hope to meet you someday soon.

FROM: *Bill Murray*, 'on the road'

Macca talks to Australians all over at Petersham Park

G'day . . .
FLORENCE

MACCA: We're at Petersham Park and Florence has just come by. Florence, do you live locally?

FLORENCE: Yes, I've lived here all my life. My family bought an old terrace here in 1922 and I still live there. I remember this park as a child, because during the war we had air-raid trenches dug here but they didn't cover them up and when it rained we used to come down and swim up and down in them. Every Empire Day on May 24 we had a ritual. We had a ceremony at the school then we'd all go home to get a glass of milk then come down here to the park, slide down the slippery dip, hit our heads or our arms and go over to Lewisham Hospital, which was functioning then, and be treated in emergency by what we called the 'blue brides', the nursing order of nuns who wore lovely blue cloaks. We had two plane crashes here in Petersham, one in May in 1945, just towards the end of the war, when we were all in school and a Mosquito bomber came over and crashed, killing both the pilot and the navigator; and the other on the railway line opposite the school.

MACCA: I remember that the Mosquitoes were just about the fastest plane of all.

FLORENCE: It was wonderful when fifty years later we had a ceremony at the school and we managed to get all the students back, and also the wife and daughter of the English pilot, who flew from England. The sister of the Australian navigator came up from Bendigo.

MACCA: What else can you tell us about Petersham.

FLORENCE: The baseball club and bowling club celebrated their centenaries two years ago, and I believe Sir Don Bradman hit a century here on this oval.

MACCA: He hit a century on every oval!

FLORENCE: So it's a very historical and wonderful area in which to live. Fanny Durack, the swimmer who paved the way for females to swim in the Olympics, and Annette Kellerman, the famous and glamorous swimmer who invented the one-piece swimming costume, lived in the area. We have a cross section of cultures and there are many interesting people here. I used to go to the Petersham Congregational Church, which sadly had to be demolished. The David Jones's were married there and they came to its centenary in 1952, and the Anthony Horderns lived in the street.

G'day . . .
ALBERT

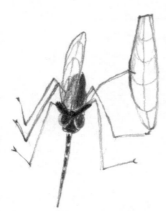

This is Albert from Padstow Heights. I was listening to the story about the Mosquito aircraft. I was the second draughtsman that De Havilland Aircraft put on during the war and eventually looked after the construction of the wing. The plane was made of spruce but the skin was of Australian-made plywood. Two of the planes crashed and it was thought that the engines were wrongly placed, causing a lot of vibration, but it turned out to be the glue holding the woodwork together. The glue was made of powder and water and whoever was mixing it would throw in some more powder and water which didn't mix with what was already in the bucket and the planes fell to pieces.

MACCA: Did you say two of them fell to pieces and that was enough for them to work it out?

ALBERT: There was a lot of worry at De Havilland about it as you can imagine but they worked it out.

MACCA: Thanks, Albert. It's great to have all the little bits filled in.

Macca talks to Australians all over at Hermannsburg, Northern Territory

FRANK: I'm a weed officer from the Alice Springs district, Macca, and I'm in the middle of the Finke River in the Northern Territory with two other blokes trying to get rid of a thing called athol pine, which is an introduced tree infesting our rivers and slowly destroying the system. It's a huge problem. We're camped on the banks of the Finke about seventy kilometres from the nearest station hut.

MACCA: I think Frank's on a satellite phone and it's a bit indistinct, but I can imagine where you are. We were out there a couple of years ago. This athol pine is just another weed isn't it?

FRANK: We're trying to destroy about 350 kilometres of it, working in complete isolation. It's a beautiful river system and I hate to see it destroyed.

MACCA: How are you trying to get rid of it?

FRANK: We're using several methods, herbicides and mechanical means, and the station people are giving us a hand. Without them we wouldn't be able to do anything at all, but it's going to take a long time. I just want to get the message across that this is the oldest river system in the world and it needs a bit of publicity so that we can get help to lick the problem. One of our huge drawbacks is that it's labour-intensive and it's hard to get people to do this sort of work.

MACCA: I'd love to give you a hand. When I go to a National Park and see how weeds are growing over everything I think that people going on holidays should be recruited. But that's probably just a pipe dream.

That call was in about 1992 and now Frank is on the line again. It's been a long time, Frank. Where are you now?

FRANK: I'm in Brisbane today, but I live south of Killarney. I'm growing flowers now.

MACCA: We're at Hermannsburg and just a stone's throw from the Finke River, which made me think of you.

FRANK: You're at the source of the athol pine problem, Ian.

MACCA: Most Australians wouldn't know an athol pine if they saw it, and that's the problem with weeds, isn't it? Are they still a problem on the Finke?

FRANK: Yes, Ian. I keep in contact with the people in Alice Springs and it's just a huge problem. I don't think enough resources will ever be put into it until they reach Lake Eyre and then people will take notice.

MACCA: Is the tree from India?

FRANK: It's from central Asia, one of the tamarisk species. It's supposed to be from the Chinese area but it's spread across the deserts of Saudi Arabia and thereabouts. It's a native tree there and doesn't cause any problems.

MACCA: I thought when you called from the Finke in 1992, here's a bloke out there trying to do his duty for all of us. It was mighty.

FRANK: I miss it. I loved my time on the river. It's debatable whether the Finke or the Nile is the oldest river in the world, so it's got a hell of a lot of heritage value.

◎

(G'day
FRANK

(G'day
FRANK

Attention! Weed Officer approaching.

G'day
TONY

TONY: It's Tony Frost from Sunshine Beach, near Noosa. In the mid-1960s, when I was working for an oil exploration company, the Finke River was up and we were stuck with nowhere to sleep except an old, roofless derelict house which turned out to be Albert Namatjira's old home. We froze for the night until we could cross the river next day.

MACCA: You're saying you slept in Albert Namatjira's house? How about that.

TONY: Yes, it was just an old stone cottage, very open and roofless, but it certainly gave us protection for the night.

MACCA: Were you there long?

TONY: Only for six months. We were searching for oil with seismic and gravity tests. There were no roads and we used to create lines of about forty miles with a dozer and then do the tests.

MACCA: That's probably where Bill Harney wrote that poem about how the blade of steel pushes back the spinifex. He probably bumped into your dozer driver in those days, back in the sixties. There's a bitumen road out here now.

G'day . . .
JOHN

MACCA: You're John Brockbank. Tell me your story, John.

JOHN: I'm a Kiwi and came here as a schoolteacher at Koolbatarra, one of the outstations about 100 kilometres from here. Koolbatarra has Lennie Namatjira, the granddaughter of Albert through Oscar. So I teach Namatjiras a few generations down the track.

MACCA: How long have you been there?

JOHN: I'm into my fourth year now. I'm the only person in the community who's not indigenous. We have between thirty to fifty people.

MACCA: Why did you choose to go and work there?

JOHN: Two reasons. My dad worked with the Aborigines at the Royal Darwin Hospital in the 1940s and he always talked about it as being one of the great experiences of his life. So when I saw an ad for a job here I thought, Oh, that's just what I want. I came for a year and nearly five years later I'm still here!

MACCA: What's the other reason?

JOHN: I like to go to places where it's really hard. I like a challenge. It's the best and the worst job I've ever had and it will probably be the highlight of my teaching career. The first six months was very hard, but the longer you're here the more it gets into your blood. You either like it very much or you don't, and I'm one of the ones who do. About a year ago I decided I'd stay here until I die or retire, so I'm hoping I retire.

G'day . . .
ANNE

MACCA: Anne, why do you work out here and why do you like it?

ANNE: It's a challenge. I worked on Palm Island with indigenous people who had been displaced because of the early days and it was lovely to come here to see the real landowners and to appreciate everything. It's just great to be in their country. We're visitors and it's a privilege to be here.

MACCA: The kids are great, aren't they?

ANNE: They're terrific and hopefully they'll develop their artwork, too, because they're in the land of Namatjira. There's great talent and great opportunity here.

MACCA: Where are you from, Larry?

LARRY: I live at Yuendumu on the other side, about 450 kilometres away.

MACCA: Why did you come back here?

LARRY: To see you!

MACCA: Larry's got his motorcycle boots and his duds on and a top beanie. What do you do at Yuendumu, Larry.

LARRY: I make sure everyone's got water and electricity and plumbing—a little bit of everything. I came over here on my motorbike for the weekend.

MACCA: Where are you from originally and how long have you been out there?

LARRY: A long time ago from the north shore of Sydney but I've been here about five years. I started a business here and I love every minute of it. It's a real honour to be with the Warlpiri people. They've taught me a lot about language, tradition, respect, how to go slow, how to be happy. They're amazing people.

MACCA: Why has it been easier for you out there?

LARRY: Just the time to look and to sit and listen to people who've been around for a long time and whose ancestors have been around for a longer time. They've got an abundance of knowledge that we don't have in the big cities.

MACCA: Well, you've certainly come the most original way today, across on a motorbike.

LARRY: It's a great run and I've got friends along the way even though it's desert. I met a bloke from Utopia on the road who was trying to get here to see you, but I had too much stuff on the bike to be able to pick him up. I don't know if he made it or not.

MACCA: We're all trying to live in Utopia, aren't we?

MACCA: Here's Roger Smitke from Taylorville on the Murray River. What are you doing here, Roger?

ROGER: Just visiting, like you! I was here forty years ago for a couple of weeks and went out on the cattle camp. In those days they ran cattle here. My cousin used to work up here and for as long as I can remember my grandfather used to pack honey, biscuits, prunes and apricots to send up to the Finke River Mission.

MACCA: What do you do, Roger?

ROGER: We're classed as private irrigators and we grow garlic.

MACCA: Garlic. I thought I could smell something! I read an article about Australian and imported garlic.

ROGER: Yes, they import somewhere around 6,500 tonnes of fresh garlic into Australia and we grow only about 300 tonnes here.

MACCA: How did you get into garlic growing?

ROGER: We used to grow lucerne as share farmers and the man we were share farming for heard about it and said we should try. We grew a couple of acres but we grew more weeds than garlic the first year and only got about fourteen cents a kilo. But in 1984 there was a world shortage and we made up to around $10,200 a tonne.

MACCA: That's amazing. Raelene, you're his wife, do you help on the farm?

G'day . . .

LARRY

G'day . . .

ROGER AND RAELENE

RAELENE: Yes, he's the brains and I'm the worker. You have to be very dedicated to grow garlic successfully.

MACCA: Is Australian garlic better than the imported stuff, Roger?

ROGER: Oh, undoubtedly, we grow the best garlic in the world. They grow tens of thousands of tons of it in America but ninety per cent of our crop is as good as the best America can produce.

MACCA: How much do you grow?

ROGER: The most we've grown is sixty-two tonnes.

MACCA: Farmers are always looking to diversify, so would it be practical for someone to say, 'I heard that bloke on Macca, and I'm going to grow garlic.'

ROGER: The cost of production is a real problem because it can be imported from China for about eighty cents a kilo landed here, and our production costs are about $3.10 a kilo, so we really can't compete. But in Australia not only can we grow garlic big, but we grow the best, because the allicin, which is really good for you, is very high here. We can get up to four per cent and the imported stuff that everybody eats is not even half a per cent.

G'day . . .
ALEC

MACCA: This is Alec O'Halloran. What are you doing here, Alec?

ALEC: I'm researching a book about a great artist, Mick Nameratu Tjapaltjarri, a Pintupi man who died a few years ago. He lived the main part of his life out west of here at Kintore, but in the 1930s as a small boy after his father was killed he came to the little school here at Hermannsburg, so I'm trying to track his life between then and 1971, when he started painting at Papunya with a senior group of men there. A lot of people say the central western art movement started, or was reborn, there. He was a very fascinating, gentle man and was one of the main painters of the Papunya Tula art movement. The Papunya Centre is in Alice Springs but the artists tend to be people out of Kintore and a lot of the outstations in the Western Desert. It's very isolated and although this is about my twelfth visit to the Red Centre I've never been out there. It's lovely country—the hills and the colours that people like Albert painted—so I'm looking to find people who know anything about what Mick Nameratu Tjapaltjarri did from the mid-1930s until about 1960.

MACCA: How did you get interested in Aboriginal art?

ALEC: In the mid-1990s I started looking at art and my attention was captured by the images and the relationship to the land. I'd never been to the outback. I think Aboriginal art has given me a new way of looking at the country and also the history. I've met lots of people and it's just a continuing journey of discovery. I invite all Australians to become more interested in Aboriginal art—it's a window into culture.

MACCA: I was at the Araluen Centre here looking at Albert Namatjira's work, which has been collected mostly from private collections but also from the National Gallery. It's touring around Australia to most of the capitals and you should go to see it wherever you are. It's wonderful, a great Australian heritage. Was your man a landscaper, too?

ALEC: He painted more dreaming stories, not the land physically. In a kangaroo story, say, he would paint aspects of the ceremony from a particular site. It might be reminiscent of body paint or of some part of the knowledge that goes with that site. It's a kind of interpretation.

MACCA: It's interesting that when Albert was painting the art critics didn't pay much attention. But who cares? The people who do things in life are the people who don't care what others say. They do it because it's in their spirit and sooner or later people will say, 'that work, that song, that cake, is a work of art and they're doing it wonderfully'.

Macca talks to Australians all over at Weethalle, New South Wales

G'day . . .

DAVID

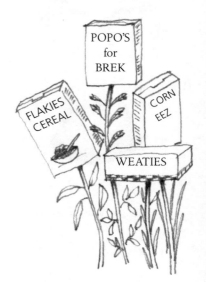

DAVID: David Lumsden's my name and I'm from a little place called Burilyang, about twenty kilometres from Weethalle. We farm there and we're copping the drought like everybody else. It's pretty well grinding us down at the moment so it's great when we've got something like the Weethalle Show and you here this morning to give people a bit of a kick along.

MACCA: It's nice to be here, I really enjoyed the Show. What do you farm at Burilyang?

DAVID: Most years we grow cereals and canola but this year's been pretty tough. At this stage it looks as though there'll be bugger-all harvest if there's not more rain. That doesn't just affect us as farmers, but also towns like this one and the wider community.

MACCA: Have you lived at Burilyang all your life?

DAVID: No, I grew up in north-east Victoria where the mountains are tall, the grass is green and the water runs all the time. Well, why the hell did you come here? Good question! I've worked all over Australia and then we came back here. It's not a bad place to be, either.

MACCA: No, it's great.

I APPRECIATED YOUR BROADCAST yesterday from Weethalle. It brought back many happy memories to me as I was a schoolteacher at a small school, Anona, in 1941 at the age of nineteen. (I was eleven miles from Weethalle.)

In those days there were small schools all over the countryside (1,800 in New South Wales alone) and six were scattered around Weethalle. The departmental requirement was that there should be an average daily attendance of at least nine pupils, and if this was not met then the school building was moved on to another location.

Jim Thompson was teacher-in-charge at Kikora Public School. When I arrived in the district everybody wanted to talk about Jim. He was not only an outstanding teacher and personality; he also captained the Kikora Rugby League team, could run one hundred yards in 10.2 seconds and was a top tennis player. The locals loved him and when they had a 'Back to School' celebration ten years ago, Jim was the special guest.

When Jim turned ninety-one I sent him a telegram. I simply said: 'They don't make them like you any more, Jim.' (And they don't.)

From:
Colin Dean,
Merrylands,
New South Wales

Macca talks to Australians all over at Port Victoria, South Australia

G'day . . .
BOB

Emergency wind power

From:
Marian Wilkins,
Torrens Park,
South Australia

MACCA: Bob Russell is here and he's a Cape Horner. Tell people what that is, Bob.

BOB: The Cape Horners as a breed finished in 1949. The requirement was that you sailed around Cape Horn on a merchant sailing ship with cargo, a ship with no engines or wireless contact with the rest of the world and was totally reliant on the wind.

MACCA: It must be a mighty thing to do, to sail around Cape Horn. It's obviously a dangerous place.

BOB: Oh, very dangerous. The thing that intrigued me about the whole operation was that we set sail from here on June 1, 1949, heading south, and thirty-seven days later at just about sixty south when I was on the wheel the old captain came along and said, 'In the morning we shall pass the Diego Ramirez.' Being quite facetious, I said, 'Oh, yes sir, about 9.30?' and he said, 'If the wind holds, yes, about then.' The next morning at almost exactly at 9.30 we saw the Diego Ramirez, a group of rocks south of the Horn. Without any means of checking our position other than the sextant and a watery sky—we hadn't seen the sun for a fortnight—we'd navigated to within twenty-five miles of a group of rocks that many ships had foundered on. The navigation skills of those people was incredible. The captain claimed he'd been around the Horn thirty-eight times, but I don't know about that!

It was a marvellous experience being in a sailing ship. It was primitive—the ship was built in 1911 and I don't think anything had been changed. The toilet for the crew was up for'ard under the fo'c'sle head and it just consisted of a pipe that went down. There should have been a clapper on it to stop everything coming back up but that had disappeared a long time ago. Every time the ship dipped its bow, we did a short arm up but still collected the lot!

JUST A NOTE TO congratulate you all on the brilliant show at Port Victoria. Talk about Murphy's Law, talk about Aussie resilience, talk about making the best of a bad thing, talk about 'never say die'!

The morning could only be appreciated if you were really there. Impossible to imagine, for example, the sight of hundreds of people, chairs, tables not to mention an entire mobile studio being completely relocated across the road, and all while most of the rest of Australia was lying lazily in bed listening to the seven o'clock news.

Impossible to imagine the wind, the cold, the confusion, the decision-making, the laughs, the cow, the jingling draught horses, the roaring sea, the grey sky, the forlorn 'One and All' in the bay, and all the rest of it if you weren't really there.

So thank you all for one of the most entertaining mornings we've had. We'll talk about it for years!

Macca talks to Australians all over from China

ROSS: It's Ross from Berwick in Melbourne, but now I'm in Guangzhou in Southern China.

MACCA: What are you doing there?

ROSS: Four of us are over here commissioning a tin smelter for the Chinese, using some of our Australian-developed technology and having a great time in a very remote part of China. In Chinese terms it's only a small town of 200,000 people and a pretty amazing place about 100 kilometres north of the Vietnamese border. There are huge mountains on either side and a lake in the middle of town with a beautiful promenade around it. It's just such a place of contrasts. We have some back streets that are old and shabby, so there's obviously a fair bit of poverty and there are some pretty ordinary places around, but there are some beautiful parts around the lake and the countryside is majestic. As I look out the window most afternoons from our office there are kites flying way up in the air, at least a thousand feet, and the old men down at the lake flying them. The kites have tails about ten feet long and when you get ten or fifteen up in the air it's really impressive and uplifting to see.

MACCA: Ross, there's obviously some sort of quarry there for mining tin. Tell us how the whole thing works in the smelter. Do we have tin smelters here in Australia?

ROSS: Not any more. We used to once upon a time and I think we still mine some tin in places. They seem to have quite a number of small mines around the area here and they supply concentrate to a smelter here. They had very old technology and we've built and installed our Australian technology, which is going to improve things a lot for their operation.

MACCA: Is that clean technology? I suppose smelters can be fairly polluting.

ROSS: Indeed, mate, that's the whole purpose of our technology. It's a totally enclosed system with almost negligible emissions and a whole lot cleaner than the old system they were using which belted fumes all over the place.

MACCA: People tell me that pollution's a big problem in China, certainly in the big cities.

ROSS: Yes, I think it's a problem for them. From time to time some of the other industries around here seem to get a bit smoggy. Now that we've started up our plant things are a whole lot better from that point of view.

MACCA: So, Ross, you're a tin smelting engineer?

ROSS: I was a metallurgist once upon a time and probably still am. Actually, I'm doing real metallurgy now so I'm sort of back to my roots. I started working on this technology at CSIRO twenty-odd years ago then went off and did other things.

MACCA: How long will you stay there?

ROSS: We've been here nearly four weeks now and we have another three or four weeks to go, depending on how things turn out. It's been a fantastic time here, a really amazing experience, and I'm really pleased I've had the opportunity. There are so many contrasts, the beautiful streets and the boulevardes and shops in the main part of the town, but then the back alleys have the markets, and the aromas from some of the stalls are just amazing. Equally, not much further along you can find some less than attractive odours, let me tell you! It's just a place of contrasts

G'day
ROSS

and the people have been incredibly welcoming and friendly. They see very few westerners, but nothing is a problem. The kids are the funniest. They're as cheeky as anything; they come up behind you and yell 'hello' and run away. But they're just having fun and perhaps they just want to test their English. Kids are the same the world over.

 G'day
JIM

JIM: Jim here, calling from Guangzhou in China—I think it used to be called Canton. I'm cracking whips in a circus here.

MACCA: Cracking whips? How did that happen, Jim?

JIM: We've got a farm at Finley in New South Wales and it was really droughty and dry, so when a fella rang up one day and said, 'Would you like to go to China and crack whips in a circus?' I said, 'Yeah, righto'. So, I packed the family up and that's where we are.

MACCA: I'm amazed! Had you been a bit of a showman in your time?

JIM: I used to do a fair bit of whip cracking years ago but I hadn't done any for a long time. My wife Anne and I ride a horse around, I do some whip cracking, and my four kids come out and do a bit in the show.

MACCA: I'm boggled! How do the Chinese take to your act?

JIM: Oh, it goes all right. But anyone who doesn't appreciate Australia ought to come over here for a while. They'd get a new perspective on things.

2

The Land is Parched and the Forecast Crook

You know the rain in Spain falls mainly on the plain.
Well, the rain in Innisfail falls again and again and again.

FROM: *Col White*, Sunshine Coast, Queensland

From:
Max Fatchen,
Smithfield,
South Australia

Round up what?

From:
Edwin Quilliam,
Smithton,
Tasmania

BECOMING UNSETTLED

The wind will blow with a furnace blast and the dust will rise in a cloud of brown
And the farmer lifts his eyes to the skies and wishes that Hughie would send it down.
The roof is as hot as a branding iron and the creaking trees in the gusts will shake
An old dog pants by the waterbag so say a prayer that the drought will break.

The land is parched and the forecast crook and the windmill rackets above its bore
And a grizzled old cocky rubs his chin and he says he's seen it all before.
The bank account is in the red and it's only money that's down the drain
The TV presenters have fancy charts but not a sign of bloody rain,

The cocky said, 'Now in the west they saw a cloud with some delight
And while we waited, filled with hope, they lost it in the flaming Bight
El Niño is the cause, they say. They must have something they can blame.'
The grizzled cocky rubbed his chin and muttered a much stronger name.

He looked across the heat-hazed plains and said, 'We need a helping hand.
You want some mates in the dried-out states when you have to tackle this hard old land.'
He whistled his dog from its dreaming paws and said, 'Get going you lazy pup.
There's a rain somewhere in the steaming air so get out of there and round it up.'

I'VE BEEN FEELING COMPELLED to write for weeks. If only we could pack up some of our cold and rain and send it to the mainland. I know we don't often hear those poor farmer souls complaining, but I'm sure every other Aussie would forgive them if they did. I'm a farmer on the rich, green far north-west corner of Tassie. I'm quite ashamed to admit it but over the past couple of months I've been guilty of complaining about the cold, wet weather that just won't go away. Our climate is such that by late spring/early summer we have such a surplus of grass that we have to conserve much of it. The mild temperatures (high teens/early twenties) and spring showers combine to quite literally give us an explosion of growth. But this year for completely opposite reasons to mainland farmers it has not happened for us, and I admit my frustration. But every time I do, I say a quiet 'sorry' to those who suffer the effects of the dry and heat. If I had it in my power to send them what I am sick of, I would gladly do it.

The mainland drought is having an effect on us too. Before too long about 20,000 cattle will have been brought into our state for slaughter or to fatten. Because the farmers are desperate to sell and the stock are poor, prices are discounted heavily, therefore pushing our prices down too. Many are searching for agistment in Tassie so that they can take them back home when the rain finally arrives.

In our district capital of Smithton last Thursday night there was a gathering to pray for the drought situation and those who are suffering as a result. So they are not forgotten, even by those of us who feel so insulated from the ravages that they endure, where a drought here is a fortnight without rain and where brown landscape is only the result of cultivation to plant the rich, succulent produce we are able to grow.

WHEN I LIVED ON the farm visitors from the city would arrive with empty two-litre bottles and plead to take my (beautiful!) tank water home. Now I'm retired in a row of linked little units and connected to the city supply of water. I miss the tanks and wrote this to celebrate National Water Week.

From:
Pat Eisler,
Traralgon,
Victoria

CONSERVING WATER

Is it true that every little drop counts?
It's been raining a lot lately.
Listening to the water
Chortling through the downpipe
As it starts its journey from my roof to the ocean
The thought occurs …

Could not all this fresh water
Be diverted on its seaward voyage
And stored in tanks
Beside my house
Or under my yard?

From there to be used domestically
Before being drained
Back into the system
And out to the sea?

Grandparents may remember
Living in houses
Where the residents were responsible

For collecting water
For their own use

This Grandma can.

I'VE JUST RETURNED FROM a visit to my research unit in the North Flinders Ranges. Needless to say, it is very dry. The last visit there was in June. It was pretty bad then and the conditions certainly haven't improved in the meantime.

Email from:
Peter Hornsby,
University of Adelaide
South Australia

For this visit, I had with me a Chinese Master of Education student, Charlotte Liu, currently studying at Adelaide University. She is a city girl from Guangzhou in Southern China. It was her first visit to the outback and decidedly a culture shock! Particularly alien was the quietness, which at times she found a little intimidating.

Between Wilmington and Quorn we encountered a mob of 1,100 sheep crossing the road and being worked by dog, something Charlotte had never seen before. The owner stopped and had a yarn with us. Charlotte found it difficult to believe that one person could own them all, which would be unheard of in China. However, she readily understood it when the owner said that in these days of almost total lack of feed they were 999 too many!

Our main task was to measure and count the number of euros (hill kangaroos) that had succumbed in the drought conditions. In a 700-metre stretch of the creek we measured sixty carcasses, all of which have died within the last twelve months.

Euros are a good indicator for drought conditions. They fall over like ninepins (as we found out) when things get bad and then rapidly breed again when conditions improve. It is mainly the big males that die; most of the smaller females (needing less food) manage to hang on. It is a very efficient survival mechanism, since when it comes to breeding up again the females are more valuable than males.

Meanwhile, the yellow-footed rock wallabies somehow manage to endure; goodness knows how, since there is little to eat except rocks! Charlotte was very dismayed when I pointed out that two small wallaby pouch young would almost certainly die within the next few weeks. It is hard to see something so hopeful and vulnerable, and to know that unless there is a quite unforeseen improvement in the rainfall, they are doomed.

I WROTE A BIT of poetry here and there and I'm sending you one that I wrote about the drought. I no longer live on a farm but I've experienced a drought or two and feel very sorry for the plight of the farmers and their stock.

From:
Marilyn Taskis,
Buderim,
Queensland

THE DROUGHT

Eyes lifted, searching, beseeching the sky
Can't remember a time when it was this dry
The laconic crow's 'cark' you've so come to hate
An expected greeting as you open the gate
Sheep forage for burr that you can't even see
(And you remember a time of grass up to your knee).

Sheep run when they hear the clapped out old ute
(And you wonder how many today you will shoot)
But they hear it and know it's their daily food sound
A tailboard trickle of oats to the ground
They bleat and come running on wobbly weak legs
And they'll stay there for hours looking for dregs.

Eyes dry, like the dam, tears no longer shed
Once water now littered with sheep that are dead
A smorgasbord laid on for the inky-plumed crow
Murky brown life's blood, but so horribly low
A poor weak sheep, mud bogged and down
A pathetic reminder of nature the clown.

Can't afford to feed them but how can you stop?
And you pray for rain, that most blessed of drop,
We need it please God please send it our way
An inch please dear Lord the next couple of days
And you ask Him what lesson He's trying to teach
You listen for answers—and put lead in the breach.

Humility, endurance ... we've learned them so well
A bad drought like this, your earthly life's hell
You wonder how much you are able to stand
Of skinny sick stock and this dusty dry land
You're awake wide with worry on so many a night
The parched earth is endless ... and there's no end in sight.

I RECENTLY DROVE THROUGH the outback areas of Queensland through New South Wales to my son in Cobar, then on through to Broken Hill and down to Adelaide. There was one thing all these things had in common, drought! It was heartbreaking, and took me back to not so long ago, around eleven years, to when my late husband and I were on the land at Augathella in the worst drought they had on record. Shovelling cottonseed day after day for over two years.

From:
Bette Wicks,
Hervey Bay,
Queensland

Then came one hell of a downpour, over six inches in a matter of an hour or so. The floods that hit Charleville went through our place, wiped out dams and fences, leaving us weeks of repair work. Yet no grass came and we went back to shovelling the cottonseed. My husband was undergoing chemotherapy at the time, and he would drive the truck and I would shovel.

My point is that no matter how bad it gets, how bad you feel, how you think you will never get through, and that you will walk off and never come back, you still keep on going, and when the rain eventually comes, you think, well what the heck, we got through that, we'll be okay, we'll stick it out. Then what happens, it comes again doesn't it? And what do you do, you go through it all again, you say the same things and you stick it out and ride out the devastation to start again.

Country people have such a love of the land, such a love of what they do, that no matter how bad it is and how bad they know it will get, they still come back for more.

It inspired me to write a poem. I feel it is how every woman on the land relates to her family and her place in the future.

BALLAD OF BELIEF

The brown earth lying cracked, hot and oh so dry,
Heat rays dancing, shimmering, in the burning sky.
No clouds on the horizon, no sign of breaking rain,
The future looking bleaker as we pray to God for rain.

How much longer can we go, how much more to take,
Before we see the rivers run, this endless drought to break.
Each day we count the cattle as we pull them from the mud,
From dried up dams and billabongs all turned to stinking crud.

The numbers growing every day, of cattle dead and dying,
I shake my head and wonder why, and then I start in crying.
Why do we stay and keep on going, trying every day
To keep our spirits bolstered and hope we'll find a way.

What would we do if we walked off, we just can't turn our back
I guess we keep on plodding on though the odds against us stack
This is our life, we know no other, what could we hope to do
We've worked to see our future grow, could we really start anew?

Maybe if we were younger we could strive to make the change,
Another start, somewhere new, our lives to re-arrange.
But as it is we'll keep on praying for that miracle to come,
And even as I say that, I see my man reach for his gun.

I see the pain in my husband's eyes as he shoots another beast
I see the carrion crow fly down to start upon the feast.
I feel the heartbreak deep inside as I go back to the truck,
I feel my dear one's misery as he curses his bad luck.

Yes, our hearts are heavy and things do look pretty black,
But who knows what's around the bend, further up the track?
We've faced these troubles all before no doubt we will again,
Each time's harder than the last, though you can't remember when.

So we will keep on going until the end draws nigh,
Until we see those storm clouds filling up the western sky.
Our faces then will wear a grin and radiance will shine
From within my dear one's heart and also from in mine.

For we are country, this is our life and we will see it out.
It WILL rain, the grass WILL grow, of this I have no doubt.
We'll see the rivers running full, the cattle growing fatter
This will be a memory, you'll see, it just won't matter.

Yes, I will believe, I can't give in, cannot let down the side
I will not sink into the gloom and say my spirit died.
From this despair nature will find a way to help us nourish
As she sends the rain to once again allow this land to flourish.

A CRYPTIC LOOK AT THE WEATHER BUREAU

From:
Ross Henry,
New Norfolk,
Tasmania

'Morning Fogg,' said Hector Pascal
The boss at the weather bureau
Nice to see you all ready to forecast
How're you going Slippery Rhodes? G'day Snow.

Ah, there's Gail Warnung. Poor Gail's feeling low
She needs a counselling session
Her kind of forecasting goes hand in hand
With a constant state of depression.

I'll let you meet Norm. He's whipped up a storm
Calm down Norm and relax
I'll take your report in a moment
When I've finished with Min and Max.

Now here's a bloke. I've known him for years
He once guarded our parks as a ranger
A hot-tempered redhead, Blue's here just in case
There's a day of acute fire danger.

And there's Miss Lorraine, with moisture in train
Always welcome in our thirsty nation
But at times during flood, when we're knee deep in mud
She should lay off her precipitation.

That's old Mr Rydge, heading straight for the fridge
We know that he's under some pressure
He'll open the door and meet a cold front
And enjoy a cool drink at his leisure.

Then in comes Vern with his equinox
As ready as ever to spring
And then at that very same moment
The telephone started to ring.

It buzzed and warbled and rang all day
The girl on the switch was Miss Frost
How has it happened, one caller asked
That my whole crop of beans has been lost?

Listen! What's that? A rattle and racket
Like a poltergeist filled with malice
But no one reacts. They all know the cause
The tea-lady Cyclone Alice.

And now let's leave the weather bureau
With their golf balls the size of hail
Where the Wayward Wind and songs like that
Are sung to the Beaufort Scale.

Oh, by the way, when their work is finished
Some feel like a quick game of keno
Or taking it easy and having a drink
In the Iso Bar at the El Niño.

No matter, whatever, they get tired of the strictures
Of watching and plotting those satellite pictures.

◎

Tea-lady *Cyclone Alice*

G'day, this is Macca

**(G'day
STEVE**

STEVE: Steve here, from the New South Wales Fire Brigade.

MACCA: G'day, Steve. You've been busy.

STEVE: Yes, mate, very busy. I'm just on my way to Tenterfield with a large convoy of trucks to assist the Rural Fire Service up there at a fire just east of Tenterfield. I was just listening to how the drought's been affecting people, and the water restrictions have put quite a different slant on our training now. Obviously, the Fire Brigade has to train every day and drill all our stations in hose handling and the different strategies that we use at fires, but because of the water restrictions we can't just waste water down the drain, so we have to find a dam on some property where we can pull water out and then throw it back in. Lately we've just had to simulate water coming out of the hoses.

MACCA: It's amazing, isn't it. It's like the army having a shortage of bullets and not able to fire their guns.

STEVE: I've just been transferred to Tamworth from down in the Wollongong area where we had no water restrictions at all, and to go out into the country and see the demands on the rural fire stations trying to keep up with their training and making the farmers and the communities happy by saving water, it's a real eye-opener for me.

MACCA: I'll bet, and they say that because of the drought the fires are worse in intensity than they've been at other times.

STEVE: In the last few weeks we've had crews from the New South Wales fire brigades in big task forces at Glen Innes, Tenterfield, Pilliga, Coonabarabran, Cessnock. The fires have been really intense. The heat out here is unbelievable and I really feel for the cockies and all the farmers. The feed is getting burnt and the water has to be used for water bombing as well. The poor buggers are copping it from both ends.

MACCA: Yes, it's like a blowtorch right across the landscape. You've got blokes from Victoria and South Australia, even Western Australia, helping you out, haven't you?

STEVE: There are crews up here from all those states and I've got what's called a task force of composites. They're a special four-wheel-drive big tanker appliance and today we're going into the rugged terrain of the national park to assist the Rural Fire Service and the CFA and the Tasmanian fire fighters to try to put a control line up there. So I thought I'd give you a ring and let you know the perspective from the Fire Brigade's point of view when it comes to the water shortages.

MACCA: Are some of these fires being deliberately lit?

STEVE: Look, I couldn't speculate on that, Macca. The Rural Fire Service has its investigators and the police have a task force set up for fire lighters and fire setters. We have a major commitment to the bushfires but we still have to look after all our towns and properties. That's the core business for the New South Wales Fire Brigade, and of late we've had quite a few house fires and we still have to go to all the big chemical spills and trucking accidents, so like every other service our resources are stretched. But we're still maintaining a really good coverage for all the towns and communities.

MACCA: Well, all Australians, mate, think you're doing a wonderful job, and if you need more money or resources or whatever—I don't know what we can do about water—but anything else, you should scream, because I'm sure everybody realises just what a crucial role you play and the wonderful job you do.

STEVE: Oh, all the fire services are being extremely well supported by the government of the day. The government's footing a huge bill for extra resources such as helicopters, extra manning, even things we don't take into account such as accommodation for the hundreds of firefighters who come up from interstate or off-duty from the New South Wales Fire Brigade.

MACCA: Where are you at the moment?

STEVE: I'm halfway between Glen Innes and Tenterfield. It's stinking hot outside and I've got the air-conditioning at full bore. I'm taking at least twenty guys up there and I think the poor buggers are going to get slogged today.

GRAHAM: I'm giving you a weather report from Kiama. It's very elegant here—light, light greys—sort of John Masefield 'the grey mist on the sea's face and a grey dawn breaking'. But there's bits of gold and yellow around the streaky clouds.

MACCA: It sounds more like Keats than Masefield, mate—'seasons of mists and mellow fruitfulness'.

GRAHAM: That's it, and the number of birds around at the moment, it's beautiful. We had the mother of all thunderstorms last night and this morning they're all singing their heads off. My wife and I went out to the Minnamurra rainforest the other day and it was fantastic. We saw five lyrebirds and one of the cocks put on a concert for us, like your music this morning from 5.30 to 6. Well, it's an elegant morning and the temperature is twenty-one and the pressure is steady.

MACCA: Nice to talk to you, mate.

G'day
GRAHAM

LYNDON: Lyndon here, at Ceduna on the west coast of South Australia. I just thought I'd give you another perspective on the drought. I was out at Cook, which is the main place on the Indian Pacific with a changeover of drivers, installing a new rain gauge for the Weather Bureau. There's a couple in Cook who look after the town and service the railway drivers and their quarters. It's only a two-man ghost town now and they haven't been doing the rain gauge for a couple of years, so we reinstalled it and they do the records for us and send them across every month. They say that in living memory they've never seen the numbers of camels coming down and licking the railway lines to get a bit of moisture. They're sitting in the middle of the railway line and the train drivers can't avoid them. These trains are doing 100 kilometres and although they blow their horns and hit the brakes they're just collecting them and causing a lot of damage to the front of the train. They cleaned up eight in one hit the other day and arrived in Cook covered in camel fat and blood and probably gave the dingoes a free feed on the way through.

MACCA: That's amazing! The droughts are obviously everywhere. You'd think that camels would be the last animals affected by drought but I suppose everyone needs a drink of water sooner or later.

LYNDON: Yes, and apparently they also like the wild hops that grow on the shoulders of the line. The people at Cook have worked on this railway line all their lives and they've never seen the camels causing so much damage and being hit by the trains. It's a bit sad, but it's another perspective on the drought.

G'day
LYNDON

Boy are those hops are wild!

MACCA: I don't think people realise the number of feral animals that are out there—camels, horses, donkeys, goats—hundreds of thousands of them, especially in that desert area of South Australia.

LYNDON: Yes, a pack of dingoes comes over to the car park of the Nullarbor Roadhouse in the mornings and there's one that's particularly friendly. He's quite a big male and he hangs around a couple of feet from you looking for scraps, I suppose.

MACCA: Lyndon, you're with the Weather Bureau. Tell us the bad news about El Niño.

LYNDON: Well, on the western side here we're less affected because it's more an eastern Australia and Pacific event, but certainly we're feeling it. We've only had six inches of rain so far this year and by now we should have had ten, and the crops are rather low. They will get a crop but nowhere near as good as last year, and in some areas towards the Mallee and further east they'll be lucky to get a crop at all.

MACCA: We're all looking for rain, that's for sure, whether it's bushfires or drought.

 G'day
SHIRLEY

SHIRLEY: This is Shirley in Mudgee. Last week everybody was whingeing about the drought, and this week we've got no fences and the grapes have nearly disappeared. We had eight inches of rain in a few hours and a lot of the vineyards have been completely flattened. We've lost all our fencing and there are big trees across the creek, but the worst thing is the vineyards. I walked through one and I could have cried for the rubbish that's lying feet deep up against the vines. We've been here thirty-odd years and we've never seen a flood like this. I'll have to get rid of my horses because I'm not up to replacing all the fences—they've just gone. Some cattle are wandering around the vineyards and up and down the creek—if they wanted to they could keep heading east indefinitely! That's the land, of course. We know that, but it's very hard.

G'day
CLINTON

CLINTON: We lost our house in Duffy in the 2003 bushfires and I can't think of any better way than through your show to thank Australia for the fantastic support that we've been given down here in Canberra. It's been quite unbelievable.

MACCA: Will you go back to Duffy, Clinton?

CLINTON: Yes, we'll go back and rebuild our place. It was demolished last week so now we can get on with the job of redesigning and rebuilding.

MACCA: Your life's changed because of something you had no control over.

CLINTON: Yes, there's not much you can do about it so you just have to get on with it. But we've had fantastic support. For example, there's a group of ladies in Longreach who decided they wanted to help a family and they chose us and they've done some wonderful things. We don't even know these people and it's marvellous.

MACCA: Clinton, I hope we see you sometime. Perhaps we could come to your street one Sunday morning and do the programme while you're building your house. You could be hammering and we could be talking.

CLINTON: Great stuff, Macca!

3

◎ *Enough's Enough!* ◎

It's just another example of greed and no service.
The big do what they want and the small do what they must.
FROM: *Cecily Coady*, Bermagui, New South Wales

From:
Jan Carroll,
Avalon,
New South Wales

WELL, IT'S THE LAST straw. Now we're being told what we can eat and where we can and cannot eat it. No, no, no. It's time for a little civil disobedience, folks. Businesses have contracted with SOCOG to be the sole providers of food and refreshments at the Olympic venue. Well, so far so good. But no one is permitted to bring any food or drink into the venue! Seems to me that's interfering with some of our basic freedoms. It's not a dress shop, for heaven's sake. How dare they!

The same thing happened in Melbourne when Premier Kennett built a grand prix raceway. Local business people in South Melbourne and its surrounds thought they would do very nicely so they supported Albert Park being decimated. Then, at the very last minute it transpired that the usual food outlets had the monopoly at the venue—surprise, surprise!

It seems to me that over the last couple of decades Australians have been regulated almost to a standstill. No horse riding here, no dog walking there; a licence for recreational fishing; dogs and cats microchipped, registered; council approval and payment required for every move; six different forms of ID to open a bank account, even if you have had an account with the same bank for thirty years and just want to open a different kind of account! It's ostensibly to make life difficult for criminals—as if! They've got lawyers for that. All it achieves is to make life difficult for all Australians. Well, enough is enough.

The majority of Australians are decent, law-abiding citizens who do not need life made any more difficult than it already is. I was under the impression that the majority ruled—well do they? Or do the minority little nitpickers and brown-shirted bossy boots?

I AM ENCLOSING MY anti-banks piece. No one hates the banks like I do. Did a one-woman crusade to try and stop an ANZ bank closing in Belmore but it was like trying to stem the tide. Inevitably it closed and of course we were all the poorer (all except the banks and shareholders) for its closing.

From:
Margaret Salmon,
Belmore,
New South Wales

Remember the institutions we once called banks
With real live tellers who used to say thanks
Nowadays with no one to greet
We do our banking in the street
Subject to attackers' pranks
Too oft a knife between the flanks
Why let the banks have their avid way
When our togetherness would save the day
Embattled customers and tellers let us all unite
To give the banks a real big fright
All done without a gun
Their ATMs we'll just shun
Armed with passbooks now maligned
And our forms all duly signed
Demanding service is our due
Not disservice paid in lieu
The banks' arrogance is a blight
Let's fix it with consumer might

PLEASE FIND ENCLOSED A leaflet regarding a rally in Ferntree Gully township. Traders and local people are very upset that their only bank is closing and have decided to support the concept of Ned Kelly and his gang bailing up the bank. Ned in full armour walking with Dan, with Steve on horseback beside him, will approach the bank and read out a proclamation that will be given to the bank staff to pass on to the management. The 'gang' will encourage people to make a stand to keep the branch open.

We did something similar in Lang Lang. The local people, although small in number, set up a people's picket line when the bank closed. It was a peaceful protest, but we feel we made our point. We now have a Bendigo Bank in the building and the other bank, the ANZ, issued notices to customers that it will not be closing.

From:
Terry Bertalli,
Lang Lang,
Victoria

ABOUT TWENTY YEARS AGO, in the 'good ol days', I was involved in a dispute at my workplace over money, wages and conditions. As an older employee, the younger people looked up to me for advice. I said, let me sleep on it and I'll come up with something.

The next day, after tossing and turning all night, I came up with the following revolutionary idea: if you want a pay rise do one of the following, or all, if you have monk-like tendencies:

1 – Stop drinking alcohol
2 – Stop smoking
3 – Stop gambling

After I suggested this brilliant idea the young walked away shaking their heads. They couldn't imagine themselves doing such a drastic thing!

I put forward the same idea now as a result of this Sheriff of Nottingham-type tax system about to hit us like a tidal wave. I and many of my friends got together about six weeks ago and agreed to put a six-month ban on all three of my suggested unnecessary pastimes, as listed above. We were amazed when we did the sums. The savings for the thirty of us was enormous even on an estimated amount saved. The true figure would probably be double as nobody likes to admit to how much they spend on wasteful pastimes!!

From:
G. Kelly,
Aspley,
Queensland

JUST AFTER YOU STARTED the programme yesterday morning you said, 'GST ... Argh!' which prompted me to send this fax.

I run a small shop on my own in Lightning Ridge, New South Wales, selling machines and powders to cut and polish the opal. When I first heard about the possibility of a GST, I thought, 'Crikey, I hope that doesn't get through.' I thought you might like this sign, which I've put on my shopfront window in bright red writing. (I gotta laugh about it or I'll cry.)

From:
Tom Fauske,
Lightning Ridge,
New South Wales

SHOP WILL BE CLOSED ON SATURDAY
1ST OF JULY (MINIMUM)
DUE TO GST UPHEAVAL/DEBACLE
AND TO PREPARE
FOR MY NEW ROLE AS
GOVERNMENT TAX COLLECTOR

Email from:
Dr Andrew Taylor,
Rosebud,
Victoria

HEARD YOU SPEAKING OF insurance and public liability this morning while eating breakfast. Nearly choked when you said it was okay for lawyers to sue negligent doctors.

Lawyers and the courts have developed a new meaning for the word negligent. It seems that if something goes wrong for someone then someone else must be negligent. In our case it is patients and doctors that end up in court. When a doctor is found negligent it doesn't mean the doctor has failed in his or her duty to care for a patient. In fact, it more often means that the patient hasn't done as well as they had expected to do, for whatever reason. The commonest reason people don't do well in hospital is the simple truth that, as we get older, we will all get sick and then we will all eventually die.

But it seems that in too many cases when a patient gets sick there is a belief that somebody has done something wrong.

The legal companies that run these incredibly expensive medico-legal actions are huge companies that each employ hundreds of lawyers and have branches in all major cities. They are not one of the small rural legal firms you spoke of by any means.

The end result of the court action is that an enormous amount of money that could open more hospitals and be used to employ more doctors and nurses is instead put into lawyers' pockets. And only a very small part of most legal awards actually compensates the aggrieved party.

I know that doctors do make mistakes. Unfortunately, the current legal system also prevents us from apologising and explaining to patients the details of any incident. We are told that if we say 'sorry' then we are virtually handing over a blank cheque. Finally, the secrecy surrounding settlements and the fear of litigation prevents doctors sharing information about errors and about near misses openly with each other. And that is why it is safer to fly than it is to go to hospital.

I would not write to you about this except that the explosion in medico-legal actions against doctors has already had a devastating impact on rural and urban fringe health services and communities. As an example there is an obstetric crisis throughout rural Australia and there are no obstetricians in Albury.

Email from:
Barry Jaques,
Urangan,
Queensland

I WAS LISTENING TO THE doctor and again hearing of the frustration with this so-called insurance crisis. Is there a conspiracy here? It's strange the way that the media, doctors, lawyers and politicians have got away with the lie for several weeks by deliberately omitting to mention the alternative for doctors and/or patients to simply sign a disclaimer that would get around the problem of legal liability.

Email from:
Graeme Martin,
Biloela,
Queensland

I THOUGHT THIS MIGHT be of interest. As of February 28th, 2002 the radio telephone service provided by Telstra is to be discontinued. After sixty years of being, it is deemed to be no longer financially viable. It is also stated in the letter sent to registered telephone users that satellite phones are now taking over from radio telephones (radphone).

I have just done a 4,500-kilometre, eight-day drive outback, and there are still plenty of vehicles, both private and government to be seen with big antennas on the front. I stopped at Winton overnight and would you believe there is still no mobile phone service out there. My outback radio contains RFDS, radphone, amateur radio bands, private 4WD and citizen-band frequencies. Satellite phones are still prohibitively expensive to buy and run and do not cover 100 per cent of the Australian land mass.

I LIVE IN SOMERTON, which is a small rural village about halfway between Tamworth and Gunnedah with a population of around 150 people.

I am writing to you because our town and livelihood are being threatened by an intensive poultry industry to be built two kilometres from our town. This development will house 800,000 chickens and will be the largest of its type in New South Wales. Despite all our objections over excessive water usage, water contamination, disease outbreak and close proximity, it seems our pleas are futile and this development is set to proceed.

Somerton is a rural farming area with many families being fourth and fifth generation descendants (myself included). We do have smaller chicken sheds that we drive past frequently on our journey into Tamworth. These sheds emit terrible odours and dust that makes us fearful for the future of our town.

The Environment Protection Authority has already refused permission twice, but somehow after yet another submission from the developers it seems they now have no problem with the development. It seems yet again that money and big business are all that matter and the community have not been taken into consideration.

From:
Donna Bennett,
Somerton,
New South Wales

I WAS GREATLY IMPRESSED by the lady (a dairy farmer) who rang in about how the soul of the country towns is being destroyed by governments that only look at the bottom line (the dollar).

Without farm subsidies the rural landscapes in America and Europe would be destroyed. Tourists could no longer visit quaint little villages—they would be ghost towns, just like many of our outback and rural centres are becoming (without assistance).

From:
Geoff Walker,
Mallabula,
New South Wales

MY WIFE AND I are travelling around the western half of this great land of ours and are staggered at the appalling postal service in this part of 'The Lucky Country'.

We have a person collecting our mail and forwarding it when I ring and tell him where we will be. I was telling him where we would be in two weeks' time, but we were missing the mail. So now I tell him where we will be in a month's time!

Australia Post makes public statements that guarantee delivery of mail from Perth in two working days to any town on the north-west coast. I would like to know where the mail is for the rest of the time!

In 1966 I worked at Dampier on the construction of the Hamersley Iron project. For the first few weeks my wife stayed in Broken Hill and during this time a letter from Dampier to Broken Hill took three working days. The return mail took the same time.

Now in 1999 with all the improvements in technology we are fortunate if it only takes three weeks.

From:
Ray Ware,
Broken Hill,
New South Wales

Global Pigeon Satellite

From:
David Roney,
Mossman,
Queensland

I AM IN AWE at the relative ease with which the mega corporations controlling the dairy industry have awarded themselves thirty per cent increases in the wholesale/retail market over the past eighteen months and now offer farmers fifty per cent less at the farm gate. All without a blink from any government or pricing authority.

And get this for a punch line. Dispossessed farmers will be helped by a government assistance package that is funded by an eleven or fifteen per cent increase in the price of milk after July 1st.

It will be interesting when the ACCC fines the government $10 million for increasing prices more than the ten per cent GST!

◎

From:
Margaret J. Gagel,
Proston,
Queensland

RECENTLY I WAS INVITED to the launch of the Queensland Ambulance Service's (QAS) First Responders, the first such group in Queensland. This group volunteered to be the first on the scene of an emergency. This happened after our ambulance officer was transferred last April. The QAS found it very difficult to get anybody interested in moving to our small town, which has about three hundred people and another six hundred in the outlying areas. (I may also add that we have had the same problem with our policeman. Our officer was transferred in November 1998 and we have only had relieving staff ever since.) These professionals feel that they will lose their skills if they move so far from the population centres of the coast. Our town is approximately eighty kilometres north-west of Kingaroy and about three and a quarter hours from Brisbane.

The First Responders had some difficulty being accepted at first as people believed that they would replace an ambulance officer. They are now aware that they are in support of the officer. At present our ambulance has to come from either Murgon (fifty kilometres) or Kingaroy (eighty kilometres). With First Responders living here they can react a lot quicker to an emergency. The QAS is still trying everything to fill our vacancy but I take my hat off to the volunteers, nine in all, who may have to confront some sights that I could not bring myself to see. Our ambulance station is very well equipped through the efforts of the local ambulance committee. The first two volunteers for First Responder came from this committee, which shows their true community spirit.

Our little town has also won the Regional and State 'Bush Spirit Award' from the Tidy Towns Keep Australia Beautiful Council. This award is for community effort in the face of adversity. The railway closed several years ago, the last bank closed eight years ago, the last major employer, a feed mill and hardware store closed three years ago, but the town keeps going.

There really is true bush spirit in this town, probably like a lot of other towns put into the same situation.

◎

From:
Toni McLeish,
Upper Manilla,
New South Wales

WHAT HAS HAPPENED TO mateship in Australia, the city–country connections of the past are disappearing fast. No longer do all the city people have relatives in the bush or vice versa. Each group has lost a connection that used to provide cheap holidays and understanding.

My husband and I own a property in Manilla, New South Wales, that we find very hard to get away from because we can't just lock the door and leave. I'm sure there are families in the city or on the coast who would love to farm-sit for a week while we went to the city or coast for a break.

Can we trust them? What about insurance? Will they look after the garden and the animals? Life has become so complicated! Where have all the mateship attributes gone?

YOU CAN BET ON IT

From:
Heather Hastings,
Launceston,
Tasmania

I came to live in Launceston
I'd planned to come for years
I'd heard 'The lifestyle's wonderful'
Which allayed all my fears.

I bought myself a Villa home
Convenient, quiet, pretty
My little piece of heaven
In a lovely gracious city.

With family members living close
Small shopping centre near
Five minutes drive to CBD
I've all I need right here.

And with a bank just down the street
The one of choice by chance
I wouldn't have to drive for miles
If I'd need a cash advance.

A bank nearby, what luxury!
And staffed by friendly folk
Yet here's the rub, my friend, with you
I'll share a small wry joke.

It's closing in September next
Our friendly Newstead branch.
Big people in high places say
'To stay it has no chance!'

Just another suburb
Just a mere statistic
Not worth mentioning at all
Though to us it seems sadistic.

I wonder how many banks
Are peopled by sad ghosts?
No sound to break the silence
And the biros still chained to their posts.

WHY IS IT THAT in banks the doors open automatically, not touched by human hands, yet the biros are always chained up beside the bank forms in neat little containers, on shelves among the walls?

Most of the pens don't work anyway (like the staff, now out of work). Perhaps these pens are dangerous, so need to be chained like dogs. I can just see the headline now: 'Fierce biro attacks bank customers'. Maybe the banks are closing because it is too costly to insure the customers against biro attacks!

Killer biro

From:
Russell,
Canberra,
Australian Capital
Territory

I IMAGINE YOU'LL RECEIVE hundreds of letters on football, and because I'm so cranky about it I have to give you mine.

When I was eight years old we lived in Bega. The annual holiday was with my grandmother who rented half a house in Mosman. We used to drive up from Bega in an old Morris. Highlight of the trip was crossing the Harbour Bridge, then following the signposts to Spit Junction and my grandmother's place.

I was aware there was a rugby league competition in Sydney. The bigger boys at school had teams they followed. Because of those signposts I decided to follow Manly. I followed them through the frustrating fifties, the promising sixties, the successful seventies, the disappointing eighties and the turmoil of the nineties. I travelled to Sydney with my brother to see Manly play. Win some, lose some more. My league team was like my country, my family.

After forty-plus years, a couple of millionaires interfere. They want my rugby league. They fight over it like spoilt children over a toy. They break it. Now they want to put the toy back together in a different way—a way that will bring them money rather than make it a part of my life. They want to replace my team and my old enemy teams with new teams. New teams that are commercial enterprises. This is fast food football. Get you in. Get your money. Convince you that you've had something good. Get you out.

I'll follow my team for as long as it's there. If Manly go, I'll have a sense of loss. Like Robert Service I'll say: '[I] feel my life has been looted clean of something it once held dear.'

I'M WRITING THIS ON April Fools Day, but this is no joke. After two and a half years of struggling after deregulation we have decided to close the dairy. Many have gone before us, and I feel there are many more to go.

Deregulation ripped the heart out of our industry, and to what avail? In 1999 Brisbane people were paying $1.30 a litre for milk and the farmer was getting fifty-four cents. Now it costs $1.59 a litre and the farmers get between thirty-four and thirty-seven cents. Did the public get the cheaper milk they were promised? I think not. And rural communities have paid dearly too, because farmers spend less in their communities. It also hurts having Centrelink payments thrown in our faces while the supermarkets profit.

There were many farms not making huge amounts of money, but they were making a living for their family and enjoying the challenges dairying brings. When you deplete their income to a hopeless level the devastation is unbelievable. The greedy top end of town is wallowing in the money that could help them survive.

Someone has to stop the rot.

From:
Jill Hopson,
Ubobo,
Queensland

FINAL CALL

From:
Max Fatchen,
Smithfield,
South Australia

They say the telephone box must go at that little country town.
It doesn't make a profit say those who know. The accountants have written it down.
The rattle of change, the coins dropping in, a call to a distant friend.
The weekend chat, no more of that, for now it all must end.

The dial would spin with a metallic din for calls weren't exactly free
To Sydneyside but the world was wide when you rang on the STD.
Those calls that you made of the family news and the kids with the chickenpox
In rain or shine you were on the line in your public telephone box.

The football scores from the local pub, the goals they tried to shoot.
The gossip you heard in the local pub, the trouble you had with the ute
So cockies told their rural news of some cows and crops and flocks
There were dreams you spoke to some girl or bloke from that public telephone box.

Time marches on and don't forget we now must rationalise.
We haven't caught up with the internet which comes as a surprise
And did you send your love today and remember the things you said
In the telephone box? … but the voices fade … for now the line goes dead.

G'day, this is Macca

📞 G'day
JOHN

JOHN: Good morning, Macca. I'm listening to the sound of waves belting on the beach at North Wollongong. It's the most beautiful view in the world, and Wollongong is also one of the most beautiful cities in Australia. I'm looking towards the escarpment over Austinmer, Thirroul and the National Park and it's wonderful. There are some misshapen clouds out on the horizon and they're going to form a backdrop to the sunrise. The fishing boats are heading north-east out to sea where the fish must be this morning and there's not a soul on the beach. It's going to be the most perfect day to go swimming.

MACCA: You're a nice way to start the program, John. I was down in Wollongong during the week and I thought again what a lovely view that is from where Lawrence Hargrave launched his box kites.

JOHN: I'm looking in exactly the opposite direction, from North Beach, and the lights are twinkling along the coast and you have that mountain background. There is no more beautiful coastal stretch in the world.

MACCA: I don't think there is. People say to me, 'What's the nicest place in Australia, Macca?', and for me Ubobo is nice—everywhere you go is nice where there are nice people—but it is really a beautiful part of the Australian coast. What do you do, John?

JOHN I'm a solicitor and I travel back and forth to Liverpool every day. Every night we come home over the mountain and it's like going on holidays every time.

MACCA: You solicitors are in the gun at the moment, aren't you?

JOHN: Unfairly, Macca. I come from the suburbs and I've been in the suburbs all the forty years I've been in practice. Over the years things have gone a bit mad, and I don't mean lawyers, but things. We've taken on the American system where they've decided you're going to get $60 million for a claim, whereas not many years ago the largest claim you'd ever get would be approaching $1 million. What's happened?

MACCA: I don't know. I think judges have got a lot to answer for.

JOHN: They do, you know. The courts themselves are part of the problem.

MACCA: When you think about it, insurance is a really crazy business. We insure everything in our houses and then people who are on drugs and stuff come in and rob us and we say, 'Oh, that's all right because we'll get the money back.' When you think about it, it's really not a good way to live your life, is it, because we don't appreciate anything we've got and if it's stolen or smashed up we can always replace it.

JOHN: I think we've got a medical system that is pretty good. I know mistakes are made, but people are doing things to achieve the best result. I just think there should be a medical system which is backed up by the government which says, 'We guarantee that system works, and if it doesn't work, be it private or public, we will look after people who have a major problem out of it.'

MACCA: And that's what we should do with society, too. I think if anyone has an accident playing football or whatever everybody in the community should rally round and say, 'Tom's had an accident, let's help him and his family.' That's the way it always used to be, but I'm really down on insurance and I think lawyers and solicitors have been sucked into that vortex, and now it's going to explode in everybody's face.

JOHN: Everyone wants to have their rights protected, and you can't blame them, but I think there's got to be a limit to those rights. There has to be some stage where you say, 'Listen, a million dollars is enough for an injury.'

MACCA: Like the one during the week: the million dollars for the kid who had a fight in the playground eight years ago, or something. It's madness.

JOHN: It is! A doctor wouldn't be game to pick you up in the street and help you. He'd walk past, because why would he expose himself to the risk of getting sued for millions?

MACCA: Last week I had an email from a doctor who said they don't talk to each other about their mistakes now because they're afraid of litigation, and that's really bad for everybody. Well, mate, it's been nice to talk to you and I'll leave you with the waves on Wollongong beach.

G'day . . .

ROBIN BLACKMORE
and TONY SLATTERY

I went to Newcastle and among other things I visited a ship called the Wallarah, *which sadly has stopped working. Robin Blackmore and Tony Slattery are both captains of the* Wallarah *and this is their story.*

MACCA: How come the *Wallarah* has two captains?

ROBIN: We used to relieve each other, three weeks on and three weeks off.

MACCA: Traditionally this ship has run to Catherine Hill Bay and brought coal back here to Newcastle. How long has she been doing that?

ROBIN: Since 1986. She's done some interstate work, but principally she's run from Catherine Hill Bay stockpiling and the coal's gone everywhere, all around the world. She's been a good ship. Both Tony and I have spent nearly sixteen years on board, and in my view it's one of the best jobs I've had. She's a well-built sixty-miler, and we're effectively the last of them. We're finishing today, actually.

MACCA: Tony, how do you feel about that?

TONY: Very sad, Ian. I'm very sad indeed, not only for this ship but for the demise of the Australian merchant fleet.

MACCA: Tell us about that. I remember I was up in Byron Bay about six years ago and a merchant man came along and said, 'Ian, you should look into the demise of cabotage in Australia.'

TONY: Yes, cabotage means that the country's coastal fleet is protected to carry cargoes around Australia but now, with the reduction of cabotage, foreign ships can have permits to travel around our coast and carry Australian cargoes. That's been exploited to quite a big extent in the last couple of years.

MACCA: Why did you go to sea?

TONY: It was a pretty attractive life in those days. A lot of us went to sea at fifteen or sixteen years of age and have been at sea ever since.

MACCA: Robin, what about you?

ROBIN: I've been at sea for thirty-odd years and master for twenty-seven years in these ships.

MACCA: There's still a mine at Catherine Hill Bay and they're going to bring the coal by truck. That's caused a lot of angst, hasn't it?

ROBIN: It sure has. It's a classic problem of economics versus the people's will and common sense, and economic rationalism is overriding the will of the people, really. People have been protesting quite strongly all the way along the route that they consider that the ships should still be running and the trucks shouldn't be. It's a complicated argument but we'd prefer to still be running coal to Newcastle.

MACCA: 'Coals to Newcastle', the old saying! They say you shouldn't have regrets in life, but one of my regrets is that I didn't get to go on the *Wallarah* down to Catherine Hill Bay and back, a lovely run.

TONY: Sometimes it could be pretty lousy, but it was a magical trip most days.

MACCA: Who's this BHP Billiton who's made this decision?

ROBIN: They own the ship. It runs for the people who own the mines and they've decided to reduce their output and they say there's no viable work for the ship.

MACCA: So what will you do, Tony?

TONY: Another seafaring job somewhere, Ian. Around the coast, hopefully, if there's anything left.

MACCA: Is Newcastle a big seafaring town?

ROBIN: It has been in the past but the problem we're all going to face, officers and seamen alike, is that we'll be competing with foreign nationals for jobs on the Australian coast. Recently there's been a ship employing Ukrainians running around the coast.

MACCA: Working for a lot less?

ROBIN: You can only assume so, and that's who we'll have to compete with for jobs.

TONY: I don't know how we'll go. Hopefully we'll get a job based on our skills, but I'm a bit expensive, I'm afraid!

MACCA: About a month ago a bloke rang us from Port Pirie about a ship that was locked up there.

TONY: She was in Newcastle two or three days ago with a Ukrainian crew, registered in Nassau in the Bahamas, loading coal out of Newcastle.

MACCA: So they didn't get to keep their Australian crew?

TONY: Obviously not.

ROBIN: It's a little hard, Macca, watching them paint over the Australian registration of Melbourne and putting on an overseas port of registry. They're human beings and we understand that they have to work, but Australians also have to work and there's no way we can compete economically with Chinese or Ukrainian wages.

We were in Melbourne doing our Melbourne Cup programme, and one of our guests was Alistair Webster who is a former MP from Macquarie. We talked about elections. Somebody's registered Felix the Cat—that's true! And Alistair talked about changes to be made to the Electoral Act to make it impossible to register to vote more than once. You know that in close elections, which we've certainly had in Australia in the last twenty years, a handful of votes have decided seats. This is an important thing because unscrupulous people could register their cat as well as themselves. I thought we should see what's happened. Alistair, can you and I still register fifteen times?

ALISTAIR: Well, it's so wide open that you don't even have to register your dog. The incredible thing is that while there's been a lot of trumpeting about changes it's exactly the same as it was over the last ten years. Nothing's changed. You can still go into the post office and get yourself a dozen or a hundred enrolment cards, fill them in yourself, send them in with a friendly address, collect the acknowledgement cards and they're all on the Roll. You just apply for a postal vote and Bob's your uncle!

MACCA: I'm laughing because it's so ludicrous. You'd know better than I that many seats, certainly marginal seats, are won by a handful of votes.

ALISTAIR: You see Macca, the thing is that it's a lot harder to hire a video at the local video store than it is to get on the Roll. Can you believe that?

MACCA: Yes, I can believe that because I tried to hire a video recently and you had to have proof of this and that.

ALISTAIR: Well, you don't need any of that to register to vote. In the current scene the government is certainly trying hard and has put out a new enrolment card that's going to make it much harder to get onto the Roll, but there's a lot of inertia by some of the states.

MACCA: But why?

ALISTAIR: I don't know. That's a good question. We should be asking it from our housetops—why? Why is it so with something as important as voting? It's quite incredible.

MACCA: And I suppose rorting has taken place over the last twenty years in Australia.

ALISTAIR: There's no question at all that rorting has taken place. The average Australian wouldn't know that in the 1993 election 53,000 people had their Senate vote registered as okay but were disenfranchised in the House of Representatives. Bear in mind that the 1993 election was only lost by 1,500 votes, and the Electoral Commission says that 39,000 people were wrongly disendorsed in terms of their vote. When you think that 1,500 decided the election—and thirteen seats were decided by only 500 votes—it becomes a very serious issue.

MACCA: I'll say, and nothing's really happened.

ALISTAIR: Nothing. It's on the agenda. The federal government is trying to do something about it but it seems that all the inertia that can possibly be put in place to stop it happening is still there.

MACCA: So when I say facetiously 'Vote early, vote often' when there's an election on, you can actually still do that.

G'day
ALISTAIR

VIDEO HIRE REQUEST

Name:...............
Address:...............
Telephone:...............
Mobile:...............
Buisness:...............
Home:...............
Driver's Licence:...............
Credit Card No:...............
Partner:
Name: ....
Address:...............
Telephone:...............
Mobile:...............
Next of Kin:
Name:...............
Address:...............
Telephone:...............
Mobile...............
Bank:...............
Health Fund:......
Address:...............
Telephone:......

ALISTAIR: Well, when you register you have to put down your residential address and it must be within the electorate, but your postal address, for the purposes of being on the Roll and getting the acknowledgement card, can be anywhere in Australia.

MACCA: It's amazing, isn't it?

PHILIPPA: It's Philippa from Jilla Jilla, down on the far south coast of NSW near Bega. I'm one of twenty dairy farmers who own Bega Cheese, and nothing's changed—we still own Bega Cheese. We're Australian farmers and that's the way it's always been.

MACCA: So, you saw the stories during the week?

PHILIPPA: Yes, I did and I was really quite annoyed that journalism could be so incorrect. We still produce our cheese. We aligned ourselves with a company called Bonland, owned by Bonlac, about eighteen months ago, purely to promote and market our cheese all over Australia. So 'better buy Bega' because it's Australian owned and produced.

MACCA: It's getting harder and harder to do that, Philippa, isn't it?

PHILIPPA: It certainly is, and I must say that it's getting harder and harder on farms to produce it at such a low price.

MACCA: Deregulation's been going for some time. How has it affected you in the Bega Valley?

PHILIPPA: We had quota into Sydney and Canberra markets. Our overall profit from the top was skimmed by 25 per cent—that's our personal income—and it's been a struggle to get on top of that.

MACCA: Who did that go to?

PHILIPPA: Six hundred million dollars a year from the farmers' pockets went straight to supermarkets and processors, and I'm not one-eyed about that. I'm wondering whether governments really want country towns, or want us to be on the land and look after it. Farmers should have subsidies for looking after the land. Where are the environmental issues – they've gone out the window too. It's very costly to keep land maintained and conserved, and if we're getting less for our product they'll be the things that will get missed along the way.

MACCA: Philippa, lots of dairy farmers are listening this morning. We were in Ubobo and I think there were three dairies in that little valley and only one or two are left now. It's happening everywhere, and dairy farming is only one thing that's affected.

PHILIPPA: You really need your heart in the land to be able to go on these days because it's getting harder and harder. They say to look at it all economically, but if we looked at our place only as a business we'd have been out thirty-odd years ago.

G'day
PHILIPPA

Definitely a better buy . . .
(Renowned cheese connoisseur)

Recipes

'My wife will bring the bread'

3¼ cups of SR flour
2 teaspoons of salt
2 teaspoons of sugar
1 can 370ml beer

Sift the dry ingredients into a bowl and pour beer in all at once into a well in the centre. Stir with a knife. The mixture will be soft and sticky. Turn onto a floured surface and knead well with well-floured hands until smooth. If two loaves are wanted divide and knead again. Place in a well-oiled loaf tin and bake for fifty minutes in a moderate oven until loaf sounds hollow when tapped. It smells wonderful when cooking and tastes even better than it smells!
FROM: HEATHER HASTINGS, ALBION PARK, NEW SOUTH WALES

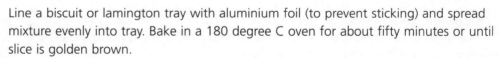

'Up the Tracks' Recipe

Into a large bowl put:
2 cups of wholemeal SR flour
2 cups of coconut
2 cups of sultanas (Bob likes some chopped dried apricots as well)
1½ cups of raw sugar
1½ cups of milk

Line a biscuit or lamington tray with aluminium foil (to prevent sticking) and spread mixture evenly into tray. Bake in a 180 degree C oven for about fifty minutes or until slice is golden brown.
FROM: JEAN WEINERT, PITTSWORTH, QUEENSLAND

The Best Fig Jam Recipe

It's tried and true! Put 4 pounds/1.85 kilograms of halved figs into a preserving pan with 1 pint/ 600 ml of water and 1 cup of vinegar (a 1/4 pound of bruised ginger may be boiled with the fruit). Boil until soft and add 4 pounds/1.85 kilograms of warm sugar, then boil until thick and set. (The fig skins are removed by covering the figs with hot water for a few minutes then rubbing the skin with cloth or peel).
FROM: HELEN O'BRIEN, THORNLANDS, QUEENSLAND

I often say I meet the most interesting people when I'm on the road. At Hermannsburg in the Northern Territory it was a privilege to have a yarn with Albert Namatjira's granddaughter, Lennie, and Helena Burns. And the kids had fun being 'tattooed' with the ABC's logo by our multi-skilled technical producer, Eddie Coleman.
In the crowd were 'the meandering Mitchells' who have been on the road for years.

Below: Part of the 'Hermannsburg Mob'.

Weethalle

Opposite: At the Weethalle Show in New South Wales we were under the 'big top'. John the truckie displayed his shaven head and beard, lost in a good charitable cause, while 'Us Not Them', Jason and Chloe Roweth, entertained.

Geraldton

Below: We broadcast from this memorial to HMAS *Sydney* at Mount Scott, Geraldton in Western Australia. It's a dome with six hundred and forty-five seagulls connected wingtip to wingtip, representing the men who were lost. Amazingly, at the sunset dedication of the site, just as the Last Post was being played, a flock of silver gulls flew over in total silence.

◎ Ubobo ◎

first met Marguerite Bradley when she called from Ubobo in Queensland to say that Telstra was going to take away their
phone box. Here we are in THE phone box—it's still there!
The peace and quiet of our broadcast from Ubobo (there's Marguerite again) was disturbed by a helicopter. We hope it was
an ABC one!

◎ Story Bridge ◎

Brisbane's Story Bridge has been the subject of urban myths, and a bride-to-be was once stranded in its 'no-movement' traffic. But a good crowd joined our broadcast underneath it.

Ebony Foster (at the back) and Tessie Lewis from Wingellina (Irrunytju) in Western Australia were 'blown away' after being told that a high school teacher in Adelaide heard their chat with me over the airwaves.

Jessica Kirkham gets 'on the blower' at Lakefield National Park in Cape York, asking 'Can I reverse the charges from a tree?'

4

◎ *It's Just a Simple Service* ◎

By far the largest amount of mail I receive concerns our Anzac traditions. It'd fill a couple of books. I think it signifies respect, most notably for those who served and those who died, but also for our country, our people and ourselves.

From:
Max Fatchen,
Smithfield,
South Australia

DAWN SERVICE

It's just a simple service in a country town I know
When steady stars are paling and the sleepy earth wakes slow
With grassy smell of morning and the bright dew on the lawn
It's just a simple service in a country town at dawn

There isn't any grand parade, or marching to a band
But just a little group of blokes who watch and think and stand.
There isn't a bugler there to play a sad 'Last Post'
But from the mist of memories the past steals like a ghost.

And all the intervening years the busy mind will bridge
To deserts harsh and beaches cold, and riven jungle ridge
To laughter, fear a thousand things, the faces and the jokes
And how it all came back again just standing with the blokes.

It's just a simple service while the dawn is breaking red
It's not the words a fellow hears but those that stay unsaid,
It's not the glow of glory that the fleeting moment lands
But just the recollections … in the morning … of your friends.

◎

From:
H.E. 'Bert' Love,
Cobram,
Victoria

I FOLLOWED WITH INTEREST the letter you read from Jan Peacock. I was on another tour and experienced the problems Jan described—trying to get to the dawn service with the road leading to Anzac Cove clogged with coaches and cars. Jan vividly recounted in her letter helping an old soldier through the crowd at the Lone Pine Memorial up to the rostrum, brushing shoulders with the Prime Minister, Kim Beazley and many dignitaries present.

I was that old soldier, 'Bert', a former Royal Marine during the Second World War.

My main reason for going to Gallipoli was to locate and photograph the grave of an uncle of mine. He was Herbert Philip Love, 1st Battalion Royal Dublin Fusiliers, who was killed in action on 7th May 1915. He was one of a family of four brothers, three of whom served in France during the First World War and were lucky to return to civilian life. Bert did not survive. I was able to locate his grave in Twelve Tree Copse cemetery, a British/New Zealand cemetery south of Krithia. I was also privileged to stand on 'V' beach where he landed on 25th April, 1915. He was killed in one of the attempts to advance on Krithia.

My other reason for going on the tour was to see for myself the condition of the landing beaches and terrain and why the invasion failed. I took part in several amphibious landings in World War Two, including the landing on Normandy beaches in France on June 6th, 1944. I have deep feelings and sad memories.

Because another member of our party, Sandy Newbury, and I had relatives buried on the peninsula, we were asked if we would like to lay the wreath at the Lone Pine memorial service which we thought a great honour. We arrived at Lone Pine with about ten minutes to spare before the commencement of the service. Although my leg was giving me great pain I was determined to be a part of the wreath-laying ceremony. We had to manoeuvre our way through the dense crowd to get near the memorial. Sandy supported me by the left arm and Jan, who had appeared from nowhere, graciously took my right arm and so the two ladies escorted me through the crowd, just as she described in her letter.

Yes, Jan, I was the 'Bert' you helped on that memorable occasion, and thank you so much. As for the medals I wore, they were the 1939–49 star, the Atlantic star with the France and Germany clasp, the Africa star, the Italy star, the 1939–45 War medal, the Malta George Cross Commemoration medal and the 50th Anniversary Commemoration medal.

◎

YOU HAD A LETTER from woman who had travelled to Gallipoli for the 25th April this year, mentioning how crowded it was, and a phone call from another traveller who had gone to the peninsula with his brother at another time and found it tranquil and rewarding because of its silence.

The problem of the crowds on 25th April has been a concern for a few years now. I went to the 75th anniversary in 1990 and it was pretty much overcrowded then. Each year since it has become worse. In a few years it hopefully will no longer be a 'must be' for backpackers and it can return to some normality.

Until then I think it is probably best to avoid going there on 25th April. I've been thinking about another idea that might appeal to travellers. There are many other significant dates for the campaign. Australians could attach themselves to a particular battle or event and link their visit into that date. For example, on 8th May, 1915, the Australians of the 2nd Brigade—mostly Victorians—attacked at Krithia, which is in the Helles battlefield on the southern 'toe' of the peninsula. In our guide book, *Gallipoli, A Battlefield Guide*, we describe the charge: 'The Australian advance along 1.3 km of fire-swept slope was one of the quintessential moments of the campaign and advanced the line to the site of the present Redoubt Cemetery at a cost of over a thousand casualties.' Travellers could arrange their visit for 8th May and would find it easy to walk the ridge along which the 2nd Brigade attacked.

Other dates stand out—the massive Turkish counterattack on 19th May, and the death that day of John Simpson Kirkpatrick, the 'Simpson' of 'Simpson and his donkey'. In early August the Allies launched the major assaults on Lone Pine, The Nek and Sari Bair. Any one of these, or all of them, could become the focus of a visit to the peninsula. With just a little background research, travellers could find out the history of the particular battle and would usually be able to retrace it on the ground.

From:
Pam Cupper and
Phil Taylor,
Dimboola,
Victoria

◎

I HEARD A LADY speaking on your programme about Gallipoli, and in particular John Simpson and the work he did carrying the wounded to safety at Anzac Cove.

Without taking anything away from Simpson, I would like to draw your attention to one of Australia's many unsung heroes, Herbert 'Bert' Latrobe. Latrobe, then twenty-one, served with the First Field Ambulance at Gallipoli and like Simpson used a donkey to ferry the wounded down from the battalion positions in the trench lines to the relative safety of the beach.

Simpson was killed on the 19th of May, three weeks after the landing, while Latrobe continued to carry out this dangerous work for nearly four months until he was wounded in the stomach by shrapnel from an exploding shell.

From:
Peter Wood,
Kangaroo Point,
Queensland

He was evacuated from the Anzac beachhead on the 14th of August. He survived the war and later joined the NSW Police Force and as a detective solved the famous 'Pyjama Girl' case, and also the Forbes murder. He died in 1947 at the relatively young age of fifty-four as a result of the wounds he received at Gallipoli.

Prior to Anzac Day about three years ago I wrote to the *Courier Mail* in Brisbane with the story of Latrobe and the same day was contacted by a couple who had lived next door to him for many years. They confirmed the story and also advised that his daughter was still alive and would enjoy knowing her father's story was remembered.

THE PARTING

From:
Connie Ross,
Cookardinia,
New South Wales

He stood in the darkening shadows, as the daylight ebbed slowly away.
Gently stroking the neck of his son's new colt, a beautiful, thoroughbred bay.
With eyes misting over, he spoke to the horse; scenes from the past flashing by—

Tomorrow, their first-born would answer the call; but somehow, well, men didn't cry!
Full of a sense of excitement, their Jack would ride off with his mate—
Ride off and enlist in the Light Horse; yet what was to be his fate?
He remembered the days of Jack's childhood, of the wonderful years they had shared.
Watched him grow, 'til now he'd reached manhood, that loveable son they had reared.

His love of the farm and his country, the cornerstones of his life—
Yet what an adventure awaited, those soldiers who would brave the strife!
For War is a terrible business, whatever the highest ideals,
And many a family face anguish, and many the lives that it steals!

He smiled, recalling the days gone by, the tasks they had shared, and when—
The neighbours scoured the countryside when Jack was lost, and then—
The day that bushfires ringed the farm—Jack didn't flinch, nor flee,
Though just a boy, he fought with men, to set the livestock free!

Jack's parents' pride was justified, for this young man so fine,
Would soon be facing gunfire from a hostile foreign line!
With heavy heart, as cold as stone, the father turns and sighs,
And lifting up the horse's head, he looked into its eyes.

'It's up to you, old fellow, to carry Jack with care,
To disregard the danger, the cannons firing there.
Leap swiftly over trenches, and never fear the strife,
Though desert sands may cling to you, please, guard him with your life!

'Tread boldly Bill, your heart so big, so swift you are, and brave;
They'll need your sort to carry men, their countries' fate to save.
Though heat and flies and thirst torment, may you and Jack be strong,
For Jess and I will find the days and nights now, very long!'

Each day, we'll pause to think of Jack, and pray he's safe and well.
He's meeting many challenges; we'll face OUR private Hell!
And Jack's old dog will yearn to hear the sound of his master's tone—
But many the months and years to pass, before he'll come back home.

I picture the city bustle, the boat that will carry away,
Our son, our dreams, our future—you'll leave at break of day.
Slowly, the man returns to the house, drawn to the welcoming light—
Tomorrow, Jack rides to the railhead, and War—
They must make the most of tonight!

MY EX-FATHER-IN-LAW is, as far as I know, the only surviving Anzac.* Alec Campbell was born on 26th February, 1899. He put his age up to get into the war. Ever since I've known him he's had an injured eye. Whether or not it was a war injury I'm not sure. His seventh child, a daughter, with whom I shared a room at Westella in 1955, told me they had a rough time in the depression and became communists and atheists.

In addition to seven children from his first marriage, he had two more from his second. He went to university and worked in the public service. He was a keen sailor and sailed the Sydney to Hobart a number of times.

Alec Campbell died in Hobart on May 16, 2002 aged 103. He was the last remaining Gallipoli veteran. A state funeral was held in Hobart on May 24

From:
Margaret Campbell,
Eaglehawk Neck,
Tasmania

I HEARD PART OF your programme and your comments about the charge of Beersheba and its commemoration. You were wondering if there were any monuments in its memory. My father's film, *Forty Thousand Horsemen*, depicted the famous charge, and is available on video. But more importantly it is good for people to know that the Light Horse is still going strong. The latest modern-day contingent of Light Horse is currently deployed in East Timor. There is a nucleus (I am not sure if it is a contingent) of traditional Light Horse in Inverell. Here, in Toowoomba, we have a rose garden and monument to the Light Horse in the Newtown Park from where local contingents left for service in World War I. In Brisbane there is a Regimental Museum at Gallipoli Barracks, Enoggera.

I am not certain whether there are any monuments specifically to Beersheba, but for any-one interested in reading of it, my father's cousin, Elyne Mitchell (daughter of Sir Harry Chauvel) wrote two books, *Light Horse to Damascus* and *Light Horse: the Story of Australia's Mounted Troops*, both of which featured the famous charge. There was also the fine old classic, *The Wells of Beersheba* by Frank Dalby Davison. I hope this might be of some interest.

Email from:
Sue Chauvel Carlsson

ONE OF YOUR GUESTS said he wrote to his wife every day while he was on service in Korea. My husband was another who all his life was very methodical, and after leaving Tasmania with the 2nd AIF in October 1940 wrote to me every day, only posting when able to. Each letter was numbered progressively so that when several letters arrived at once, as happened, they could be read in their correct order.

He was called up for war service on 3rd September, 1939, the day the war was declared. He transferred to the AIF in May 1940, leaving Tasmania in October. While in the Middle East until his return in March 1942, he wrote 156 letters, all of which I still have.

P.S. I don't know if I should mention this, but we had a code by which I knew, roughly, his whereabouts.

From:
Peggy Harrison,
Summerhill,
Tasmania

From:
John Josselyn,
East Albury,
New South Wales

AS THE TEACHER-IN-CHARGE at Girilambone Public School (thirty-nine children from kindergarten to third year) in 1960 I was asked to give an address to the gathering at the Girilambone Anzac Day service.

At the age of nineteen and in my first year of teaching I found the task a little daunting. Girilambone's population of sixty was sitting in front of me. Nervousness increased when I realised that there were six World War I veterans in the audience. But I managed to give my speech.

After the service one of the veterans approached me and shaking my hand he thanked me. 'I could relate to your comments,' he said. 'I was watching the kids and they were genuinely interested.' What a relief!

Next thing I was approached by the 'Unelected Mayor', the president of the P and C, tennis club and everything else. 'Unfortunately, John, I can't invite you to the RSL Club—you're underage.' What a downer!

Every man, woman and child and even one or two dogs was heading to the RSL Club, which was pretty basic—one-car garage wide and two garages long, without electricity. The whole town lacked that commodity except the pub, which had a lighting plant.

Joe the publican drew me to one side: 'I knew this would happen,' he said. 'I've put on a keg. You go over to the pub and help yourself. I'll be there as soon as I've done a bit of PR at the Club.' I was lucky to have Joe as a landlord. The pub was the only accommodation available for a single male teacher. Joe, the good bloke that he was, had gone to considerable trouble to make sure I could have a beer. At the pub I found, under the bar, a freshly tapped keg with a wet wheat bag draped over it and a middie glass on the bar!

One memorable Anzac Day for me.

P.S. In his official capacity as the president of the P and C, the Unelected Mayor met me at the station the previous Australia Day. He told me he would prefer it if I lived in a tent with the relieving stationmaster rather than at the pub. He reckoned it was a bad influence!

◎

From:
Audrey Ridley,
Bigga,
New South Wales

YESTERDAY MORNING I FOUND myself relating to so much of the discussion on your wonderful programme. It has prompted me to ask, 'Who are the real war heroes?'

The disappointing revelations coming out about international cricketers, the take-over of organised sport by big business, allied to the increasing interest being taken in the sacrifices of our troops in past wars has made me think of Eric, a friend for nearly forty years.

Eric grew up in Canterbury, where he and his three brothers participated enthusiastically and successfully in sport, particularly cricket and rugby league. All four went into the Army. We can only imagine what their mother suffered during those dark days. Her husband had fought and been wounded in the Battle for the Somme during World War One and did not see his first child until the baby was twelve months old when he was invalided home.

All four sons came back, but with disabilities that haunted them for the rest of their days. Eric died in 1997 but in his later years sport held no interest for him. He said he'd left the world of business behind. He wanted entertainment.

During the Borneo campaign Eric wrote poetry. As he put it, 'When no-one was actually trying to kill me.' His love of Australia, the beauty of nature and his hope to return home found expression in verses he considered insignificant but are treasured now by his widow.

Like others who knew the real meaning of war he never complained, but had enormous sympathy for others worse off than he was. He often expressed deep sorrow for the Korean veterans who were being treated at Concord where he spent so much time.

Of course, we of the older generation all knew an Eric, and we all know 'who the real heroes are'.

I THOUGHT THIS MIGHT be of interest. I am eighty-three years of age and I was a member of the Royal Navy unit bound for the Pacific on board the Dutch-manned troop carrier *New Amsterdam* in 1945. We celebrated as best as we could VE Day while in the Red Sea. Also on board were wounded Aussies, mostly RAAF, and many of them ex-prisoners-of-war. We were dumbfounded one morning to see these poor souls being wheeled out onto the foredeck by Dutch crew members, as we had at least eight to nine hours of sailing before reaching Fremantle. We were to learn later that the strong breeze from the east was like the 'Fremantle Doctor' blowing in reverse direction, and it carried the lovely odour of eucalyptus to Aussie nostrils, letting them lie and envisage the gum trees of their homeland, a thoughtful gesture by the Dutch captain.

I wonder how many of these wounded boys are now old guys like me!

From:
George Teare,
Ridgehaven,
South Australia

COULD YOU PLEASE ADDRESS the enclosed letter and seal it for me. It is to the man who rang in about the Boer War, his computer efforts and the Internet. I am eighty-two, so my knowledge of computers is nil.

I have told him about one of the best war memorials in the country, which is in Longwood (of course) and includes photocopies of a VC citation awarded in the Boer War to a local soldier.

Our district has been awarded three Victoria Crosses and three Military Medals. Not bad for a small country town, but not enough to make the Olympic torch procession stop, for they went through here without blinking an eye!

From:
Ildie Houston,
Longwood,
Victoria

Macca talks to Australians all over

At around the sixtieth anniversary of the first air raid on Darwin in World War II, I recalled my talks with some of the people that I've talked to who were there on that fateful day.

TED AMBROSIO: I was the main electrical supplier in Darwin and I was an ARP warden at the time. I was due to lock up to go to the post office to post my mail, but a couple of chaps came in for some goods. I said 'Hurry up, I've got to get to the post office,' and while I was giving them the stuff they needed we heard boom, crunch and ran outside. We looked up and you could see the planes coming out of the sun, with the dive-bombers and the heavy bombers and the Zeros coming in waves. They looked really beautiful. Then someone said, 'Look, they're dropping leaflets.' And I said, 'They're not bloody leaflets, they're bombs, mate.' (laughs). I reported to ARP headquarters and they said, 'Ted, there's an unexploded bomb outside the Taxation Office,' and I said 'I hope the bloody thing goes off!' I ran on towards the harbour where I could see they were trying to beach the *Neptuna* and the dive-bombers and Zeros were having a go and I watched the *Neptuna* go up. It was incredible. We had never been in this sort of situation

G'day
TED AMBROSIO and
MEL DUKE

before and we didn't realise that these damn things could kill you. You just dodged them, and if the Zeros saw you they'd have a go at you. I used to be one of the fastest runners in Australia—I used to do about 9.8 in the 100—and I reckon I was breaking nine. I could have beaten Lewis or anyone!

MEL DUKE: The crew had been up all night and the captain had told everybody to take it easy, so we were sitting up on the fo'c'sle near the anchor chain when somebody looked up and said, 'Oh, here comes the air cover that Roosevelt promised us.' And somebody else said, 'It's air cover, but it's not ours.' About that time the bombs started to fall and the captain gave word to heave up the anchor. A bomb hit for'ard and I was caught in the middle of it. The ship was going down by the stern and we took a couple more hits so there was nothing to do but go over the side. It was chaos, but everybody was trying to do the best they could. I'd like to say that we went to the War Memorial in Canberra and I was surprised that they'd removed all the memorabilia of Darwin. I was shocked, really, because that was the first time that Australia had been under attack.

Mel, who passed on last year, was on the 'USS Peary' which was bombed in Darwin harbour and ninety-one American sailors were killed. But a bloke who wasn't killed is Ben Greer. He's here from America with his wife, Betty, who is a little Aussie, and they're here for the sixtieth celebration. Have you been back to Australia before?

G'day . . .
BEN and
BETTY

BEN: Oh, yes, we come back every two or three years to visit Betty's relatives.

MACCA: You cad! You took her to America and she's dying to get back to Australia, I can tell. The only thing that's changed about her is her accent, but we can fix that.

BEN: Well, it's a great country and I consider it my second home, because I was here for about four years in navy supply depots in Melbourne and Sydney.

BETTY: We got married two years after the war. I was officially a fiancée so I had to wait until the war brides all got to America and then I was allowed to go over in 1947.

MACCA: You've done well for yourself, Ben.

BEN: Well, I think so. I couldn't find a better person to marry. I've got to say that, you know! (all laugh). We got married in Washington DC on August 29, 1947.

BETTY: I was from Randwick in Sydney and we met on a blind date at a Policemen's Ball at Sydney Town Hall in 1943, and every time we go back there just to see where we met.

BEN: The table's still there, where we sat!

MACCA: Were you in Australia for the duration of the war?

BEN: Yes, after the bombing in Darwin we stayed around up there for about two weeks at a US Army station, and they said 'If you want to eat you have to work,' so we spent two weeks digging trenches and unloading gasoline drums from the ships that got through. The last day we were there we unloaded rotten potatoes from Hong Kong, so it was a beautiful finish to Darwin.

MACCA: How old were you then? How long had you been in the Navy?

BEN: I was twenty-three and I'd joined the Navy when I finished my university courses.

MACCA: It's hard for someone like me who was born after the war to imagine what it must have been like. What is your recollection?

BEN: We'd been on a mission before the raid and we got back to Darwin about 6 a.m. It was just routine business on board ship and we weren't expecting anything, and all of a sudden I saw the bombs dropping on the harbour. The captain called for general quarters and we tried to get the ship going again but all of the power had been shut off, so we just had to sit there and take whatever the Japanese were going to give us. Five bombs hit the ship from the stern on up to the bow, and I found a life jacket and got off from the bow. The ship was on fire so the captain's mess cook and I paddled away and we were picked up by a lifeboat. I was so exhausted they had to use a boathook to get me out of the water. They took us to a little harbour boat—I believe it was the *Southern Cross*. We still have to thank the sailors on board for looking after us during that time, because they were really nice to us and took us ashore about 6 p.m. They wanted to take my life preserver but I said, 'No, this is mine, get off!', although I was hoping I wouldn't have to use it again. Even though bombs had been dropping all over the place they had a cake with candles and they were singing 'happy birthday' to a fellow by the name of Bluey, so it was quite unusual. I'd like to thank them all for rescuing me from the waters and Bluey in particular, because I enjoyed his birthday party.

MACCA: Betty, coming from Randwick, how did you adapt to living in America?

BETTY: I was very lucky because I went to Washington DC and we had our Australian and New Zealand embassies there. There was a large influx of war brides because a lot of their husbands were still in the military, attached to the Pentagon or somewhere, so I walked into a much nicer setup than a lot of Aussie girls. The embassy were very supportive and had an afternoon tea so that we could all meet and we still have our club in Washington called the Southern Cross Club for Australians and New Zealanders. I think there were about 10,000 marriages. The ambassador gave a talk one night and told us they had a very low rate of divorce. He thought one of the reasons was that it was too far to go home to mother! I think that might have had quite a lot to do with it.

MACCA: I thought you were going to say it was because Australian girls are so resilient and strong.

BETTY: Oh, they are.

BEN: I can vouch for that!

ON SUNDAY 17TH FEBRUARY you had a guest who was a survivor from *USS Peary* which was sunk in Darwin harbour on 19th February, 1942. I don't know if your guest knew that the *Peary* was raised in 1959, together with the tanker *British Petroleum* and three other vessels, and towed to Japan for scrap metal.

I am old enough to remember the *British Telegraph* newspaper headline, 'Darwin bombed—9 killed at post office', and have read as much as I could on this and the other sixty-two raids on Darwin, Wyndham, Broome and Katherine. A good reference on the subject is Douglas Lockwood's *Australia's Pearl Harbour—Darwin*. The Adelaide River War and Civil Cemeteries also contain a lot of information on their various memorials. Lockwood states that there were ten killed at the post office whilst the cemetery memorial lists nine staff (the postmaster Hurtle Bald, his wife Alice and daughter Iris, together with Emily Young, Eileen and Jean Mullin, Freda Stanisowski, Arch Halls and Arthur Wellington) killed in the raid, and Walter Rolling 'who was fatally injured'. This would explain the discrepancy with the headline 'nine killed'.

I hope this is interesting to you.

From:
Ray Walters,
Birkdale,
Queensland

From:
James (Bob) Haddock (9),
Gymea,
New South Wales

WHAT AUSTRALIA MEANS TO ME

What Australia means to me is hard for me to say,
Although I can feel it every year on Anzac Day.
It's sunset on the mountains, a gum tree growing tall,
Baby lambs playing and a kookaburra's call.
But it's more than just the beauty of a country proud and free,
It's a special kind of peace that the soldiers gave to me.

A soldier looks down from a photo, a proud look in his eye,
He joined up with the Lighthorse, he was prepared to die.
I wonder how he did it, left home and went to war,
Across the sea to Borneo, the horrors that he saw.
I hope one day I'll ride for him, I'll hold my head up high,
Then I'll see my country through great grandfather's eyes.

5

Gross National Happiness

I expect GNH is the sum total of all individual 'happiness'.
Sometimes hard to find, definitely hard to measure (just ask Treasury),
but we go looking for it on Sunday morning.

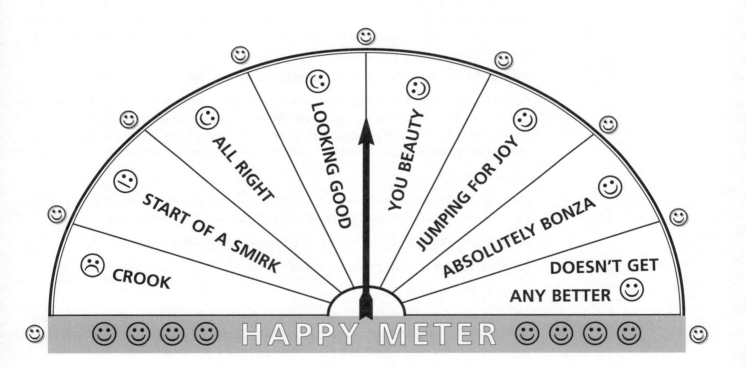

G'day . . .

JOHN HEAD and

COLLEEN KANE

MACCA: John and Colleen, good morning. You're trekkers, is that what I call you?

JOHN: Yes, travellers, trekkers.

MACCA: John's brought in a photo album of his. It's of Kilimanjaro and the first thing I saw was these little flowers that look just like everlasting daisies. That's on the foothills of Kilimanjaro, is it?

JOHN: As you approach the foothills. The vegetation is very interesting, some of it very reminiscent of home. A lot of African vegetation has similarities to ours and you can feel that at some point there was probably a connection.

MACCA: And they're everlastings—like ours?

JOHN: Yes, and there are millions of them. They're very beautiful.

MACCA: Isn't that amazing? It's almost disappointing to think that other people have them. I thought they were uniquely Australian. It's a fairly harsh climate, I suppose, at the foothills of Kilimanjaro.

JOHN: It is. You go up through rainforest at the base of the mountain and eventually you come out into a much more arid landscape with hardy plants, succulents similar to those in our own desert, and then you break through to a point where there's very little vegetation at all. It's quite like a moonscape.

MACCA: So, how long have you been trekking, and where do you go?

COLLEEN: Well, John's a great traveller. He's been trekking for years. While I was at uni he was marching around the world going everywhere. We have some friends we travel with quite frequently. We've been up to Bhutan, which is an extraordinary place. The people are fantastic and it's completely unspoilt because it doesn't have any technology, really, no television.

MACCA: Shock, horror!

JOHN: Yes, we like Bhutan because the King, who's a very well educated man but likes the traditional life, talks about *gross national happiness* rather than *gross national product.*

MACCA: GNH! That's great isn't it? You can't measure GNH, unfortunately.

JOHN: But you can see it on the people's faces.

MACCA: Where's Bhutan?

JOHN: It's sandwiched to the east of Nepal and south of Tibet. The people have a lot in common with the Tibetan people but, of course, they've been independent forever. They wear traditional costumes and they don't cut down a tree without permission. It's not a bureaucratic place but they know how to look after their country.

MACCA: Do they appear happy?

JOHN: Oh, yes, it was just the most marvellous experience.

COLLEEN: They're well educated, too. It's not like they keep them in the dark—there are big schooling programs there. It's fantastic.

MACCA: That's great. As my old friend, Gilbert, says, 'I practise contentment', and we all should try to do that. It's pretty hard, though, in the modern world.

COLLEEN: I think Australia's got a lot of gross national happiness, mostly.

JOHN: One of the great things about travelling to these places is that you see other ways of life. When I first started travelling I was rather an angry young man but as the years went by I've always been happy to come back to Australia. You see these wonderful places and it just reinforces what a great place we live in.

MACCA: You've been to Kilimanjaro and it's sort of adventure trekking, isn't it? There's lots of places in Australia where you can do that sort of thing, too; some are really dangerous and you're only a bottle of water away from starvation and death.

JOHN: A couple of years go we did the overland in Tasmania from Cradle Mountain to Lake St Claire and that's awesomely beautiful, as wild as any place you could go, and you realise there that even in January or February the weather can really catch you out. You're out there in your shorts and T-shirt and bingo, things can change in a moment.

MACCA: That's what happened to those poor snowboarders. The weather just turned unbelievably bad. I think most of us don't realise that Australia can be just like that—one minute beautiful and the next fifty degrees of heat or minus twenty.

COLLEEN: I think that's partly what's so beautiful about it, though. It's so harsh, and it tones you down, reminds you of who you are.

MACCA: Where were you on September 11?

JOHN: We were up on the side of Kilimanjaro, and had it not been for a couple of the Tanzanian porters carrying their transistor radios with them we probably wouldn't have known about it for more than a week. It was quite strange, really, to be so distant from such a huge event in the world.

MACCA: Just imagine what it was like in the fifteenth century!

COLLEEN: Well, they say you go up to the mountain and you come back changed, but we went up the mountain and we came back and the world had changed. It was bizarre.

I WAS INTERESTED IN your comment about the Australian of the Year and how many Australians are never recognised for what they have done. Ask the average Australian who wrote the national anthem and they would not know. Most people don't even know the words. Peter Dodds McCormick was a Scotsman who came to Australia in 1854 when he was twenty-one. He loved Australia so much his mother, sister and two brothers also came to live here. He was a lover of music, conducting choirs at large public gatherings, composer of songs, published author and poet. He was upset that Australia had no patriotic song and wrote 'Advance Australia Fair' in 1878. He knew Edmond Barton and Sir Henry Parkes.

I am amazed that Peter was a carpenter/joiner when he arrived in Australia and had a major career change, becoming a teacher at age twenty-eight. That would be an achievement today, so just imagine how difficult it would have been in those days.

Peter was married twice. His second wife was a distant relative of mine, hence my interest. She was a Dening and her parents lived at Five Dock. In Drummoyne there are streets named after the Dening family. His second marriage lasted fifty years.

Peter's first teaching appointment was at Stoney Creek (St Mary's). He also taught at Five Dock, Dowling Street, Surry Hills and other schools in Sydney before he resigned from teaching in 1884. He then gave religious instruction in schools for the Presbyterian Church. He left

From:
Jennifer Burgess,
Coorparoo,
Queensland

the royalties of 'Advance Australia' to the Presbyterian Church and this money continued for some years.

In the 1970s someone claimed 'Advance Australia Fair' was written by their family, who Peter was friendly with in the 1860s. From my research this seems unlikely as the father of that family died in 1866 and there is no music to support the claim. 'Advance Australia' was a slogan used through the last half of the nineteenth century, and advertisements to sell clothing and beer featured the words.

There is continuing controversy about our anthem, and people want to change it. Peter wrote it because he loved Australia. We all loved it when Julie Anthony sang it at the Sydney Olympics. Perhaps some day this man will be recognised for his legacy to Australia.

THE SPIRIT OF A COUNTRY TOWN

From:
Dorothy Watt,
Briagolong,
Victoria

There's a little town in Gippsland with a heart of solid gold,
The people there show how they care, their story should be told.
When early-comers staked their claims and aimed to settle down
The Avon flowed through virgin bush, which soon became a town.

A church was built and roads were formed, the council formed a plan
To build a bridge across the stream, and work there soon began.
The life was hard, rewards were few but Stratford forged ahead,
The land was tamed and sown and grazed, the population fed.

In times of trouble all pitched in to give a helping hand
And this is still the rule today, enthusiasm fanned.
When fire destroyed the work of years, townsfolk did not despair
They rushed to see how they could help, the damage to repair.

They did not whine, nor plead for help, but help came just the same,
Vic. Government announced a grant and many without name
Sent cheques or cash or volunteered to help clean up the mess
And bingo, raffles, balls and plays were planned to ease the stress.

And at the same time gather funds to help replace what's lost,
The vehicles, equipment, shed bought at enormous cost.
The local traders offered goods, the hotel lent its bus,
To take the old folk into town, for shopping without fuss.

And that is why a country town is friendlier than a city,
And if that spirit should be lost—'twould be an awful pity

Email from:
Rosie

I LISTENED WITH AMUSEMENT to your comments about leaf blowers. I am certain that I live in the area with the highest ratio of leaf blowers per head of population in Australia. When they get going the noise is akin to that heard on the tarmac at Sydney Airport. But I have another claim to fame—I live next door to the most leaf-intolerant person in the world. I know this because she uses her leaf-blower to actually blow the leaves off the trees. She used to beat them off the trees with a broom but has recently graduated to the mechanised version of autumn. Makes you sad doesn't it?

THE BACKYARD OF MY YOUTH

From:
Cynthia Hallam,
Springwood,
New South Wales

A dog sleeps at his kennel door,
And a rabbit in its hutch,
A cat sits watching fireflies,
While a hen nods on her clutch.

A castle in the sandpit stands
Protected by its moat,
And half an inch of water keeps
The sovereign's fleet afloat.

A moonlit clothesline shines like silk
A forgotten sock upon it,
And a hessian peg bag, hooked nearby,
Has painted daisies on it.

The grass is full of bindies
And a dandelion or two,
While a track, worn bare by anxious feet,
Signposts the outside loo.

Two boxes and a cricket bat
Await tomorrow's matches,
And where the bowler makes his run,
There's lots of dusty patches.

A swing moves gently in the breeze
Beside a rope-hung tyre,
And a pram and scooter lie beside
A roll of chicken wire.

And propped up on the paling fence
Is a red homemade canoe,
And even in the evening glow
It oozes derring-do.

There's a mulberry tree way down the back
With branches wide and low,
A sanctuary where two best friends
Who share their dreams can go.

A garden tap with a constant drip
And a puddle underneath,
A coiled red hose with a sprinkler for
Some summertime relief.

A mower lurks in the woodshed's gloom,
With the catcher hung outside
Near the cubby house with fruit-box walls
That the choko vine can't hide.

There's lettuce, beans and radishes,
And dahlias staked up tight,
While a sweet-pea trellis fragrance wafts
So gently through the night.

I smell it in my darkest hours,
For I've realised the truth,
That my favourite comfort zone is still,
The backyard of my youth.

◎

RATHER UNIQUELY, I GUESS, my Christian names are Donald Bradman. My father played A-grade cricket in the thirties and on occasion played against Don Bradman's team in City versus Country matches so I was named after the great man. This is just one occasion when I unavoidably became intertwined with the famous man's name.

Being a Justice of the Peace in New South Wales I am sometimes uncomfortable using my full name. Such as the time in the country town of West Wyalong where I carried out my local court responsibilities as a JP selecting locals to fill the jury listings. I was called urgently to the bench at the local Court of Petty Sessions to formally remand a prisoner to the next sitting of the circuit magistrate. The accused was a big, rough-looking bush character, handcuffed and escorted by two equally burly police officers. The man had been charged with murder and showed hostility to the whole proceedings. I could feel his deep resentment.

The police officers stood the prisoner up in the dock and the Clerk of the Court commenced the formalities. 'The West Wyalong Remand Court is now in session. The presiding Justice of the Peace is Donald Bradman Douglas ...' The accused let out a cry of protest. 'Hey, hang on a minute! Donald Bradman, it's not bloody fair. This bastard's gunna hit me over the fence for six!'

We all broke up with laughter. The huge smile on the prisoner's face revealed several missing front teeth. The Clerk somehow managed to restore decorum and, quite reluctantly, I also did my duty by holding the accused over in custody until the next regular sitting.

◎

From:
Donald B. Douglas,
Temora,
New South Wales

From:
Judi Cox,
Kenmore,
Queensland

We cockroaches are denigrated
Cursed and sadly underrated
Traits for which we're killed and baited
In sportsmen would be praised and feted

Our skills at leaping and at running
Swerving with such speed and cunning
Playing dead with legs a goner
Like some football prima donna

So what! Our playing field's your larder
We don't get paid, and we work harder
Than those blokes that bowl and bat
Oh no! there goes me mate! how's that!

We may not play much on TV
Or spill champagne for all to see
But we are winners, all the same
And in our own way, play the game

We've learnt our sports for a million years
And played upon your hate and fears
Left little calling cards behind
As are some footie blokes inclined

Roach rage is very 'in' this summer
Spray and baits make life a bummer
So now I wait with baited breath
Alas, an almost certain death

R.I.P.

Here lies a cockroach, who's coming back
To be a sportsman, without the flack
Then he can swear and spit and chew
And be a god-like hero too.

HAD LOVELY SURPRISE, a care package from my adopted Aussie folks in Western Australia, Audrey and Don Jackson. It contained Milo, Violet Crumbles, brown sugar (necessary for baking and unavailable here in Germany), and other vital necessities of life. No Vegemite—haven't adjusted to that! Having spent a year in Perth, I love the country of my heart.

Email from:
Erika Schulz

G'day, this is Macca

EILEEN: This is Eileen, and I live at Glenroy in Victoria. I'm ringing about a shearing story. We've got six sheep. We used to have about twenty but because of the drought we had to get rid of them. We decided to shear them ourselves and my husband bought a machine and it took us six hours to shear the first one and six weeks to shear the whole six. My husband bought the machine and sent me back to school to learn how to shear, so we rounded up our sheep into the yard and my son said, 'Here, Mum, it's all ready for you to go.'

MACCA: Would you class yourself as a gun shearer now?

EILEEN: Oh, definitely! I think I'd be better off shearing by hand.

MACCA: The sheep must have been traumatised. If they could have spoken they would have said 'Haven't you finished yet?'

EILEEN: Well, when I got onto the third one, three weeks later, I decided to shear it by hand and did a fantastic job because the sheep went to sleep.

MACCA: Spring used to be shearing time but I suppose you can shear any time, can't you?

 G'day
EILEEN

EILEEN: Yes, and usually we'd have a shearer in but with only six we decided to have a go ourselves.

MACCA: Would you do it again, or would you get the shearer back?

EILEEN: If they went to sleep I might have a go, but no, if we have a number of sheep we'll go back to our shearer.

EILEEN, THE GUN SHEARER

You know that times are hard dear, with this drought upon the land
We can't afford a shearer, you'll have to lend a hand.
Our flock is much diminished dear, there's six left in the yard.
You'll have to go to school and learn to shear, it can't be hard.

So Eileen took the challenge and learnt the shearer's art
Then she cleaned the shed out, prepared to make a start.
She told her loving husband, I want to do it right.
To save the sheep from heat stress I'll only shear at night.

She started up the donkey, prepared to strike a blow.
Then she put the blades in and blood began to flow.
Aghast, she screamed in terror this machinery's not right.
It's far too bloody noisy, and it gives the sheep a fright.
There has to be a better plan to get the clip away.
With value added pampering I'm sure our wool will pay.

The shed became a dormitory for tired and listless sheep
Eileen found it easier to shear them in their sleep.
While the sheep were dreaming of pastures wide and thick
Her scissors timed their snoring with a sharp and rhythmic click.

She gave each sheep the treatment, three weeks for every one,
Then the word passed around, Eileen was a gun.
Macca on the radio, was first to get the call,
He relayed it on the airwaves, it was heard by one and all.
It was heard in town and city, from Darwin down to Dover,
on Macca's show we're proud to call Australia All Over

With a lot of rearranging to that rural shearing shed,
she opened up a salon for only sheep well bred
The deal is by appointment, and the stands are always full
of sleeping sheep in curlers, and ribbons in their wool.
Eileen's wool emporium has become a household name
And Australia's riding proudly
on the echo of her fame.

And now out on the boards are ladies in demand,
clasping only scissors in their long and dainty hands.
Eileen looks around, to see the shampoo flow,
and is smiling at her husband who is raking in the dough.

From:
Gregory Dillon,
Zillmere,
Queensland

Snip go the scissors girls, snip, snip, snip
The aeroplane is coming in to take away the clip.
Stock exchange is ringing in, shares are on the go,
Keep the scissors snipping girls and watch our money grow.

WHEN YOU MENTIONED THE stars at night you made my day. My grandfather and my mother both loved the night sky. My grandfather's favourite was the Southern Cross. He is long gone now, and my mother, too. Myself, I am almost seventy-not-out, and I love all the stars. On a clear night I put out the house lights, sit out in my backyard, and watch the Southern Cross rise in the sky to a certain point where the cross moves across the sky to the west and it turns completely over. With the two pointers above the Southern Cross it sinks gracefully into the western horizon. A wonderful sight—certainly beats television viewing.

From:
Laurel Genrick,
Mackay,
Queensland

A POEM TO MOTHERS SEEN AT CABRINI
NURSING HOME, WESTMEAD, NEW SOUTH WALES

From:
Bob Moore,
North Rocks,
New South Wales

She was a child
Before we were born,
Now she is helpless
Alone and forlorn.
She was a bride
Long years ago
Walking in beauty
Cheeks all aglow.
She was a mother
Babes at her breast
Caring for others
Giving her best.
She is a woman
Salute her for this
Now she is withered
And hard to kiss.
Speak to her gently
And nurse her with pride
And now as she waits
To sail with the tide!
Ours are the last hands
She'll ever hold
Let her know love again
Now she is old.

◎

From:
Christine Meijer,
Point Vernon,
Queensland

GERRY, MY HUSBAND, IS THE Director of Anaesthetics and Intensive Care at Hervey Bay. He has taken two weeks leave to go as part of a team called SMILE to operate on the cleft lips and palates of Filipino children from two months right up to late teens. They have been several times before.

Some weeks before the team arrives a banner is stretched across the street informing the locals that they are coming. The people come from outlying areas with children who are terribly disfigured. Some of them have never been able to eat or drink without regurgitating their food, let alone being able to speak clearly and be understood. In some cases the parents have hidden them away from society.

The SMILE team takes all the medication, anaesthetic drugs, and theatre gear right down to the last swab. Some thirty-odd suitcases of equipment and supplies accompany them. Approval is required from both the Australian and Philippines authorities to take such equipment. The hospital they operate from is fairly well equipped, but the lack of good anaesthetic monitoring equipment has given my husband some very stressful days. They start work at about 8.30 a.m. and sometimes exceed twelve hours operating.

This is truly a humanitarian trip. I just thought you might be interested that there are people out there still plugging away at making the world a better place.

◎

From:
May Jones,
Noble Park,
Victoria

TO GILBERT

It was great to hear you, Gilbert,
On the radio today
And I'm sure that Ian's listeners
Will join me, when I say:
'Happy birthday, Mr Bennion—
It is so good to know
You remain a good role model
Though years may come and go.
You are so very positive
And happy. Furthermore—
It is really wonderful to know
You have reached *one hundred and four*!'
It's time to charge our glasses
To wish dear Gilbert well—
A really good Australian
Who has no parallel.

◎

From:
Judi Cox,
Kenmore,
Queensland

AS MENTIONED ON AAO, shopping trolleys are to be tracked and returned to their rightful owners.

As you know, I have close relationships with trolleys, and one of my acquaintances tells me the trolleys are very distressed at this news. It reckons that after years of service and metal stress they deserve to be left alone in their selected groups by creeks, under trees, lolling in comfort on top of traffic lights or on roofs with a view. It hadn't been easy to find these locations and they seriously hope the wheels fall off the whole idea. They are, however, prepared to co-operate with you if you set up a Macca Tracker Trolley programme where listeners from all over Australia report sightings. Those sighted will then hand themselves in.

What do you think?

I WAS WORKING IN a remote part of Cape York and came across two shopping trolleys on a very remote beach They were in Bathurst Head in Lakefield National Park, about ten hours by four-wheel drive from Cairns. One was exposed at low tide on a mudflat. Its partner was rusting away on the beach.

From:
Phil,
Cairns,
Queensland

Submitted by:
Jack Arnold,
Armidale,
New South Wales

GET IT WRITE

Aye have a spell ling chequer
It cam with my pea see
It plain lee marques four my revue
Miss steaks eye can knot sea

When aye strike the quays and right a word
I weight fore it two say
Weather I am rung or write
It tells me rite a weigh

As soon as a mist ache is maid
It nose bee for two lait
If en e thing I rote is floored
Its really, really grate

Iv run this rime write threw it
I yam shore yaw pleased too no
It 'tis let a perfect inn its whey
Mi chequer tolled me sew.

Sauce Un no en

THE PREAMBLE

This is a tale
Of a bloke from Coonamble
Who dropped into the pub
To write a preamble.

He pulled up a stool
And sat at the bar
Thinking deep thoughts
… But they didn't go far.

By instinct he knew
What was basically wrong
Why at this rate the whole thing
Would take ages too long.

From:
Ross Henry,
New Norfolk,
Tasmania

He needed his skills
To be in top gear
So he called to the barman
For Bundy and beer.

Thoughts soon took the form
Of phrases galore
As the tip of his biro
Moved across the A4

(The A4, of course, is not an expressway
But to draft a preamble, it's one of the best ways.)

We the people, he wrote
As he warmed to his task
Welcome all comers
But first you must ask.

You can't hit the beach
In any old boat
Then head for the scrub
That's just acting the goat!

Australians'll spot you
The scene won't look right
Whether you try it
By day or by night.

Did I hear someone say
Hang on matey—fair go
Trying to get to Australia
Takes most of our dough

OK—fair enough
Well, here's some advice
Listen with care
I won't say it twice.

You'll slip in—no worries
Between you and me
In morning peak hours
At Circular Quay.

More Bundy and beer
Cried our bloke from Coonamble
As he penned those last words
To his stirring preamble.

He'd given to mateship
A brand-new dimension
He'd have been the star turn
At the Canberra convention.

The short A4

Macca talks to Australians all over

MACCA: Ladies and gentlemen, Letty Katts, a great Australian songwriter and contributor to our culture. Letty's father came from Russia.

LETTY: My mother and father were interested in music. My mother had never learned but she played the piano by ear, and my father played in a balalaika orchestra in Russia. He came to Australia many years ago and we had musical evenings at home with my mother accompanying my father. I started music when I was about five and I always loved it. Then I found that I could play by ear, and I'd find a melody that I liked and I hoped I hadn't heard it before. This is one of the things that affects people who write music, because when you first start to write you think, Oh, I might have heard that somewhere, that's too good to be mine! So I started to write songs and the only way I could learn about it at that stage was to study sheet music and see what it consisted of—you know, so many bars this, so many bars that—and I worked it out for myself.

MACCA: We're playing your Hit Parade song, *A Town Like Alice.*

LETTY Thank you. I remember there was an Australia-wide contest for a popular song with a classical and a pop section so I sent *Never Never* into the pop section and it won. Nowadays the song is considered a ballad and it's usually sung by a choir, but then it was a pop song and it was on the Australian Hit Parade.

MACCA: Is songwriting addictive?

LETTY: Well, not exactly. I just have to have the idea, or find a tune on the piano and then it will set me off.

MACCA: I know you've written songs that have never seen the light of day, like The Sun Upon My Shoulders, which you've sent me, and there's probably some other little gems there as well.

LETTY: To be quite truthful, I sometimes go through all my own music at night and I think, what a shame that nobody heard this one or that one, because I rather like it, but it was very hard to get anything published. Because *Never Never* won a competition the publishers approached me and that made life a lot easier, of course. Then the ABC used to have orchestral music at night and I sent them *A Town Like Alice* and that was also very well received. I got letters from three different publishers wanting to publish it, so that went ahead and did quite well.

MACCA: When writing a song did the music come first or the words?

LETTY: Sometimes it was the music. I'd just be wandering around the keys and something would appeal to me, and then at other times I'd get just a sentence in my head and think, that'd make a good song, so I'd start fiddling around for rhymes with what I already had and a melody would be forming in my head. Later on I started to study music more seriously with Dr Lovelock, who was the head of the Conservatorium in Brisbane and was teaching privately.

MACCA: How many songs do you think you've written?

LETTY: I don't know, I suppose about fifty or maybe more. Some of them are only half finished. And there's always, of course, the musical show that I was going to write. I've got about eight songs for that.

MACCA: What was that about?

LETTY: Oh, well, that will never see the light of day because it's waited so long that the words of the songs are now hopelessly out of date. I didn't realise how things had changed until I started

G'day . . .

LETTY and STAN

looking through the music the other day and I thought, oh, nobody would sing that nowadays! To my knowledge *A Town Like Alice* was the first all-Australian song on the Hit Parade, so that was fun. The most fun of all, though, was one morning when I was out walking in an area where nobody knew me and there was a little boy sitting on a fence whistling *A Town Like Alice*. That was really very enjoyable, very nice.

MACCA: This is Stan Mellick, a great Australian who's spent his life serving Australia and helping other people. He's married to Letty Katts.

STAN: My father married an Irish girl so I was born in Londonderry, Northern Ireland and at the age of three months they exported me as a security risk! I grew up and was educated in Brisbane and was always interested in Australian literature. My father instilled in us a love of the Australian bush. Every school holidays we'd go overland, and I really mean 'overland,' in an old Overland car. We'd sleep in the bush, we'd wake up in the morning, we'd see the frost on the ground, we'd see the kangaroos and the flocks of emus, and Dad would be boiling the billy. He married us kids to the land irretrievably and forever. Night time was the time I liked the most. You'd climb into your blanket and you'd look up and see the tips of gum leaves dancing in the heatwaves coming up from the fire, and when the fire died down there was the velvety-dark feel of the night sky, and embedded in this a myriad of twinkling lights. People who've camped in the bush will know what I'm talking about.

JOAN: Hello, it's Joan Blake here.

MACCA: Joan Blake, the singer?

JOAN: That's right! I'm calling from Melbourne

MACCA: Ladies and gentlemen, if you've just got up, I played a song earlier this morning which is called *Say a Prayer for the Boys Over There*.

JOAN: That's right, with George Trevare and his orchestra, of which your father was a member.

MACCA: Yes, he was one of the Trevares. Do you still sing, Joan?

JOAN: Occasionally at parties when they can't shut me up.

MACCA: Joan, it's a lovely song, and I think they released an album of yours.

JOAN: Yes, I've got it all on CD now, thank goodness. Everything that Trevare ever did is out on CD, which is wonderful.

MACCA: He was quite a bloke, wasn't he? You met him, obviously.

JOAN: Oh, yes, but not socially. I was only a kid then, about eighteen. Those songs were recorded during the war out at Homebush.

MACCA: I remember Dad telling me about being out there at EMI at Homebush. That's all gone now.

JOAN: Well, of course, isn't everything?

MACCA: Yes. So, Joan, are you still involved in music in any way?

JOAN: Oh, yes, I listen to a lot of music and I belong to one of the websites here in Melbourne, *Australian Dance Bands*, and I'm still doing computer work. I'm 78 and a great-grandmother now.

G'day

JOAN BLAKE

MACCA: Can you take us back to those times during the war when everything was very patriotic. That was originally an American song, wasn't it, and we changed the words to suit Australia.

JOAN: I think so. We got the music one Monday morning and had to perform it the next Monday morning. Nobody consulted you about what key you'd like it in, especially George. You'd start to record it at 9 a.m.—can you imagine what your voice would be like at that time?

MACCA: It'd be hard. It's like asking a trumpet player to play at that hour.

JOAN: Well, your father was a trombone player and that's what he had to do.

MACCA: They were interesting times, Joan. How do you look back on that time?

JOAN: With a great deal of pleasure and joy and thinking how lucky I was, and I've got something to play to my grandchildren and my great-grandchildren.

MACCA: It's lovely stuff. Somebody was telling me that you do voice-overs and things, as well.

JOAN: Yes, when they want on old Aussie female.

MACCA: I remember my Dad telling me that when you were recording there was only one take. If you mucked it up you had to do the whole thing again.

JOAN: Exactly, particularly with a song called *Johnny Zero*. I can't remember why, but we had to do it eleven times.

MACCA: When we come down to Melbourne to do the program you'll have to come in, Joan, and maybe you can sing us a song.

JOAN: If the voice is still working I'd love that.

◎

Macca talks to Australians all over

MACCA: I'm with John and Glenys Wolfe. We're here at Harold Park in Sydney and they're the owners of a wonderful horse, Shakamaker.* It must give you a big thrill when you hear people yelling that and going nuts!

JOHN: 'Shaka—Come on, Shaka'. It's a wonderful feeling, Ian, and tonight the Sydney people really responded well for us.

MACCA: John, tell me about yourself. Where are you from?

JOHN: Originally from Horsham, then Ballarat, and we moved to Melbourne in the early sixties. I got interested in harness racing in Horsham about sixteen years ago and have been dabbling in it ever since. Shaka is by far the best horse we've ever had that's any good. The thing is, Ian, that once you get a horse like Shaka you think that maybe you can get another one, but I guess what you end up doing is investing in the industry. You buy yearlings and you give them a chance and it's just as pleasing to win a $4,000 race at Oodnadatta as it is to win the Miracle Mile at Harold Park.

MACCA: I don't think they've got trots at Oodnadatta but I know what you mean.

JOHN: That's probably right. But we used to go a fair bit at Horsham and that's what started me

G'day . . .
JOHN and GLENYS

in it and we've raced at Horsham and Hamilton and Ballarat. Recently Shaka won the Ballarat Cup, which was a great thing for us because Glenys comes from Ballarat and we promised we'd go back and try to win it and we did this year. It was great.

MACCA: Glenys, are you a reluctant trotter, or do you enjoy it?

GLENYS: I love it just as much. I'm just so proud of what Shaka does and it's such a wonderful feeling. It's amazing how you feel, having such a great horse. As John just said, we probably won't ever again have a horse as good as Shaka, but you never know—we keep trying! He's given us such a big thrill. It's been amazing.

JOHN: No one else wanted him at the yearling sales and it was just like, 'I'll have a punt on this one,' and we bought him for $3,500. But I don't think that's the big thing, because you can pay $3,500 or you can pay $35,000 and you never ever know when you're going to have a good horse. It's just a big gamble and we're a bit like that. I enjoy doing it and if it's wrong, it's wrong, and if it's right sometimes it's good.

MACCA: It's a lot of fun, obviously, for both of you.

JOHN: Oh, we've had a magnificent time. Shaka's run in every state and the people around Australia are absolutely marvellous. And tonight, to break the track record at Harold Park in the first event was absolutely magnificent.

JOHN: When will this be on the air so I can tell my family to listen?

MACCA: Well, you're on now!

*Shakamaker retired after the 2003 Inter-Dominion in New Zealand

G'day . . .
FATHER BRIAN
GLASHEEN

MACCA: I'm talking to Father Brian Glasheen. They call you 'the pacing priest'—is that right?

BRIAN: That's right, Ian.

BRIAN: I'm the parish priest of Bacchus Marsh.

MACCA: Well, first of all, how did you become a priest?

BRIAN: I came from a family of practising Catholics, and I suppose some of my role models were great priests. I worked for eight years as a company secretary and a civil engineer before I studied for the priesthood

MACCA: 'The pacing priest'?

BRIAN: My family's been in trotting or harness racing continuously for 120 years. My grandfather was a professional trainer/driver and had his first winner in about 1880. He drove half a dozen winners within a month of his death in 1946. He had three sons and they were all hobby trainers and drivers and I was brought up with the sport and just loved it, so I had a driver's licence before I left school.

MACCA: And does that sit all right with the priesthood?

BRIAN: A Jesuit came to the seminary during our training, and he said 'Any sort of knowledge in any field will be of use to you as a priest,' and that's true. Lots of people are in harness racing and I don't find it in any way a conflict. In fact, it's often a good way of meeting people. The pastor, I suppose, is one who looks after the sheep and my sheep are the people in my parish, but a lot of people in harness racing use me as a priest too.

MACCA: Travelling around I meet a lot of priests who listen on Sunday morning. Do you happen to listen?

BRIAN: I listen to your show either before or after my shower on Sunday morning and often when I'm driving to a little church we have in the bush about twenty kilometres from Bacchus Marsh.

MACCA: Well, I suppose if you're called 'the pacing priest' you should give us a tip for the Inter-Dominion. It's a great time, isn't it, all the champions together.

BRIAN: Yes, it's like the Melbourne Cup for us. People from all over Australasia come together and the Inter-Dominion means between the Dominion of New Zealand and the Dominion of Australia, and it's been going for over fifty years.

MACCA: Is it hard to be a priest these days?

BRIAN: Oh, I think that wherever you've got people there's a need for priests because people need to be cared for, and not only in the context of baptism, birth, marriages, death, reconciliation or counselling. I think the role is just as important as it's ever been. People have a need for priests and we're delighted to be able to serve them.

MACCA: And priests have a need for people.

BRIAN: Of course. It's all about relationships and it's a privilege to be able to meet people, not only on the exterior but inside their shell. It's a privilege to be a priest.

ANTHONY: Hello Macca, it's Anthony Costello at Middlemount I'm a coalminer.

MACCA: Where's Middlemount?

ANTHONY: Two and a half hours inland of Rockhampton in Central Queensland in the Bowen Basin. I've just come out from doing a twelve-hour shift in the colliery.

 G'day
ANTHONY COSTELLO

MACCA: Tell us all about it, Anthony.

ANTHONY: I've been coal mining now for sixteen years and I'm currently working for SBD Services. We go probably about 200 feet underground and six and a half kilometres in.

MACCA: Did that take much getting used to? Do you like it?

ANTHONY: The first time I went underground it was very strange. I had a light on my head and it was very dark and it took a little bit of getting used to, but once you get it into your blood ... well, as I said, I've been there for sixteen years now. I really enjoy coalmining.

MACCA: It must be a bit like working in a submarine, you either get used to it or you get out.

ANTHONY: Well, I think the money helps us stay in the business, Macca. It's extremely good pay but you work for it and you suck a little bit of dust. Last night we were stone dusting, putting calcium lime on the coal to stop friction ignition and to keep the pit from going up.

MACCA: How deep is the pit you work in?

ANTHONY: We're in about six kilometres. We go through an incline shaft down through a portal off a high wall and we're about 200–250 metres underground so it's a fair haul if there was something wrong and you wanted to walk out. This is one of the larger and older pits in the Basin.

MACCA: Anthony, last weekend in Cessnock there was a commemoration service.

ANTHONY: That was for the lost miners. If you ever go through Cessnock there's a big plaque there. Years ago that's where they had all the big strikes and the big fights and a lot of people lost their lives in that area, Macca. It's got a very interesting history.

MACCA: In about a month's time I hope to be going down to Mount Kembla, where in 1902 they lost ninety-six people. It's called the Mount Kembla mining disaster, but that's happened everywhere. Do miners think that one mine is more dangerous than another? Is that in the back of your mind all the time?

ANTHONY: Years ago it probably would have been, Macca, but today we've got so much technology and a lot of government rules and regulations that cover you, so it's become a lot safer. But you look after yourself and you do the right thing and you'll come out of it.

MACCA: I'm looking forward to doing our story down at Mt Kembla.

ANTHONY: You'll meet some of the most colourful men you will ever see in your life, Macca.

MACCA: After they come up from the mine covered with coal dust, you mean?

G'day
BAZZA

BAZZA: I wanted to talk to you about the Harbour Tunnel. I mentioned the last time I spoke to you that it isn't actually a tunnel. Eight sections of it were made in Port Kembla and towed up there. The company that I work for, Leightons, dug a casting basin, like a big dry dock, and when the sections were cast they towed them up to Sydney where the floor of the Harbour had been dredged and prepared, lined them up and sank them into position.

MACCA: Engineers are pretty clever people, aren't they?

BAZZA: Yes, they are. So now, when you drive through the Harbour Tunnel, remember that it was made in Port Kembla.

MACCA: I never go through the Harbour Tunnel—I get claustrophobic. I still go over the Bridge!

G'day
EVE

EVE: This is Eve, an elder of the Gubbi Gubbi people of the Sunshine Coast in Queensland, and I wanted to share some good news with you. Our country extends from just north of Brisbane right up to Maryborough and takes in the Glasshouse Mountains, which are our very special, holy mountains. We've been meeting in Brisbane, and for the first time in the history of Queensland the government has offered to return some bora rings to our people. All the clans surrounding the Gubbi Gubbi people have got together and are accepting those bora rings. It's great!

MACCA: Tell people what bora rings are.

EVE: It's a ring where indigenous people have a lot of celebrations—ceremonies and corroborees and sometimes initiations—and it's also what you might call a council ring, like a boardroom, where people sit around and discuss serious things as well as celebrations. There are several along the coast but these are very important ones. One's near Noosa and one's closer to Brisbane, near Bribie Island. So all the clans have agreed to accept our custodianship of these for the future. It's nice to know that the Queensland government, which hasn't been famous in the past for its treatment of indigenous people, is going to hand back some things to us. There's a lot of paperwork to be gone through yet, but we're all very happy.

MACCA: Eve, that's great news. Keep in touch, won't you.

GARY: Gary Nairne here, federal member for Eden Monaro. It's nice to talk to you on the last day of the millennium and I'm looking forward to tomorrow, the first day of the new millennium, January 1, 2001.

MACCA: Now, Gary, you've got some interesting facts and figures because in a former life, before you became a politician, you were a surveyor.

GARY Yes, I spent twenty-five years surveying, fifteen of them up in the Northern Territory and about three years overseas. Using that survey experience we did some calculations on determining exactly where on the Australian mainland you will see the first dawn of the new millennium. There's been some debate about this for many years. I think the people in northern New South Wales have always claimed it would be Mt Warning.

MACCA: But you've got a different story.

GARY: Yes, it's scientifically possible to determine exactly what the real situation is. I must stress that I'm speaking of the mainland, because actually down in Tasmania they beat us all, but on the mainland the first dawn will be seen on top of Mt Imlay, down south of Eden, which actually beats Mt Warning by about eight minutes, a fair slice of time.

MACCA: I remember some people telling me that they were going to climb Mt Warning one New Year's Eve and ring in the dawn up there. They said it was quite a climb and so many people wanted to do it that they had to rope it off or something. Does the same thing happen on Mt Imlay?

GARY: No. I'd originally thought that we'd try to be up Mt Imlay for the dawn, but when I went there with the National Parks people I realised it's a pretty decent sort of climb and I decided it really wasn't all that practical to try to do it safely. You'd have to be up well before dark on the night before and there isn't really an area suitable for camping overnight. It's very rocky and pointed and really quite unsafe, so it's the sort of thing that should be done in a well-planned climb during the day.

MACCA: Do you know the time in Tasmania?

GARY: Down in Tassie, dawn on Cape Barren Island will come at the same time as Mt Imlay, but on Tasman Island it will be 4.31 EST and 5.31 daylight saving time, so it's a few minutes ahead.

MACCA: Gary, it's interesting that last year lots of people hopped on the new century/millennium bandwagon but as this year's gone further along I've noticed that they're coming back and quietly expressing the view that the millennium century starts tomorrow and today is the last day.

GARY: It used to irritate me and I had many an argument about it. As far as I was concerned there was actually nothing to argue. The millennium doesn't start until January 1, 2001, and anybody who gave any sort of mathematical thought to it would have to come to that conclusion.

MACCA: And you're a surveyor, and surveyors think like that, don't they?

GARY: Well, we get a bit finicky about this sort of thing, I suppose. I think it's part of our training.

Back in 1991 I was at the Theatre Royal in Hobart doing a concert. Murray Ling was up on the third tier so I ran up with my radio mike and had a talk to him. Sadly, he passed away in 2002, but this is Murray's story about the night a boat hit the Tasman Bridge and a whole arch disappeared.

MURRAY: We parked the EK Holden with our two boys in it on the edge of the bridge the night she broke. We were just about coming on to the bridge when suddenly in the drizzle the lights

☎ G'day
GARY

☎ G'day
MURRAY

went out. I thought, oh, it's a blackout. Our two eldest girls were at home and I thought we'd better hurry to get there. We were doing fifty going up the bridge and I looked over and saw the lights of Lindisfarne on and I thought it was funny that there was no blackout there. It wasn't until we got right to the crest that you could see the lights were still on everywhere else and I realised that it must be the bridge and there must be something wrong. I braked just as a large yellow car flashed past me and disappeared with a thump and we pulled up within inches of the edge. My wife said, 'Back up!', and I saw lights behind us, and when you've got trouble stopping you can bet that behind you they've got trouble stopping, too, so I said 'Get out'. She jumped out where the passenger rail was and tried to lift the five-year-old over, and I jumped out in the middle of the road and tried to stop traffic. As she was lifting his brother over the rail our eleven-year-old boy said to her, 'There's nothing there except a lot of water.' The water mains broke behind the car and two of them were gushing. My wife ran up the bridge with the two boys and tried to stop traffic and a lot of cars turned round and went back but others kept coming and one ran into the back of mine and knocked the front wheels over the edge. I waved furiously at another one and he just drove straight around me and over the edge. Within two or three days at least sixteen people had contacted us and thanked us for saving their lives. A big Continental bus wouldn't stop and I got alongside him and said, 'The bridge has gone, there's a span missing, get off!', and he managed to turn it around like a Mini Minor. (laughs).

MACCA: How long ago was that?

MURRAY: That was on 5th January 1975.

MACCA: A day you'll never forget, I'll bet.

◎

From:
Robyn Reid and
Matthew Taylor,
no fixed address

MY FRIEND MATTHEW AND I are travelling this beautiful country of ours on horseback, followed by two ever-patient pack donkeys who carry all our needs and desires, which are few. It is not often that we know the day, the date or time for that matter, but when we do realise it is Sunday we make an effort to listen to at least some of the programme. A few Sundays ago, just after we'd broken camp from a tiny township called Muskett Flat in south-east Queensland, we realised what day it was and Matthew had a brainwave. We dug out our small shortwave radio, fiddled with the dial until we found you, dropped you into a canvas bucket which hangs amongst our things on one of the donkeys, and proceeded along a gravel road. Unfortunately, by the time you made your way out of the canvas bucket and into the din of sixteen hooves clip-clopping along the gravel, we could only catch a word or two or hear the faint melody of a tune. You also distracted the donkeys from keeping up with us. At times you were as far back as thirty metres whilst they tried to make up their mind as to whether or not they liked what you had to say.

6

◎ *. . . and on the Road* ◎

Many of us cannot travel due to work and/or family commitments,
but come Sunday morning we can all be 'on the wallaby'.
FROM: *Catherine (Herring) Williams*, Hornsby Heights, New South Wales

Macca talks to Australians all over at Geraldton, Western Australia

G'day . . .

JOAN WALSH-SMITH
and
CHARLES SMITH

We're on top of Mount Scott at the site of the memorial to HMAS *Sydney*. The people who designed it are here, Joan Walsh-Smith and Charles Smith.

MACCA: Do I detect an Irish lilt, Charles?

CHARLES: You're very observant at this hour in the morning!

MACCA: Tell us about this memorial.

CHARLES: Well, we were approached about three years ago by the Rotary people of Geraldton who were looking to memorialise the *Sydney*. The whole concept was to create a precinct, a space, to try to fill the emptiness left by the great mystery surrounding the total loss of all men and the ship—no wreckage, nothing. I think of the people they left behind; they never had anywhere to go or anywhere to lay wreaths, so this is, in a sense, a sort of closure.

MACCA: It's a dome with six hundred and forty-five seagulls connected wingtip to wingtip, representing the men who were lost, and you can see it from almost anywhere in Geraldton. I'm sure you can see it out to sea as well. Joan, tell us the seagull story.

JOAN: It was really the heart of the whole complex when we started work. When we talked to the committee they told us about the incredible thing that happened on the night they had the dedication of the site. It was at sunset, because the ship went down at sunset, and just at the minute's silence when the Last Post was played, a flock of silver gulls flew in total silence over the assembled crowd. It was amazing because seagulls are always such noisy creatures. So the seed was in our mind from that story and we now call it our 'dome of souls'. We've been back here many times and I think our souls, too, will always be wandering around here.

G'day . . .

JESSIE
CUNNINGTON

Jessie Cunnington is here. Tell us your story, Jessie.

JESSIE: I'm a Victorian but I went to live in Toronto, Canada, in 1976 and have been there ever since, with yearly trips back to Australia. I heard about the memorial to the *Sydney* quite by accident and decided I had to come, do, die or bust. I needed to come. My father was on the *Sydney* and my mother died last year, having spent all these years expecting to see him walk around the corner. I'm here for her. He was on the *Canberra* first and then the *Hobart*, then he was transferred to the *Sydney* not long before she sailed. Someone became ill and he was the replacement.

MACCA: So the lady watching and waiting on the sculpture—was that your mother for the rest of her life?

JESSIE: Yes, especially for the first ten years. She was always talking about him being a prisoner of war and sure to come back. His mother was forty when he was born, an only child, and when I was ten I looked very much like him and every time she looked at me she burst into tears. So it was traumatic for her, just seeing me, because by that time she was quite old. It was a hard time, and I just had to come today. I'm most impressed with the memorial and with the people here who did such an incredible amount of hard work for their dream and their vision. It's absolutely exquisite and I thank them.

MACCA: I'm talking to Ray Parkin, who is the author of a book about the *Endeavour* and also *Wartime Trilogy*. Ray is now ninety-one and lives in Melbourne. He was on board HMAS *Perth* in Sydney Harbour when he heard the news about *Sydney*.

RAY: We'd just come back from the Mediterranean and had bomb damage, so we were refitting in dock alongside Garden Island. A very good mate of mine was the fleet signal officer and he came quietly alongside me and said, '*Sydney*'s gone.'

MACCA: How did the news affect the people on board your ship?

RAY: Well, I suppose one of the surprising things was that a light cruiser could be knocked off by a merchant ship raider. It was a bit of a shock as she was one of the family and when part of the family goes it has an effect on you.

MACCA: It happened to you on the *Perth* a year later, didn't it?

RAY: Yes, less than a year later. We'd only just got refitted when we were sent up to Java and we didn't come back.

MACCA: I know you were involved in finding where the *Perth* lay in the Sunda Straits. What do you think of the attempts to find where the *Sydney* lies?

RAY: I think it's futile. *Perth* sunk fairly close to shore and we had some idea of the approximate position because it was a night action and the navigator was keeping track of the ship. But the ocean's too big and too little is known about where the *Sydney* may be to be able to find her. She's a mystery, one of those unsolved things—with not a murmur from the whole ship's company the ship just vanished. How does that happen? In an emergency they would be preparing to abandon ship but there's no evidence at all of that taking place. The last seen of her was by crew on the *Kormoran*, the ship she sank and that sank her. She was moving westward, on fire, and didn't seem to be under control at all.

MACCA: Everyone loves a mystery, I suppose.

RAY: Oh, well, people aren't satisfied until they've solved a mystery, but in my opinion she's gone. The blokes that went with her went down. That's their tomb and resting place. Why disturb them?

MACCA: Here's Steve Lodge, who runs the Geraldton fish markets. How long have you lived in Geraldton?

STEVE: For twenty-seven years. I went into the fish business about eighteen years ago. We make ice as well. We started up to service the cray factories and now we're the biggest ice-maker in Western Australia.

MACCA: I went to the ice factory yesterday and I now have much greater respect for people like Shackleton and Mawson, because within thirty seconds we were just about frozen. I've never wanted to climb Mount Everest because I think there's nothing worse than being cold all the time. I believe you don't have electronic locks on the doors.

STEVE: We don't have auto doors on the freezers for safety reasons. Lee, that friend you brought

G'day . . .
RAY PARKIN

G'day . . .
STEVE LODGE

with you said, 'Don't worry about Macca. He'll feel cold because he's only got a heart the size of a pea!'

MACCA: Steve's known for his jokes! He's trying them out on you all—if you laugh he's going on the road. Steve, I'm told that a lot of your ice goes out into mining camps. Why's this?

STEVE: Instead of water they put ice into the concrete and that keeps the heat of the concrete down so that when poured it doesn't cure as fast and you don't get cracking.

MACCA: It's amazing to think of all those semi loads of ice going out all over Western Australia from here.

STEVE: The thing with ice is that it turns back into water. It's a very environmentally friendly product and within the industry everyone calls it 'white gold'.

Macca talks all over at Ubobo, Queensland

UBOBO: Township, island and railway siding in Calliope Shire; derived from 'dhabubo' meaning 'rough, scrubby country.' (*Aboriginal Place Names of Southern Queensland* by Rod Milne.)

UBOBO ALL OVER

Every man and his dog will be heading for Ubobo
For they've heard that Macca will be there
Broadcasting his programme 'Australia All Over'
Yes, Ubobo's going on the air!

How I wish I too could be heading for Ubobo
I'd give anything to meet Macca there
But instead I'll have to be satisfied
To get to know Ubobo over the air!

To Macca, as you and your team are heading for Ubobo
I'll be thinking of you and I'll say a little prayer
That your programme in Ubobo will be extra special
As you meet all kinds of characters there!

From: Carole McGuffog, Forster, New South Wales

G'day . . .
MARGUERITE

MACCA: This is sweet Marguerite. When I first came through Ubobo in 1987 the name intrigued me, and some time later Marguerite rang up and told me Telstra was going to take their phone box away because it wasn't paying. Can you believe it? Marguerite, tell us how it all started. It's really about small towns, I suppose.

MARGUERITE: We were never actually informed that the phone box was going to be removed. There was just a little sign inside the box. We thought they were just going to move it across the road because we couldn't believe they'd take it out of the town. We contacted Telstra, who told us that it wasn't making any money so it had to go, so we phoned you and the papers and it snowballed from there. The frightening thing was that we discovered it wasn't just Ubobo; every little place in Australia was going to be affected, and that's why it became such a big issue. It was unbelievable that small rural places were going to lose their only form of telecommunication. But because of your coverage and the community getting behind the issue, Telstra changed their whole policy and the phone boxes remained throughout Australia.

MACCA: I think that big companies don't understand that they're part of the community.

MARGUERITE: Everyone's aware that telephone companies do make a lot more money with mobile phones, but we have no mobile coverage here.

MACCA: So there won't be another assault on your phone box.

MARGUERITE: I don't think they'd be game, do you?

GIL: My name's Gil Irwin and I used to be a butcher in Ubobo. I came back here looking for the rest of my finger!

MACCA: And you did that butchering? What did you do when you cut your finger off—scream?

GIL: Oh, it was all right. It never went into the mince. The foreman just said, 'Get that apron over it, there's enough blood on the meat now!'

G'day . . .
GIL IRWIN

UBOBO LAMENT

His Honour, Mister Justice Gobbo,
Said to a dog named Hobo,
'For not chasing foxes
And messing phone-boxes
You're banished for life from Ubobo.'

From:
Paul Neville

MACCA: Where are you from, Graham?

GRAHAM: We started out in Perth and we've been on the road for five years, just travelling around, signwriting. It pays enough to keep the wheels going round.

MACCA: So you're a gypsy?

GRAHAM: We sold the house, kicked the kids out, bought an old bus and hit the road and I guess we'll keep doing it until we drop dead.

G'day . . .
GRAHAM

I've never been to Ubobo
But it's definitely on the list,
For when we travel the wallaby
Either this year, or maybe next.
We'll take the Burnett Highway

From:
Cathy Ylias,
Mylneford,
New South Wales

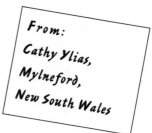

And hang a right at Monto,
Then travel the pretty back roads
To the famous town of Ubobo.
The first thing I will look for
When we arrive in town,
Is that very famous phone-box
Known the whole nation 'round.
I'll make sure that it's a Sunday
So I can make a call,
I'll reverse the charges to Macca
And tell him about it all.
It will be a day I'll look forward to
And one I'll never forget,
As I become part of the program
That I really love the best.
So while I won't be there this weekend
For your 'Back to Ubobo' show,
I'll listen in from home
And learn all there is to know.
So when I do finally get there
I'll know just where to go,
So can call 'Australia All Over'
From the phone-box at Ubobo.

AN ODE TO UBOBO

There was a young man from Obobo,
Who blew long and loud on his oboe,
'Keep that up' said his Mum
'You'll be out on your bum
To tramp the road like a hobo.'

Macca talks to Australians all over at
Daly River, Northern Territory

G'day . . .

PETER

MACCA: Peter, tell me about your brush with a crocodile.

PETER: About ten years ago we were camped on a fairly high bank about 200 kilometres from here, going west to our family's traditional homeland. It was a really bad day because Essendon got beaten by Collingwood! About eleven o'clock at night a croc came out of the creek and up onto the bank. Mum heard it and woke us up. The croc ran the last four or five metres, straight through the side of the tent.

MACCA: They're quick, aren't they?

PETER: Very quick. Mum pushed Dad to one side and the croc grabbed her right across her body and they landed in front of me. I grabbed it by the head and stuck my fingers in its eyes. It whirled around and dropped Mum to the ground. The croc stayed for a minute and we wondered what we were going to do if it came back, but fortunately it went back to the creek. It took us an hour to get Mum back to a homeland outstation where we rang Air Med. She spent about two weeks in ICU.

MACCA: You got a bravery award, didn't you?

PETER: Yes, an Australian bravery medal, and Mum did, too.

MACCA: Why did you go for its eyes? Were you thinking rationally?

PETER: My father was a professional croc shooter and knows crocodiles. He always told us to go for its eyes. There's another part but that was a bit too far away!

HARRY: Harry Philips here, from Canberra. I thought I'd give you a ring because you're at Daly River and you might be interested to know that during the war, in 1942, the B platoon of the Second Fourth Independent Company was stationed at Daly River at the Crossing. Our company was spread across the Northern Territory and we used to patrol the river because they thought the Japanese might use it to bypass Darwin. We set up observation posts on platforms because of the crocodiles, big fellers they were. The mosquitoes were nearly as big—we reckoned we could hear them changing gear as they approached! Our headquarters was at the Crossing under a big banyan tree, which I believe has since been destroyed by flood. The Daly's a marvellous river, tidal as you probably know, and when there was a full moon we'd get a bore of water anything up to six feet high when the tide came in.

 G'day
HARRY PHILIPS

MACCA: Here's Dick Perry. Where are you from, Dick?

DICK: We've got a property on the western bank of the Daly. I came up thirty years ago to a conference in Darwin, fell in love with the temperature and the people, and so eight years ago we bought a property. You hear lots of stories about crocodiles and most people say that saltwater crocodiles only get up as far as the Daly River Crossing. But that's not right. I once came down from Katherine in a canoe after big floods and there were monstrous crocs. To see people in the water upstream of the Crossing is frightening. On that same trip I saw a freshwater shark about six or seven feet long and as thick as a man, an unbelievable size. I believe that this species of freshwater shark is only found in the Daly and the Swan River in Western Australia. So whatever you do, don't go swimming there because you've not only got the crocodiles to worry about but sharks as well!

G'day . . .
DICK PERRY

MACCA: When Ted Egan heard we were coming to the Daly River he told me to talk to Miriam Rose, and here she is. They say you're the community leader here.

MIRIAM: I'm just a layperson, but a lot of people think I'm a nun although I'm married with a sixteen-year-old boy! You went up the river in a boat yesterday with my husband, Ken, and when you asked him if he knew me he was going to say, 'Oh, yes, I've slept with her a couple of times!'

MACCA: That trip up the river was great. Ken's lived here for a long time and he told me about

G'day . . .
MIRIAM

all the things that have happened and the changes to the area. Sitting next to Miriam is Paul, who manages a property here, Elizabeth Downs. Paul, you're a chopper pilot. Tell everybody about prickly acacia.

PAUL: Well, it's one of those noxious little weeds that seem to get into places where you don't want them. It's starting to cover the flood plain area that a lot of Aboriginal people use for traditional hunting. We've got a Landcare group going now and we're going to try to open up some of the area on Elizabeth Downs, and on their own country to bring some food source back into the community. We get quite a lot of community people coming out onto the property, which is really good because they educate the kids on nutritional hunting.

MACCA: Miriam, how has the place changed since you were a little girl growing up here?

MIRIAM: It has changed, I hope for the better. I'm really glad that I was born in this era where there are still a lot of traditional aspects to the way that I do things. But I'm still comfortable in a western-type situation. Ken is from the Gold Coast and if I had to move I could live there comfortably.

MACCA: This is a great place and congratulations on your lovely community.

Macca talks to Australians all over from Moscow

G'day
DON

DON: I rang you six months ago to tell you I was going to Moscow. I'm in the suburbs of Moscow now.

MACCA: What are you doing in Moscow, Don?

DON: I'm on a project for the Department of Foreign Affairs, the refurbishment of the Australian Embassy in Moscow, and it's going really well.

MACCA: Is it cold in Moscow now?

DON: Just a little bit. The other day it was minus two with a wind chill factor of twenty-five, but it started snowing last night and we've had about five inches, so it's covering everywhere. It's very picturesque at the moment because it's dark with a lot of neon signs and lights reflecting across the snow. It's very beautiful.

MACCA: Don, you seem to get around the world a fair bit. Can you tell me about your work there in Moscow?

DON: I'm a project manager working in all sorts of areas, mainly renovating and restoring buildings to their originality and doing restoration work. I'm very fortunate in the type of work I do.

MACCA: How long will you be in Moscow, Don?

DON: Well, when I finish this project I'll go the ambassador's residence, which was built in 1901. One of the rooms is called the Bolshoi Room. People might be interested to know that Bolshoi means 'very big' so when you say Bolshoi Ballet you mean a very big ballet! The window in that room is eighteen feet high with five double-glazed panes going back to 1901, which was very clever then. During the Revolution it was the Chinese Embassy and there are actually bullet holes in the glass and we can't replace that glass because it's part of the Embassy's history. Since Perestroika, it's fantastic coming here and seeing the churches being renovated and restored to their natural colours, with the gold domes and the pinks, the blues, the yellows, the reds, the whites. A lot of the city's buildings are being restored to these colours, too, so the streets are very colourful. I think people think of Moscow as a very dark and drab place, but it's not, it's a very vibrant and exciting city with a lot of colour and light. The Kremlin is absolutely superb and I remember standing in Red Square and saying, 'Somebody pinch me—am I really here?' It's a very interesting place to visit. You have a lot of freedom to walk about as long as you carry your passport and do the right thing. We live two minutes' walk from the Moscow River in an apartment on the twelfth floor of one of seven buildings built by Stalin called the 'Seven Sisters'. The river isn't frozen yet and when we arrived here in the summer we did a couple of river cruises. It's absolutely brilliant, passing all the historical places and monuments.

MACCA: Not dangerous, Don?

DON: No, not at all. I was concerned about my wife at one time but she feels just as safe here as she would in Australia. If you went out at night and wandered the streets drunk you might be in trouble but otherwise there's no problem. Like in any other city there's a lot of poverty here. They're trying to catch up with the commercial world that we have and I think we're very fortunate in Australia. It's the best place in the world.

Macca talks to Australians all over
from the Ivory Coast

KEVIN: Kevin Chaplain here from the Ivory Coast, West Africa. I'm over here working in the cotton industry, about 700 kilometres north of Abidjan, setting up factories for African companies

MACCA: Kevin, how did you get there and how did you find out about cotton?

KEVIN: I was working in the cotton industry in Australia and somebody asked me if I wanted to go to Togo to help there. So in 1999 I went over there and then I worked in Greece for a while. I came back to Togo for seven months and I've just moved to the Ivory Coast two weeks ago to start up a new plant.

MACCA: Where are you from?

KEVIN: I'm from Wee Waa, north-west New South Wales.

MACCA: And what's it like living in West Africa?

KEVIN: It's not too bad. It's a different way of life. You have to adapt to their way—nothing's quick, nothing's done easily, nothing's simple. You have to adapt, otherwise you'd go crazy. You can't force something onto them that they've never had.

MACCA: And what actually do you do?

KEVIN: I teach the workers the safety aspect of the factory, set the machines and teach them what to do when I go so they'll be competent to run the machinery without any problems. The language is difficult because they speak French. I can speak a little bit to them but other than that you just have to show them what to do and sometimes they understand and sometimes they don't.

G'day
KEVIN

MACCA: Does Africa seem as big to you as it does to us, looking at so many countries and so many millions of people?

KEVIN: Yes, you could drive for hours and hours and see nothing or you come across little villages where they've hardly ever seen a white man before. It's fascinating, the little kids five or six years old that haven't seen a white man, like some kids in Australia who haven't seen rain.

Macca talks to Australians all over from Irian Jaya

G'day

GEOFF HOCKING

GEOFF: It's Geoff Hocking from Irian Jaya. I spoke to you about five years ago, and I just got a call up here to get in touch.

MACCA: I was going through my files and with all the problems in Indonesia remembered your call. Where are you and what are doing?

GEOFF: I'm calling you from about eight thousand feet up in the Irian Jaya highlands. I work for Freeport Mining and it's a massive operation, an unbelievable place up here.

MACCA: How long have you been there, Geoff?

GEOFF: About four and a half years. Freeport Mining runs the biggest copper and gold mine in the world. We mine at about twelve and fourteen thousand feet and sixteen thousand people work at the mine, including one hundred Australians.

MACCA: Have any of the troubles in East Timor and Indonesia been reflected in Irian Jaya?

GEOFF: Not so much because we're a five-hour trip by plane away from Jakarta. We're on the end of Papua-New Guinea and we don't see the problems here like in other places.

MACCA: Geoff, after I spoke to you all those years ago I got a letter from David Baker at Tea Gardens asking me to ask you if the two glaciers are still in the mountains or have they melted?

GEOFF: Yes, they're slowly melting but they're still there and they sit over the top of the mine. They're the most magnificent things and you wouldn't believe that in a place like Irian Jaya there could be glaciers. The terrain where we live is very beautiful with mountains towering up to about sixteen thousand feet. We live at eight thousand but we've got to climb up through nine thousand feet to get into the town where we actually live.

MACCA: I never thought of glaciers in Irian Jaya.

GEOFF: Well, that's just a part of this place. As far as the mines are concerned we've got the most incredible technology in the world. The throughput is about 200,000 tonnes a day with about $5 million worth of concentrate going down the hill each day. It certainly is a most amazing piece of technology here, yet there are penis-gourd guys in the town next to where we all live.

7

◎ *Little Possums* ◎

I first met Aaron and Gerard Maloney at our Melbourne outside
broadcast in 1992. Sadly both have passed away, victims of cystic fibrosis.
I feel a better person for having known them.

From:
Daisy, Phoebe,
Dena and Jade,
Vaucluse Public
School,
New South Wales

Use No. 2: for the rain gauge

I THINK ...

As I PUT MY toes in the great Pacific Ocean, full of life, I think. What about all those people who depend on water? Their life, their work, their soul. If only we could spread the water evenly among everyone. Who are we to be hogging it all!

As I am drinking a cool glass of water, I think. What would it be like to live in the outback, ridden with drought? Being parched daily and watching the cattle drop to the hot, sandy, ochre floor.

As I watch my mum serve up dinner, I think. How would I feel if I just sat there watching my business die before my eyes? The crops dropping in their tens. I stop and feel sick. No dinner for me tonight, Mum.

As I am running the water for my bath, I think. With a limited amount of water, nightly showers would not be possible. Dehydration would be common. Isolated, alone, sick. Praying, hoping for rain. I stop and turn off my bath. Why does Mother Earth work this way? Where is the rain? Why is it hiding?

As my Dad is tucking me into bed, I think. We are so fortunate in the city. We are able to put our toes in the Pacific Ocean, we are able to drink a cool glass of water, we are able to watch our business prosper and we are able to have nightly showers. As I am drifting off to sleep, I hear the dark thunder of a storm, the slow trickle of water dripping off the window and I think. We are so lucky.

From:
Rose Taylor,
Vaucluse Public
School,
New South Wales

DROUGHT

IN THE COUNTRY AREAS of Australia, the beautiful home of many, is a lack of water, food and crops. Wildlife, cattle and sheep dying and hoping for a change.

Farmers are desperate; their produce is failing; their source of life is scarce. We the city dwellers must sympathise with them and understand the hardships that their homes are going through and try to help. You know we can for we are provided with resources that country dwellers work up a sweat to receive and at the moment they are often coming up empty-handed.

The riders and their horses too weak to take a ride. The shepherds and their sheep too tired to run from danger. The herdsmen and their cattle too thirsty to produce their milk.

Do we want our children and theirs to grow up in a hazardous world? Of course not! Do we want our national heritage to perish under flame? I should hope not! Do we want our native wildlife to die from lack of nutrition? NO! So help us save our rural areas, for nature provides us with life, therefore we should return the favour.

From:
Louise Minney,
Underbool,
Victoria

THE UNDERBOOL PRIMARY SCHOOL has an annual end-of-year concert. We chose our theme to be 'Australia All Over'. We would like to invite you to come. It is on the 8th of December. It starts at 8 p.m. It is held at the Underbool Linga Memorial Hall.

Underbool is a small town so you cannot get lost. Underbool is in the north-western Mallee, west of Ouyen. The school has forty-two pupils. It is very small. We would really like you to come. If you cannot come, please ring the school. After the concert you will be asked to come out the back of the hall to meet us. We will probably want your autograph so come with a pen.

'Australia All Over'

By Geoff Brown (Teacher)

PERFORMED BY THE UNDERBOOL PRIMARY SCHOOL, VICTORIA

Introduction: Magpie calls on tape

OPEN CURTAIN

Song 1: Australia All Over

CLOSE CURTAIN

MACCA (Ashlea) – Hello and good evening, this is Macca. We're coming to you right across Australia from this great little hall in the Mallee. A place where everyone knows everyone and if they don't they'll find out. A place where grain, sheep and that Aussie pioneering spirit lives on. And what a show we have for you this evening. We're going to talk to you about birds, the land, cricket and, of course, the weather.

I've heard a whisper that some local Underbool folk are going to ring in so we look forward to that. Nine triple three ten twenty's the number, o-two's the code. You can reverse the charges.

What have you been doing? Tell us something we don't know. Where are you? How are you? What have you been doing? Love to hear from you.

Here's a song while you think about it. It's called 'Welcome to All People'.

Song 2: Welcome to All People

CLOSE CURTAIN

[*Macca's Table and Phone Box*]

OPEN CURTAIN

Cricket is a great Aussie game. Who hasn't grown up with an innings or two in the backyard or played along side that great cricketing legend from Torrita, 'Daryl Elliott'. Yes, we sure were privileged to have been a part of his side, that schoolboy champion.

Talking of legends and cricket there is a letter here from Mr Peter Lockett …

LETTER 1 – Rhys

Dear Macca, you might be interested in this cricketing story. Quite some years ago in Ouyen, the local barber, known as 'Jonesy', used to also be the SP bookie on the side.

One very hot February afternoon the gaming squad police came down from Mildura and created a terrible panic. Jonesy ran out of his shop, over the street, through the fence, across the railway, over the highway, through the bowling green and onto the cricket oval.

By this time he had just about had it and wished he had jumped on his motorbike instead. But he staggered onto the field, pushed the umpire out of the way, and stood there, gasping for breath. Just then the wicketkeeper appealed 'Howzat?' and Jonesy replied 'Not Guilty'.

Ring, ring

MACCA – G'day this is Macca, hello.

MOBY – Yeah Macca, Moby here.

MACCA – G'day Moby, Where are you calling from?

MOBY – I'm ringing from my 'elsewhere' property near Underbool. Apart from being a farmer I'm the local weatherman. People ring me from far and wide just to hear my predictions. I'm surprised you haven't rung me.

MACCA – Well, sorry about that Moby. Look, why do you say 'elsewhere'?

MOBY – Well, when they say 'rain and showers in the south, elsewhere dry' they must be talking about here.

MACCA – Okay, thanks for your call, Moby from 'elsewhere'.

Did you hear 'Waltzing Matilda' at the Olympics? Some say it should be our national anthem. While other countries sing about being in the land of the free and home among the brave, we sing about some bloke who roams the country, stole a sheep and broke the law! I reckon it's a great song, so here it is.

CLOSE CURTAIN

MATT – [*Walks out to the front of the stage*]

Song 3: Waltzing Matilda

CLOSE CURTAIN

[*Put chairs out for Wedge-tailed Eagle Rock*]

MACCA (Koby) – G'day, this is Macca. I've got a poem here about our feathered friends, the magpies, sent in by a well-known bird lover, Murray F. Lockett.

'Magpies sing like violins or piccolos or flutes, perhaps that's why they always fly in dinner suits. They dress up like musicians, in white tie, shirt and tails and give their own renditions of serenades and scales.'

SWOOPING RUN (Kaine and Lauren)

MACCA – Yes, I reckon we have a terrific variety of bird life in this country, especially those magpies. We've even got a football team named after them. They are a beautiful bird with a lovely sounding call and perhaps the most accurate swoopers in the country. Another great Australian bird is the wedge-tailed eagle. Here's a tune we should all remember.

CLOSE CURTAIN

Song 4: Wedge-tailed Eagle Rock

CLOSE CURTAIN

[*Front of stage (phone box)*]

Ring, ring

MACCA (Matt) – G'day this is Macca

MARIE – G'day Macca, this is Marie Kilpatrick here. How are you?

MACCA – Good thanks Marie, how are you handling the weather, Marie?

MARIE – Well it's getting pretty hot. Mind you, last night I got so cold I had to turn off the fan and pull up a sheet.

MACCA –Well, thanks Marie.

MACCA – I have a letter here sent in from Mr Brown.

LETTER 2 – Jason

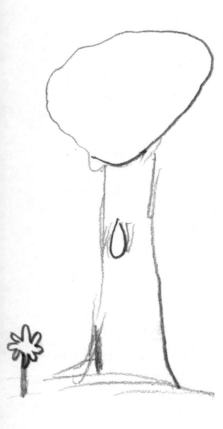

Dear Macca, this true story happened a few years ago when our local reverend was delivering a somewhat lengthy sermon to his congregation. During his talk he noticed an elderly lady sitting near the back of the church take a small item from her handbag and place it in her ear.

Always conscious of how people responded to his sermons and assuming that the ageing parishioner had resorted to using a hearing aid, Reverend decided to deliver the last two pages of his sermon, which were optional depending on the reaction of his congregation.

He felt encouraged when he saw that the dear lady had a gentle and happy smile on her face. At the end of the service, while greeting his congregation as they left the church, Reverend told the lady he was delighted that her hearing aid had helped her enjoy his service so much.

'Hearing aid?' she said, 'Oh no, that was my little radio's earpiece. You were so boring today I tuned into "Australia All Over".'

CLOSE CURTAIN

(*Take phone away*)

OPEN CURTAIN

MACCA (David) – Hello this is Macca, if you have just joined us, where have you been? Ring in and tell us what you were up to. Is there anything you would like to tell us? Nine triple three ten twenty's the number, o-two's the code. You can reverse the charges.

We've been talking about magpies and cricket and life in the Mallee. Hope you enjoy this next song, 'Home Among the Gum Trees'.

SONG 5: Give Me a Home Among the Gum Trees

MACCA – G'day this is Macca, give me a call, nine triple three ten twenty's the number, o-two's the code.

CLOSE CURTAIN

(*Phone out*)

OPEN CURTAIN

Ring, ring

MACCA – G'day this is Macca, hello.

SKIN – G'day this is Skin here.

MACCA – G'day Skin, how are you?

SKIN – Good thanks Macca. I was just ringing to read you a poem about getting up early.

MACCA – You don't like getting up early?

SKIN – Yes I do, but that's not why I'm ringing. I just want to read you my poem, now.

MACCA – Okay Skin, go ahead.

SKIN – Early to bed and early to rise
Makes a man healthy, wealthy and wise
Birds prosper too, if they're quick out of bed;
It's the earliest bird who is the best fed.
But think of the worms on which the birds dine and sup,
They'd be much better off if they didn't get up.

SONG 6: Macca in the Morning

MACCA (Terry) – G'day this is Macca, give me a call. Nine triple three ten twenty's the number, o-two's the code. Reverse the charges.

Matt comes on to stage to ring. Looking for some money in his pocket. Mumbles to himself …

Ring, ring

MACCA – Hello, this is Macca, Hello, Hello …

Matt throws his arms in the air, mumbles off stage.

Ring, ring

MACCA – (*Macca sighs a little because he is a little annoyed*). Hello

COL – Hello Macca, Col here,

GEOFF – Hello Macca, Geoff here.

COL and GEOFF (together) – We are the Lockett brothers and we have a ripper of a poem for you.

MACCA – Okay, boys let's hear it.

COL and GEOFF – *Poem*

MACCA – Thank you, boys.

As Col and Geoff leave the stage

COL – Couldn't give me a ride, Geoff?

GEOFF – Yeah, okay

CLOSE CURTAIN

(*Take phone away*)

OPEN CURTAIN

MACCA – Fishing is a great Mallee sport. You can always find a spot by the Murray, the dam or the resi. And everyone has a story about the one that got away. Here's a short song written by 'Jake-the-fisherman' Brady from Underbool.

Song 7: *Fishing song*

MACCA – There's a lot of the Mallee that's not on the east coast, in fact none of it is. So I thought we would have a song about how large this country is.

Song 8: *Out the back*

MACCA – I have fax here from Shirley requesting a song be played that was written by her husband, the great Greginardo de Vallincio. It's called 'Song of Joy' and will be played live in the studio by the students of the Undeboolian Primary School.

CLOSE CURTAIN

OPEN CURTAIN

Song 9: *Song of Joy*

CLOSE CURTAIN

MACCA – With Christmas just around the corner, it's good to sing a few Christmas carols. The songs that aren't about the frost, winter or snow, but rather heat, flies, utes and cricket. This next one's a favourite.

Song 10: I Made a Hundred . . .

MACCA – Well, it's great to have had your company this evening. Have a good week and a great Mallee Christmas everyone.

(*All Maccas come on stage for this*)

ALL MACCAS – See ya later, from all of us.

Song 11: Rusty's Holden Ute

Song 12: We Wish You a Merry Christmas

Song 13: Jingle Bells

THE END

My name is Jesse Gerard Edwards and I am eight years old. I live in Merimbula at the Pelican Motor Inn. I was born in Mount Gambier, South Australia, and I go to the Pambula Primary School. I am in 2 MC.

I am visually impaired and I enjoy music. I have lots of CDs and old records (33s and 45s plus a few 78s). I know about you because my Nanna Shirley has some of your tapes and I have listened to them. I like 'Murphy and the Bricks', 'Ring Macca', 'Bundaberg Rum', 'The Rabbit Trapper' and lots more. My Dad and Mum think the 'Bundaberg Rum' song is funny. My sister's name is Chloe and she is ten. We have a dog called Scally.

I am learning guitar and when I can play well enough I will send you a tape. I am learning Braille at school.

Bye for now.

> *From:*
> *Jesse Edwards,*
> *(dictated by Jesse and typed by his Nanna Shirley)*
> *Merimbula,*
> *New South Waleas*

I am Jessica from Yarralumla in Canberra. I am thirteen years old and I love listening to your program! I thought you might enjoy this poem I wrote. Enjoy and keep giving Australia the best radio coverage every Sunday morning!

Through all the darkness comes a smile
Happiness, peace, laughter, from a child.
He smiles on, embracing love,
Although he will never be able to release a dove,
His voice will never be heard,
Out of his mouth, not a single word.

Never will he speak his mind,
Never will he not be kind,
Never will he chase a ball,
But he is not worried, not at all.

He takes his life day by day,
Never angry for his fate.
Never thinking that it's too late,
Never not taking the extra mile,
Never not sharing his wonderful smile.

> *Email from:*
> *Jessica Saunders,*
> *Yarralumla,*
> *Australian Capital Territory*

Stuck in a wheelchair,
He doesn't seem to care,
He lives each day like it was his last,
And never focuses on the past.

Yet he is not perfect,
He has his faults,
But he is pure,
And will conquer all of life's vaults.

… smiles …

If everyone had his perspective on life
There would be no war, no killing, no strife.
Why can't we all regard everyone as equal?
Why do we always have to wait for the next sequel?
Why can't we share a smile?
It might bring happiness, if only for a little while.
Why can't we follow his lead, I plead.

His smile shows a thousand words.
Bringing happiness, laughter, in this time of curse.
What a wonderful gift,
To bring joy with a twitch of the lips.
We all have this power
And we should release it in this hour.

Through all the darkness comes a smile,
Happiness, peace, laughter, from a child.

◎

Email from: Judy Walsh

YOU WERE SPEAKING WITH a fellow about city kids spending time on a farm. I was fortunate to be a child like that. Thirty years ago when I was five my family holidayed at the Sunshine Coast and in the unit next door was a family from the bush. Each Christmas for around thirteen years we would holiday side-by-side. During the Easter holidays of those years we would then travel out to their farm. They had pigs, grain and cattle, and it was a great experience for my brothers, my parents and myself.

We learnt about conserving water and where meat, milk, grain and eggs came from. We terrorised their chickens; as soon as we heard a cluck-cluck one of us would race over to collect the eggs. We would stand back in amazement at calves being born, branded and sent off to market. We would go into the pig sheds and cuddle piglets and help the farm cats catch rats. We would help out at harvesting time, chase mice during the plagues, and that is where I learnt to drive a car and motorbike.

◎

From: Honi Reifler, Glenreagh, New South Wales

I ASSIST AT A SMALL north-coast country school and I have been focusing on the drought this term. Although the rural children see the effects of the drought they don't understand. Drought creeps up slowly and children grow slowly—so what they see is a normal part of life for them.

However, on our way home from a school excursion to Canberra recently, I think that they finally gained an understanding of the drought.

How many Maccas can you see? And how many hundreds have you hit in your backyard? This end-of-year concert by the kids at Underbool Primary School in Victoria was just mighty. (You can enjoy the whole script in the book.)

Above: Word got around that we were visiting Fitzroy Crossing in Western Australia. The long-drop dunny at Mary's Pool was used to announce the show because it's the only permanent building for miles!

Below: Monica and Dave Taylor's caravan was directly in the path of this 'stampede' at Mary's Pool, but at the last moment the leader headed towards greener pastures!

ore publicity for our visit to Fitzroy Crossing. There was plenty of good music under a gum tree with Brian Young, and
om the Pulsford kids, Katherine, Tom and Jack.

Narrandera

Above: I caught up with Bill Oliver at Narrandera in New South Wales. He reckons over two thousand were there! The readings on the programme from his book *Sugar in the Blood* were very popular, and we had letters from several listeners reminiscing over the old days of LPs and great tenor singers.

Several bush poets from all over Australia joined us at Narrandera, including 'H' who spent a lot of time busily forgetting his lines!

We stopped at a little village, Caroona (west of Tamworth), to refuel the bus after battling strong winds and 'willy willies' all the way from Dubbo. One of the girls went to the toilet behind the church and ran back with a dead baby koala in her hands. The children were visibly grieved, as I examined the still warm little furred body with ants crawling around its face. The local ladies serving us were also sad. They pointed out the mother koala still sitting in the solitary gum tree. They said that they had been watching her and her growing baby for weeks. That particular day was incredibly windy and the baby koala must have been blown from its malnourished mother's back. We all sadly looked at this little victim of the drought and grieved for the suffering mother, wondering if she would survive this relentless scourge.

WHAT AUSTRALIA MEANS TO ME

It's the kookaburra's laugh at dawn,
The feeling of wool freshly shorn,
The taste of damper, billy tea,
The golden sand and crashing sea

Great Barrier Reef, Uluru,
The emu, koala and kangaroo,
We pray for rain, but dread the flood,
We breathe the dust and curse the mud.

The lucky country wide and free,
Given to us at Gallipoli,
It's a spirit, a feeling of pride,
So many have fought, so many have died.

It's the rising sun on an April morning,
The 'Last Post' plays as the day is dawning,
It's mateship, honour, the freedom to be
An Australian. My country was given to me.

From:
Patrick Haddock,
Gymea,
New South Wales

MY OUTBACK POEM

The outback
Where people are not slack
People grow crops
And have cattle stops
They sometimes muster sheep
And hardly have any sleep
Sometimes cattle
Are a really big battle
And our dirt roads
Don't have toads
Wheat
Is hard to beat

From:
Mark Currey (11),
Walgett,
New South Wales

Pigs
Can't eat any fruit like figs
And lambs
They sometimes get stuck in dams
Ploughing up dirt
That is a job of getting grease on your shirt
Burr chipping I hate
Because it means I'll be late
Why be in the states
When you can be opening gates
This is where the kangaroos
Don't wear any shoes
And wild dogs
Hide under logs
Some rivers
Give me the shivers
Most trees
Have bees
Some city slickers come to ride horses
But have to take lots of courses
Out in the outback girls think horses are cute
But boys say they're not as good as a ute
Sheep and cattle are dying
And city slickers aren't even crying
Hay is a treat
To keep them on their feet
Dad has to get in the wheat bin
To fill up the feeding tin
The water isn't very deep
For us, the cattle and the sheep
Cotton growers are in trouble
Because they need water on the double
Mum and Dad feed till late
That is what they hate
Most foxes are mangy
And acting strangely
All the fish are dead
Lying in the bottom of the river bed
Some people cart water from the Walgett water tower
So they can have a nice clean shower
Our garden is dead
Because there is no water in the dam and the river bed
We had to dig a well
And now the water is starting to smell
Steak, lamb and chops
That's all we can really afford at the shops
Dust storms everywhere
Now I've got dirt in my hair

8

◎ *Keep on Keeping on, Macca* ◎

Your show is the next best thing to rainwater.

FROM: *Ray Purches*, Wangaratta, Victoria

I never want the programme to end. I have my own name for
ten o'clock on Sunday morning: IAO—'It's All Over'

FROM: *Cas*, Hayes Creek, Northern Territory

Email from:
Lyn Ketter,
Thornlands,
Queensland

I WAS INTRODUCED TO *Australia All Over* many years ago when I was helping my parents with cleaning their pet motel.

The radio in the kennels and the radio in the cattery have been permanently tuned into ABC radio for the past twenty-six years. My mother says that animals feel more comforted listening to the ABC than commercial radio!

I don't particularly like cleaning the kennels except on Sundays. I feel so proud to be an Aussie when I listen in and hear people from all over ringing in with their little piece of whatever.

Keep on keeping on, Macca — luv ya mate!

From:
Lorna Melbourne,
Warragul,
Victoria

DON'T EVER STOP DOING what you are doing on your Sunday morning program. During my sixty years I have travelled to Adelaide once, as far north as Deniliquin, across to Canberra to the coast and back to Gippsland. My other travels are with you, through your programme. Whenever possible I listen in and although I've never ever seen you in person or in a photo, I feel like I've known you all my life. You talk about things that interest everyone, not just a special group. I have thought about phoning in, but I am sure I would become tongue-tied whilst on air, although my husband doesn't think that's possible! Macca, when you mention certain things it starts the memory racing and most often I can relate to the same experiences in my childhood.

Email from:
Bill Hawkins

I LISTEN TO YOUR show every Sunday but this is the first time I have thought of contacting you. I have worked and lived at some time or other in every state of this land. I must say that your show brightens up my Sunday morning and when I hear it I know that I have only a couple of more hours of work. I sit in a guard box and look down the road towards town for nearly twelve hours so tend to let the old mind wander a bit. I have worked since the early sixties and have done the following jobs that I can remember: shoe salesman, electrical apprentice, labourer on the WA main roads, hospital orderly, shed hand, sewer worker in Kojonup, truck driver, national serviceman, Telecom linesman, uni student, uni tutor, computer technician, council ranger and now a security guard.

Well Macca I must go now, as I need some sleep, but please keep up the excellent show.

From:
E. Bird,
Lidcombe,
New South Wales

WE ENJOYED YOUR OUTSIDE broadcast very much last Sunday, as usual another successful programme.

You said at the end of the programme how your production team breathed a sigh of relief when you completed another long stint at the microphone without any problems. I imagine most of your listeners would not appreciate how stressful it is to do a unique programme like yours. Maintaining interest for four and a half hours without a break is a tribute to your talents.

I might add, you come over as smooth as silk with no hint of pressure, and I just thought I'd like to express our thanks to you.

I AM UNABLE TO listen without agitation to the trivialised nonsense and ego-drenched out-pourings of the commercial commentators on talkback programmes. So your programme gives me respite and fills my Sunday morning with its intelligent, informative and at times undoubtedly amusing and practical views of your Australia-wide participating audiences. It is about real Australians in real environments from every walk of life.

Again I congratulate you Macca and all those involved in your production.

From:
Jim Hammond,
Drummoyne,
New South Wales

COMING HOME

Over the waves and through the foam
A solitary bird comes flying home,
Of all the birds present and past
This lonely creature is the last,
With forests gone and climatic changes
Rancid water and barren ranges
Polluted oceans rank with oil
Dying fish and poisoned soil
No living thing will stay alive
No earthly creature can survive.
'Til there's found a real solution
To the growth of foul pollution.
Polluted government, polluted wealth
Polluted land, polluted health
Polluted politics, polluted tradition
All is pollution and all perdition.
And this prescribes the time that comes
When the fathers' sins will visit their sons!
A famous poet once did say
What is writ won't go away
Nor all our tears or all our wit
Can ever change a word of it!

WE CAME UP TO see you on Australia Day and really enjoyed your Hyde Park broadcast. I came home and wrote this short poem.

We listen to you each Sunday from the comfort of our bed
But on the 26th January we saw you for real instead
We hit the road at four forty-five
Up to Hyde Park we went for a bit of a drive
We love your style and the way it does flow
And hearing from people and the places they go
You're a fair dinkum Aussie, Macca, and that is for sure
And next time you're in Wollongong we'll be there again for sure.

From:
Margaret Anderson,
Figtree,
New South Wales

JUST A SHORT MESSAGE to say thanks for your efforts to support harness racing in your program. Many people associated with harness racing, or trotting as we oldies say, heard your interview with me.

Email from:
Fr Brian Glasheen

Your show is a show that ordinary people can identify with. It is not a show you put on for big business, or to sell things produced by the big multinationals. Your show is a show for the ordinary people and it was a privilege to be a part of the wonderful service you provide for thousands of Australians. Congratulations, well done.

From:
Hilda Baillie,
Lipson,
South Australia

CONGRATULATIONS ON PRESENTING SUCH a wonderful programme. It would seem that it would be relatively easy to present a radio programme in a first-class fashion for a short while—and then give up. But, to present 'Australia All Over' for as many years as you have and maintain its popularity with so many people is nothing short of remarkable. A noble effort indeed.

In this fast-changing world we all need some things that are constant, that we can rely on, that make sense.

From:
Kathleen Silver,
Box Hill,
Victoria

EVERY SUNDAY MORNING FOR a long time I do, as instructed, 'switch on and lie back in bed' and listen to Macca. As an elderly person (eighty-seven by the time you read this!) I cannot tell you how much pleasure and information I have derived from your programme. Often, I just close my eyes and visualise the scene: I follow the routes taken, I smell the gums, I see the wildlife, the dramatic gorges, the sandy beaches, or I'm on a ship, etc.

I feel so privileged to have participated and it is just wonderful. Also, I enjoy the humour and I sing along with the songs I know. No wonder I am in such a good mood on Sunday mornings!

From:
Rev. Dr John Bunyan,
Chester Hill,
New South Wales

I SHOULD HAVE WRITTEN long ago to thank you for a wonderful programme. The gratitude in this case is very deep. For some years earlier in the nineties I had severe clinical depression, always worse in the mornings and especially Sunday mornings when I had to continue to take services. The ABC dropped a cheerful hymn programme for a religious programme that often seemed to feature some gloomy subject, but fortunately I discovered *Australia All Over* which certainly helped to cheer me up on a Sunday morning and I appreciate that very much.

Email from:
Brian Durell,
Cheltenham,
Ontario, Canada

OUR GOOD FRIENDS Marion and Jim on the Gold Coast have been taping *Australia All Over* for us for years since our visit to your great country in 1990. Saturday evening in Ontario, Canada, is Sunday morning in Oz. So here I am listening to your delightful programme live (or close to it) through my computer as I type. Fantastic. Love the program. It makes the desire to return all the greater.

Email from:
Michael McNaughton

THANK YOU FOR YOUR program. I think it is a great way to bridge the gap between city and country. To listen to your programme on a Sunday morning is so soothing compared with the testosterone-charged intensity of programmes on weekdays. I really enjoyed your broadcast from Wollongong and it was pleasing to hear so many of the listeners you interviewed express their enthusiasm for the natural beauty and potential of that wonderful city. Together with Newcastle, Wollongong has wonderful natural assets that are greatly underrated. They are a 'bridge' between the madness of Sydney and the tranquillity of the country.

9
Those Weeds Must Have Powerful Genes

I hate cocos palms. I think there ought to be 'palm police' to audit landscapers' designs and not allow them to be planted.

FROM: *Ron*, Elizabeth Bay, New South Wales

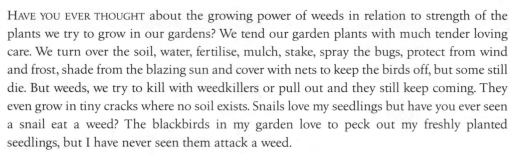

From:
John Gill,
Surrey Hills,
Victoria

Ugh! Weeds! The fast food of the garden

From:
Shirley Svensson,
Buccan,
Queensland

From:
Val Vansittart,
Warragul,
Victoria

From:
Lorna Murray,
Mount Ommaney,
Queensland

HAVE YOU EVER THOUGHT about the growing power of weeds in relation to strength of the plants we try to grow in our gardens? We tend our garden plants with much tender loving care. We turn over the soil, water, fertilise, mulch, stake, spray the bugs, protect from wind and frost, shade from the blazing sun and cover with nets to keep the birds off, but some still die. But weeds, we try to kill with weedkillers or pull out and they still keep coming. They even grow in tiny cracks where no soil exists. Snails love my seedlings but have you ever seen a snail eat a weed? The blackbirds in my garden love to peck out my freshly planted seedlings, but I have never seen them attack a weed.

All I can say is that weeds must have some powerful genes.

I WAS JUST LISTENING to the gentleman talking about going to Lord Howe Island to weed. I didn't catch what sort of weed he was going to eradicate. While I probably couldn't afford to do that, I think I may join Landcare or some group. I went up Mount Tambourine recently for the first time for a long time and was horrified at the extent to which convolvulus (morning glory vine) and yellow cassia (Easter bush) had taken over the beautiful rainforest on the drive to the summit. Once you could see beautiful tree ferns and lovely gum trees. I will be writing to the local council, too. In fact, I was about to do so when I heard your programme. Maybe some interested people will get out there and do some weeding. Mount Tambourine is only a short drive from Brisbane or the Gold Coast. I'm at present working on a very large and neglected garden at home so won't get much time to do my bit!

YOUR PROGRAMME HAS MADE me aware of the weed problem sweeping Australia, from coastlines to the outback. During a recent tour of the Flinders Ranges, as our coach was heading down a gorge, I noticed a rare patch of colour in a dry creek bed, rare at this time of year, the temperatures being in the mid-thirties. When we moved closer, I was able to identify three sturdy oleanders in three different colours—double pink, double white and a deep rose. They were centred as though planted by a caring gardener. Further into the ranges I saw another oleander growing wild near a creek, also well-established prickly pear bushes on hillsides. As you probably know, oleanders are poisonous and easily propagated. I suppose floodwaters were the means of spreading them into the wild. This goes to show how careful we should be about disposing of garden rubbish, not dumping things near creeks or waterways.

I felt like leaping from our coach, shovel in hand to destroy these pests.

I WAS VERY INTERESTED to hear your comments in the programme this morning concerning the problems with weeds in many parts of Australia now, and the need for all Australians to appreciate the unique floral heritage we have in this country.

It is heartening to hear of the work being done by many groups to try to eliminate weeds in certain areas, but I would like to highlight the need for all Australians to become aware of the potential for many more introduced plants to become serious weeds in the environment, and thus the need to remove such plants from gardens and park plantings. Prevention is much better than cure.

In the south-east Queensland area, for example, there are problems developing with lots of plants still being planted, such as asparagus, Singapore daisy, camphor laurels and jacarandas. This list could go on for pages. There are many species of local plants that could easily fill the same role in horticulture as these weedy exotics.

I would like to mention here the Australian Plant Society (APS) or the Society for Growing Australian Plants (SGAP) that is active in every state of Australia, with branches or groups in many country areas. The federal umbrella body is the Association of Societies for Growing Australian Plants (ASGAP), to which all the state regions belong. There are almost 10,000 members throughout Australia, and among the members, including enthusiastic amateur naturalists, botanists, and arid native plant nurserymen, there is a vast amount of knowledge of our indigenous plants.

One of the main activities of the Society now is trying to convey to the general population the message about the damage being done to our native environments by the spreading of exotic weed species. In this regard our members often work with local councils and other environmental groups, but the message about weeds is getting to the general public only very slowly.

Our members were instrumental in persuading SOCOG that the bouquets to be presented to the winning athletes at the Sydney Olympics should be composed of native Australian flowers.

KIERAN KELLY was speaking about following in the footsteps of Gregory and of the difficult terrain they both encountered. Tall, prickly spinifex made the going even tougher and more painful.

Spinifex is actually the botanical name for a grass that grows on some sandy dunes of the coast but the name is commonly applied to the spinifex country of inland Australia.

Spinifex, or porcupine grass as it is also known, is the dominant ground cover over huge tracts of the inland. This type of country occupies nearly a quarter of our landmass and is generally referred to as the hummock grasslands. However, for the moment, spinifex will do.

It can also occur on a range of soils and landscapes—everything from plains, sand dunes, rocky slopes and mountain ranges. It's a long-lived grass that can grow well over a metre in height. Each plant typically grows in a circular hummock shape to a metre or two in diameter. In older plants the centre of each hummock dies and the plants take on a ring shape.

The spinifex grasses occupy all our major deserts as well as other areas including the understorey in mallee communities in southern areas. The deserts they occupy are the driest places in Australia and may only get a couple of inches of rain a year. These extremely tough plants are obviously very well adapted to their hot, dry environment. Even fire, a regular occurrence in spinifex country, poses no problem because they readily regrow from their extensive root systems.

One of the most remarkable things about the spinifex country is that it supports the richest assemblage of reptiles anywhere in the world. The dense, spiny porcupine-like nature of the leaves makes an ideal safe haven from potential predators and the soft sandy soil underneath the plants is a great place to construct burrows. In rocky places the plants provide extra protection for animals sheltering in numerous nooks and crevices.

Lizards, geckos, skinks and snakes are not the only tenants to have successfully made this seemingly inhospitable country their home. The spinifex bird, the spinifex pigeon and the spinifex hopping mouse all rely on the plant and its environment for their survival.

From:
Roger Oxley,
Deniliquin,
New South Wales

While this environment is not particularly user-friendly for people, most of the native animals that live there are completely in tune with it.

From:
Val Strange,
Beverley,
Western Australia

I GUESS YOU HAVE been besieged by letters and calls from Western Australians about the caller who was fairly derogatory about the Stirling Ranges.

According to my atlas Mount Dandenong is 2,078 feet high. It is an old atlas and the measurements are in feet. There are seven (at least) peaks in the Stirlings that are higher than that. Blue Knoll is 3,640 feet high, which (if my maths are right) makes it 1,568 feet higher than Mount Dandenong. I once tried to climb it and made it about a third of a way to the top!

I presume the lady also visited the Porongurups, which are about twenty miles away and have lovely karri trees, which are the third-highest species in the world. It is always amazing to me how the two ranges which are so close together can be so different, the Stirlings covered with low bush and the Porongurups with huge trees, but both have lovely wildflowers.

I have also been to the Dandenongs in Victoria and thought they were quite beautiful with all the tree ferns in the gullies. I am sorry your caller was disappointed with the Stirlings but I think they are like the rest of us over here—different!

From:
Ruth Lipscombe,
Innisfail,
Queensland

IN THE RECENT PROGRAMMES you have mentioned building monuments to commemorate events such as the Childers fire.

Could I put in a plea for consideration to be given to the planting of a plot of indigenous trees instead. We have enough 'daggy' (your word) monuments and not enough trees. Planting trees would be more meaningful to commemorate all sorts of events.

I loved your cassowary song—several walk through my property to access their bush food. They'd appreciate trees instead of concrete too.

From:
Roger Oxley,
Deniliquin,
New South Wales

WELL IT'S BEEN ONE of those years again. I remember that a few years ago I wrote to you and said that the river red gums were flowering like nothing else. Well, this year they have even passed their last record. Perhaps it was the relatively mild winter and summer we've had to date, but the fact is that the red gums have gone berserk. They flowered like it was their last hurrah.

Once January came, the male bits of the flowers dropped off and it rained stamens—they're the bits of the male flower that contain all the pollen that fertilises the female bits.

I reckon that the blokes who bring their beehives into the red gum forests would have had a five-star year. The trees were a mass of flowers. The red gums that are in my back paddock were so laden that they were overstressed and were a mass of bees.

First of all were the buds, then came the flowers, billions of them. And then came the bark. Huge sheets of it. Normally red gums shed their bark every summer but this time they did it like there was no ever after. Great sheets of bark have been dropping off and covering the ground with a huge layer of litter.

The amount of bark that the red gums are shedding is unbelievable. A reasonable sort of red gum, say about a couple of feet diameter, probably sheds about fifteen square metres of bark. Multiply this by a minimum of three to allow for all the smaller branches and you get a figure approaching forty-five square metres of bark per tree. When you multiply this by the number of red gums growing in a reasonable sort of forest you get a figure of about thirty square kilometres! Amazing isn't it.

What happens to all this bark? Well, it gets recycled and it breaks down and provides some of the essential nutrients for the next generation, assuming our rivers and creeks are allowed to run free.

The bark of river red gums takes a while to break down and to be recycled. A lot depends on the sort of weather we have. If it's a wet year then it breaks down fairly quickly but if it's a dry one it takes much longer.

Whatever happens I hope the cycle goes around and that the majestic red gum forests are allowed to keep on keeping on.

THE GREATER BLOWER ANNOYUS
or SUNDAY MORNING IN THE SUBURBS

The kookaburras chuckle and the magpies gurgle too,
Joined by the raucous chorus of a cockatoo or two,
But hark! I hear another bird not easy on the ears,
Sounding like a learner driver cranking up the gears,
It's the Greater Blower annoyus, the leaf-dispersing bird,
It's migrated fairly recently to the suburbs in a herd,
This flocking early-rising bird has overthrown the broom,
Like the parasitic cuckoo sending nestlings to their doom,
On and on the droning voice drowns the Sunday song,
Shut the windows, close the doors, why does it take so long?
The noise has stopped, the great bird sleeps, I glance out at the stack,
I really can't beleaf it. Those leaves have blown right back!

From:
Judi Cox,
Kenmore,
Queensland

From:
H. Anne Link,
Petrie,
Queensland

I'M RESPONDING TO THE letter you read out from Alison in Canberra. When I was a little girl in primary school in a Sydney suburb in the 1950s, we always celebrated Wattle Day. It was the first of August and every pupil received a little sprig of yellow wattle to pin on their uniform. Every year when the wattle trees are in bloom I wonder why the idea was abandoned. It gave us a lot of pleasure and was one thing we could all enjoy together.

While we're on the subject of sprigs, I also have pleasant memories of Anzac Day when we all received a little sprig of rosemary to pin on our lapels. Rosemary is for remembrance and the fragrance always takes me back to crisp April days, and my mother's birthday (25 April).

Prickly pair

From:
Vic Groves,
Ravensbourne,
Queensland

THIS MORNING YOU ASKED 'What sort of Christmas tree?' I felt the answer 'Just a pine' left you wanting, so I'd like to tell you what we used. It's the native cherry Exocarpus cupressiformis, a well-known forest fruit, known also as wild cherry, forest cherry and cherry ballart. Ballart, by the way, comes from a Victorian Aboriginal word for the native cherry. It has drooping foliage made of pendulous, cypress-like stems. It has affinities with the primitive mistletoes and the desert quandong. They are root parasitic, tapping the root systems of adjacent plants to draw off nutrients. I chose this tree as it is a native. It fruited at Christmas and its colourful fruit is like built-in decoration.

1 0

◎ *In the Wake of Flinders and Cook* ◎

The problem was we hit three gales going across Bass Strait, with calms
in between. We couldn't go anywhere. Four of the crew were in the hatch for
two hours—they couldn't get out. The sea was breaking over and I was back
aft on my own. It was scary. It was the worst experience I've had in
sixty years at sea, but the *Norfolk* survived.

FROM: *Bern Cuthbertson,* Captain of Flinders replica, *Norfolk*

Email from:
Pam Jacobs

WHILE THE FOCUS IS on the bicentenary of Acting Lieutenant Murray's entry into Port Phillip Bay, and Matthew Flinders' circumnavigation of Australia, it is worth remembering the naval surveyors who followed in the footsteps of these famous pioneers of hydrography.

The extract from a letter written by a naval officer to his mother in Melbourne paints a splendid picture of life in the navy as a surveyor in 1953:

I am quite astonished at the amount one can do in five weeks. Join the ship, get her out of dockyard hands and fully stored, be inspected by an Admiral, sail her from Sydney, survey Pine Peak Island, take astrolabe sights at Dayman Island, take soundings at Booby Island, and in doing all this steam the ship over 2,000 odd miles through some of the most difficult navigational waters in the world. The Barrier Reef, the treacherous tides of Torres Strait, and across the top of Australia and down to the narrows of Clarence Strait, poorly marked in the way of navigational aids—which is just outside Darwin, and then into Darwin itself. There the harbour wharves are falling down, the tides rise and fall twenty feet, the waters are littered with wrecks and the sun rises blood red on the water.

As I told you in my last letter, the trip up the Reef was very pleasant, despite the narrowness of the waters and the difficulties of navigation. One night, the navigator and myself were on the bridge all night, from seven in the evening to eight o'clock the following morning, which is a long time to be at full stretch.

We anchored off Dayman Island just around from Cape York and it was here over a period of six days that we took our astrolabe sights. Dayman Island is about half a mile long and a quarter wide surrounded by a reef of dead coral that comes out a hundred yards from the shore and shows pale green under the water. The island itself rises pretty steeply to 300 feet, to a long flat-tish ridge at the top. It was up the slopes to this ridge that we transported our camp and instruments. Walking and climbing was difficult, particularly when carrying a load. We normally start our astrolabe sights about 7 p.m. and work through until 5 a.m. the following morning, interrupted sometimes by rain, sometimes by the sky clouding over.

Booby Island, where we went next, is a lonely rock rising out of the sea with a white lighthouse perched on the top of it. We were there for twenty-four hours taking soundings to see if there had been any siltation in the channels. We anchored off the light that night. As the sun went down the lighthouse keeper flashed 'Good night' to us. In the morning we sailed for Darwin.

From:
Ray Roberts,
Mount Eliza,
Victoria

I SHARE WITH YOU a deep admiration of men like Matthew Flinders and James Cook. My admiration of Flinders was heightened back in 1972, when I was involved in a mining feasibility study that called for a deep water, open sea ship loading facility to be located in the Gulf of Carpentaria, about seventy kilometres north of the mining port of Weipa. The only hydrographic chart available for that section of the coastline was one prepared by Matthew Flinders.

Much of the sea floor in that part of the Gulf is gently sloping so a jetty would need to be very long in order to reach deep water. It would also be very exposed and costly to construct. Our only hope was to locate a depression in the sea floor extending close in to the shore. There were no physical features along the coastline to suggest any variation of the sea floor. However, a detailed examination of Flinders' chart showed that he had located and taken soundings of a 'gutter', a depression running at right angles to the shore at a point south of the mouth of the Pennefather River.

I was amazed that Flinders should have taken detailed soundings of a minor depression in the sea floor in such a remote location. There is little doubt that we were the first people to make use of his soundings. We were concerned that the depression may have silted up or moved, so arrangements were made for a hydrographic survey vessel to carry out a check survey. Sure enough, the depression was exactly as the Flinders' chart showed it.

The experience made me think long and hard about the character of men like Flinders. Even in 1972 the area was isolated and unforgiving. Yet 170 years earlier Flinders had located a minor depression in the sea floor in the Gulf of Carpentaria and had delayed his voyage to take detailed soundings. He did this despite the fact that it would then have been some eighteen months since he left his home in England and possibly six months since he had left the last outpost of civilisation at Sydney. The work must have taken him several days during which time the *Investigator* would have been most uncomfortable pitching in the 'slop'. I can only conclude that men of Flinders' calibre were more hardy, more dedicated and prepared to make more personal sacrifices in the discharge of their profession than most of us know anything about these days. And to cap it off, the French held him prisoner in Mauritius for over six years on the way home.

I HEARD PART OF your conversation with a naval officer regarding Matthew Flinders' visit to the Pennefather River in 1802. I am an historian based in Brisbane and I have had a thirty-year association with the Western Cape York Peninsula region.

Email from:
Geoff Wharton

The Pennefather area is a very important Australian historical site. As you are probably aware, it is the place of the first recorded sighting of the Australian continent by Europeans (Willem Jansz in the *Duyfken* in 1606) and from an indigenous perspective, probably the site of the first sighting of Europeans by the indigenous people of this land.

The river was thought by Matthew Flinders to be the Coen River, which was actually a river farther south. From Flinders' time in November 1802 until the late nineteenth century, it was noted on hydrographic charts as the Coen River. One of the early Dutch navigators had named the original Coen River in honour of a Governor-General of the Dutch East Indies, Jan Pieterszoon Coen.

In June 1880, Captain Charles Edward de Fonblanque Pennefather, skipper of the Queensland Government Schooner *Pearl*, explored the Coen River and wrote a report to the Queensland Government. In either the 1880s or the 1890s the river's name was changed from Coen to Pennefather, probably to avoid confusion with the other Coen River, which commences in eastern Cape York Peninsula and runs westward to join the Archer River.

Captain Charles Pennefather was born in 1848 and first joined the Queensland Government Service in 1879. He became Comptroller General of Queensland Prisons in 1893, serving in that capacity until 1919 and possibly died a few years later in Fiji.

G'day, this is Macca

JOHN: It's Commander John Maschke ringing from Cairns. I was interested to hear you read a letter about surveys up around the Pennefather River. Many years ago I was involved in surveys up there and also I've found in my career in the Navy that a lot of the charts that Matthew Flinders did in his time are still very good.

G'day
JOHN MASCHKE

Stuffed cat

MACCA: Yes, it's amazing to think that he did them all those years ago. Apparently, the *Investigator* was a pretty leaky old tub, John.

JOHN: It certainly was. I think he nearly sank a couple of times. I was actually commanding officer of HMAS *Flinders*, a survey vessel the Navy had which was decommissioned in 1997. We carried a stuffed cat called Trim that was named after Matthew Flinders' cat, but I think ours was a lot uglier than Trim!

MACCA: What are you doing now, John?

JOHN: I'm Seagoing Commanding Officer up in Cairns where our survey fleet is based. We're still doing surveys around the place to update our nautical charts. It's interesting to note the comments that were made about the Pennefather River. In 1996 I had on board a maritime history author called James Henderson, and during my time on *Flinders* we retraced the steps of William Jantz, who went through the Pennefather River in about 1602. That's right along the west coast of Cape York and it was quite fascinating being part of that sort of history.

MACCA: Your job sounds wonderful to me. I think a hydrographer has an interesting job, too. You're the sort of blokes that can tell the rest of us landlubbers just what it's like out there. Do you spend much of your time in that northern area?

JOHN: I've spent time all over the place, mainly in the northern areas but also around Tasmania and the south-west Pacific—Papua-New Guinea, the Solomons, Vanuatu, all those sorts of places. It's very interesting, a little bit like being Captain Cook or Matthew Flinders, especially in areas that are uncharted, and there are quite a few of those because we mainly concentrate on the approaches to harbours and the main shipping routes and finding new passages.

MACCA: I remember talking to a bloke who was up there, and New Guinea sounds a wonderful place to be—really interesting geographically and, I suppose, hydrographically.

JOHN: I did some work on the coastal strip between Wewak and Madang quite a few years ago and it was fascinating. We went about a mile into the Sepik River and passed a couple of volcanoes and took the opportunity to climb up one of them. It was funny because when we were climbing up I asked one of the locals how often the volcano erupted and he said, 'Oh, only during the dry season,' and I said, 'When's the dry season?' and he said, 'It's right now, actually.' It was a bit of a worry after that but we got back safely.

MACCA: Sounds scary!

JOHN: Actually the Dutch, as well as Flinders, managed to chart quite a lot of the northern part of Australia between 1500 and 1600 and some of their charts are still quite good. The only problem they had in those days was making sure their calculation of longitude was correct and it wasn't done very well most of the time because they didn't have a very good timepiece to do it. It was only after James Cook sailed round with one of Harrison's chronometers that the longitude started to be worked out correctly.

MACCA: John, it's really interesting to hear about your admiration for Flinders and Cook. I'm reading a book at the moment, *King of the Australian Coast*, which is about Parker King, another great navigator, and it makes me think about how in 1999-2000 Bern Cuthbertson had rebuilt the *Norfolk* and followed in the wake of Flinders. What he wished to do was to rebuild the *Investigator*, which is just as important in lots of ways as the *Endeavour*, but of course it would have cost millions of dollars. We rebuilt the *Endeavour* and it's a shame that it's left up to people like Bern who had limited resources. We really should be doing that as a nation.

◎

ON 4TH MARCH 1802 Commander Matthew Flinders recorded in his journal after sighting three or four Aborigines near the place he named Port Lincoln: *Such seemed to have been the conduct of the Australians and I am persuaded that their appearance on the morning the tents were struck was a prelude to their coming down.*

As far as is known this is the first use of the word 'Australians' to describe the inhabitants of the continent whatever their ethnic origin.

Flinders used the word again about a year later up in the Gulf of Carpentaria when he was comparing the Aborigines there with those that he had seen down south.

It is well known that Flinders wanted the name 'Australia' to take precedence on his chart of the continent, but he was forced to put it after 'Terra Australis'.

It was near Port Lincoln, about two weeks before this entry, that one of *Investigator*'s boats was lost with all eight crew including the master, John Thistle, who had sailed with Flinders on HMAS *Reliance* and on the *Norfolk*, and with George Bass in his whaleboat voyage from Sydney to Westernport. Flinders named Thistle Island after him, seven other nearby islands after the others, and Cape Catastrophe and the Memory Cove after the event. They are all just south of Port Lincoln.

It was also near Port Lincoln that in the 1840s Sir John Franklin, then Lieutenant-Governor of Tasmania, who was Flinders' cousin and a midshipman on *Investigator*, raised the first memorial to Flinders.

From:
Peter Poland,
Woollahra History &
Heritage Society,
Double Bay,
New South Wales

IT WAS INTERESTING TO hear John the naval commander speaking from Cairns. This year we are celebrating the 200th anniversary of the circumnavigation and charting of Australia by Matthew Flinders in the *Investigator*. I have heard on radio and television that this was the first voyage in which Australia was circumnavigated. Not so!

Abel Tasman achieved the first recorded circumnavigation of the continent of Australia in ten months in 1642–43 on his voyage of exploration of the Great South Land, during which he discovered Tasmania (which he named Van Diemen's Land) and New Zealand. A full account may be read at http://www.lexicon.net/world/tasman/bhouse.htm. This was read before the Royal Society of Tasmania on the 25th November, 1895 by James Backhouse Walker, FRGS.

Flinders' contribution of 1802 was important in three ways. Firstly, he mapped a great part of the coastline. Secondly, he proved that New South Wales and New Holland were joined together, to form one continent. Thirdly, he named this continent 'Australia'.

Earlier, with George Bass, Matthew Flinders had proved that Tasmania was an island separated by what was then known as New South Wales by Bass Strait.

It is right to commemorate the activities of Flinders and his crew in 1802 but let us not forget the contributions made by earlier discoverers including Abel Tasman.

Email from:
Richard Num,
Adelaide,
South Australia

A FEW WEEKS AGO I was touring around the south-west of Western Australia and on my return was able to catch up on the TV series about Flinders and Baudin, *The Navigators*. It was particularly interesting to watch the programme, having just visited places such as Geographe Bay and Cape Leeuwin. After seeing the series one could not help but be filled with admiration for the Frenchman whose navigating feats were in many respects as great as those of Finders. At the end of the programme it was revealed that in France Baudin is unknown, and

Email from:
Don Radford,
Bilgola Plateau,
New South Wales

indeed Napoleon would have hung him if he had not died on the voyage home! I did not see any monuments to Baudin during my travels in Western Australia and wondered if his feats have been celebrated anywhere along our coasts. If not, it's time to acknowledge his feats against tremendous difficulties.

WE VISITED ALASKA SOME YEARS ago and were delighted to find a wonderful statue of Captain Cook in Anchorage, looking out to the west (to the midnight sun when we were there).

Cook travelled through the area seeking a north-west passage, and had Vancouver as his second-in-command and William Bligh as a crew member. Before sailing through Prince William Sound and the Anchorage area they had sailed into the Turn Again Inlet, thinking that it was a strait. Fortunately they managed to get out before the tide turned and stranded them on the 1200-foot deep mud in the inlet exposed by the thirty-nine foot tide, and which is deposited powdered outflow from the glaciers. Bligh Reef was named during the voyage. (It was on Bligh Reef that the *Exxon Valdez* foundered and caused so much environmental devastation some time back.)

We have also seen the memorial to Cook on Hawaii where he was killed. He lost his temper over the theft of a boat and miscalculated the way the Hawaiians would react to his demand for its return.

We took a trip to North Queensland as far as Cooktown and stayed in a motel opposite Cook's Landing. We enjoyed seeing all of the commemorative features in the area, especially the wonderful James Cook Museum with the anchor and one of the cannons from the *Endeavour* on display. The cannon was dumped when the ship was holed on the reef in 1770.

At St Kilda in Melbourne there is another lovely statue to commemorate Cook on the foreshore. It was donated by someone in 1904, and has the typical stance of Cook looking out to the bay and has the names of the crew members on the base. It is great to find memorials to Cook and his wonderful skills as an explorer and sailor in various parts of the world.

I HEARD YOU TALKING about Captain Cook's illness and how it might have led to his change of character and then his death. I thought you might be interested in these extracts from a chapter in the book produced for the Cook Exhibition that toured here in 1988. The chapter was titled 'The Effect on Health of Cook and his Crews' by Surgeon Vice-Admiral Sir James Watt, a former Medical Director General (Navy).

'During the second ice-edge search of the second Voyage, in December, 1773, Cook had developed loss of appetite, anaemia, vomiting and constipation followed by acute intestinal obstruction from which he almost died. It was relieved spontaneously after seven days and the evidence appears to point to a heavy ascaris infestation. At Easter Island in April, 1774 he had been adversely affected by sunlight which had caused darkening of the exposed skin and ulcerated lips. He evidently recovered in England when Nathaniel Dance painted his portrait but had lost weight again as Webber's painting suggests by the time he arrived in New Zealand on the third Voyage in February, 1777.

'The most likely explanation is that Cook suffered from a parasitic infestation of the intestine interfering with the absorption of thiamine and niacin, vitamins of the B group. Symptoms include prolonged ill health, fatigue, loss of appetite and weight, constipation or diarrhoea, digestive disturbances, loss of interest and initiative, irritability, depression, loss of concentration and memory, change of personality and sometimes sensitivity to sunlight. They were all symptoms from which Cook suffered and which were attested to by six independent observers, two of who were his surgeons. There is absolutely no evidence that Cook ever suffered from venereal disease.'

The Admiral says that Cook's change of character was probably brought on during his third voyage by a combination of his health and his realisation that these voyages of discovery were bringing disease to the natives, and explains his increasingly severe punishments to crew and islanders, his rampaging and destruction in the Society Islands and his poor handling of the events in Hawaii that led to his death.

WE STAYED FOR TWO weeks in Cooktown some years ago. Our time there was in the same month that Lieutenant Cook (as was his rank then) had been there repairing the *Endeavour*. Each day I went into the library and read copies of Cook's journal for that day. It made history come alive.

I remember that one particular day the crew managed to get the bow of the *Endeavour* up onto some barrels—a primitive kind of 'dry dock' I suppose. The problem was that as the ship was upended the water went to the stern and that was where the bread pantry was. Disaster! All of Mr Banks' botanical specimens collected at Botany Bay were in the bread pantry for safe keeping. When I went over the *Endeavour* replica in Sydney the first place I asked for was the bread pantry, and no one knew where it was!

Every time I visit Canberra I visit the National Library, hoping to see the original Journal that Cook wrote. Often it is out on loan. Or it's 'resting' and only the facsimile copy is available. In 1997 I struck gold and was able to see and read some of James Cook's original journal! I had my seven-year-old granddaughter with me and I wanted to plant in her memory the importance of the book on the stand in front of us, so I told her that the book we were reading was written by Mr Cook but it wasn't a cookbook. It was a book by Cook! She read a whole sentence and still remembers that big book by Cook!

The part of the journal that I asked to read was from what became known as the Cooktown sojourn. The day that they saw a kangaroo and tried to describe it in terms of animals that they knew. It was a 'greyhound' (that was crossed out), it was it a 'bear' (that also was crossed out) and the word 'kangaroo' was inserted.

Gungarde is what the local Aborigines call the site of Cooktown. Lieutenant Cook did not do so well in his relationship with the local Aborigines. Having caught a heap of turtles on their patch, when they came for a share as their law demanded he refused them. So, Cook broke the law of the local Aborigines who sentenced his camp to be torched that night.

Does this make Lieutenant Cook the first white criminal in Australia? His crew had fished in the territory of the Aborigines and their law laid down that catches be strictly portioned out. When in Aboriginal territory should Cook have done as Aborigines do?

*From:
Irene Shanks,
Mareeba,
Queensland*

G'day, this is Macca

BEV: Hello, Macca, this is Bev in Portugal. I just wanted to let you know that there's a couple of Pommies here who enjoy listening to your programme.

MACCA: Bev, is it? And you're a bloke?

BEV: I'm afraid so, yes. You'd have to ask my mother about that. She and my sister live in South Australia and I'm the only one in my family still left back here in Europe.

MACCA: So what are you doing in Portugal?

BEV: My wife and I run an astronomy observatory and that's why we're up so late on a Saturday night. People visit and use the telescopes. They mostly come from Britain, because the sky is a lot clearer here and it's a lot warmer.

MACCA: We think we've the best of everything here in Australia but our night skies are legendary. What are they like in Portugal?

BEV: They're pretty good. We get something like 3,000 hours of sunshine every year so there's lots of clear skies, and being a bit closer to the Equator there's more to see down into the southern sky, which has all the best things in the astronomical field. We're bringing a planeload of astronomers to South Australia in December, hopefully to witness a total eclipse, which will go from Ceduna across Woomera.

MACCA: What are astronomers like? In the media we have dramas like an asteroid's just passed within 750,000 miles from the earth and if it had hit it would have killed us all.

BEV: Pretty laid back. The ones we get here are mostly from Britain. Because of the climate you have to have a sense of humour to want to see the sky in Britain! But most astronomers live to a ripe old age so it's obviously not too stressful. I'm wondering why Australia isn't searching for these asteroids like everybody's furiously doing in the northern hemisphere.

MACCA: It's because those people have nothing better to do, mate, fair dinkum. They go on and on, saying 'We can get rockets and we can blow them up out in space'—it's just such nonsense. I suppose I'm a great fatalist. I believe in what's going to happen, not in sending nuclear bombs out to blow up asteroids that might hit the world and put big holes in the place.

JOHN: Hello Macca, it's John Ryan here, ringing from Althorpe Island. I rang you about a month ago when we were fixing a lighthouse up in the Coral Sea. Today we're doing some work just off the North Peninsula, about ten kilometres off the mainland and if we turn around we're about thirty kilometres from Kangaroo Island.

MACCA: So, John, you've travelled a bit since the last time I spoke to you. Have you been home since then?

JOHN: I've been home for a couple of weeks. I'm not down here on my own, I've got Laurie Campbell from Melbourne and Darryl Payne from Adelaide with me and we're just doing some maintenance on the light on this island.

MACCA: And what's Althorpe Island like?

JOHN: The light is about 120 years old and it's about 400 metres up off the water so when you walk up from the landing it's a pretty hard climb. It's got low scrub and there's an old airstrip and a helipad. It's actually a muttonbird roosting island so there's plenty of birds morning and afternoon.

MACCA: And it's obviously adjacent to the shipping channel.

JOHN: Yes, the shipping channel appears to be between here and Kangaroo Island. There are two lights on this island, the main light and the lead light, which comes from the west.

MACCA: What do you do to the light, John? Maintenance and polishing and that sort of thing?

JOHN: Not so much polishing these days. That used to be the old keeper's job. We're staying in one of the keepers' residences but we're here just to do maintenance on the light, just to keep it in working order.

MACCA: It's amazing that boats still go aground in these high technology days, isn't it?

JOHN: Yes, there's a little notice here that says there are about six shipwrecks around this island in various spots. If you go up here at night you can see three lights flashing in the area that we look after, so a lot of navigational aids are maintained just for shipping.

MACCA: I've got my map here. Althorpe's only a little island. I can see Stenhouse Bay and Marion Bay.

JOHN: I'm not sure what size Althorpe is. There's a strip for light aircraft but you wouldn't want to land too much these days because it's like a wheat field and full of muttonbird holes. We came out by helicopter this time and it took eight or nine trips to get our gear out.

MACCA: Gee, the things that people do that you don't know about. John, thanks for that and a good geography lesson.

I WAS LISTENING TO your show last week about the Australian coast and in particular your guest talking about his exploits during the war years. You spoke about the British naval ship's near tragedy and your guest mentioned how close he came to losing his ship on a reef in New Guinea. That story highlighted to me the need of those who venture out to sea to retain our navigation skills.

Today we have a wide range of tools to assist us in navigating our waters, such as the global positioning system (GPS). Many people use these tools as their only means of navigating the sea. The adverts say 'key in your destination' and the GPS will guide you there. But the 'old' navigation skills are vital. We never know when our tools will break down and we must protect ourselves. Everyone at sea should know how to plot their course onto their charts and be able to obtain a fix of their position without these tools so they understand what the tools are doing.

Email from:
Eric Taylor

SOU' WESTERS

There's a stiff sou' wester blowing inshore and it ruffles the open bay
And it rushes along the jetty's stretch and sings of another day,
Of ketches and blokes with singlets of blue and wheat stacks and cockies and farm
And tall ships anchored on swinging chains and safe from Cape Horn's harm.

From:
Max Fatchen,
Smithfield,
South Australia

The bay is empty where whitecaps paint their foaming erratic lines.
The wind will sweep the esplanade and rattle the parking signs.
The caravans on hilltop quiver, a creaking in jetty planks
There fishermen scowl with their tangled lines and give the wind no thanks.

No wheat stacks now where the mice once went in their squeaking, hungry hordes
Where farmers discussed the season price with agency overlords.
There flat-swinging sailors from foreign climes with landlubbers disagreed
For life under sail on the swaying yards created a hardy breed.

The bollards capture no mooring ropes, no horse-drawn truck arrives
On the rusty lines of the jetty's deck, reminders of long-gone lives
But over the waves comes the ghostly sound and toll of some ship's bell
For there in the breeze from the seven seas are the yarns sou' westers tell.

"... and on the Road Again

I always call into Captain Moonlight's grave up on the hill in Gundagai's cemetery, sit in the shade of a big gum tree and soak up the beautiful countryside.
FROM: *Bob Moore*, North Rocks, New South Wales

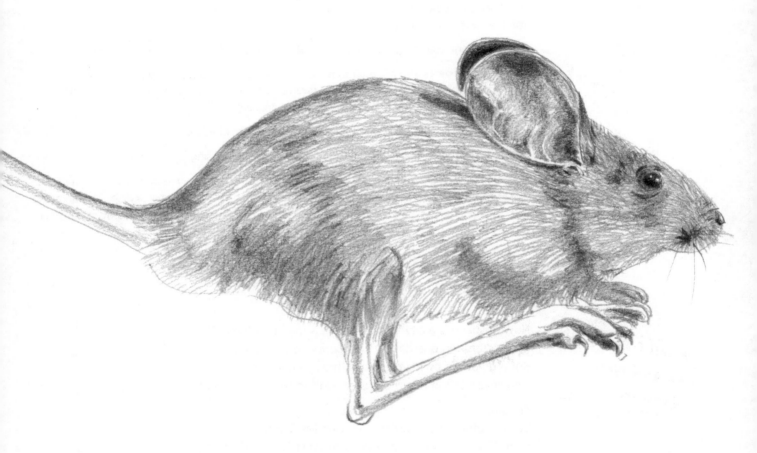

Macca talks to Australians all over under the Story Bridge, Brisbane

G'day . . .

HUGH LUNN

and

RAY WEDGEWOOD

MACCA: We're under the Story Bridge this morning and with me is Hugh Lunn. You have something to tell us about the bridge, Hugh.

HUGH: Dr Bradfield wrote a book about how he designed and built the Story Bridge, which he presented to the Premier. It's in the Premier's office but unless you can get into the office you can't read it. This is what he said:

At the beginning of time the foundation fabric designed to form the stars, the sun, the planets, this earth of ours and all the radiation which has been poured out from the sun and the stars ever since, was a chaotic mass of gas, a fire mist diffused through the whole of space. Mythology tells us that we owe steel, the most potent factor in the building progress of the world, to the goddess of the Pole Star. This goddess descended from the firmanent, became enamoured of a mortal, Siderite, but he, loving none but his brother Sidere, repulsed her. In her wrath she transformed the devoted brothers, Siderite into lodestone and Sidere into iron.
One force can draw it from the star above
Iron the symbol of fraternal love

MACCA: Thank you, Hugh. Ray Wedgewood's here too. Did you have a comment on that?

RAY: Well, engineers are supposed to be fairly non-poetic, but Bradfield wrote stuff like that about the Harbour Bridge, too. Steel has given way to concrete now in our big bridges. It's cheaper, more flexible and it requires less skills than steel.

MACCA: You built the big Anzac Bridge in Sydney. Is that mostly concrete?

RAY: Yes, but there's steel in the stays that hold it up. We're using steel in a more efficient way.

HUGH: Bradfield said that he wanted a bridge that with its lofty towers and powerful river arms would harmonise with the picturesque and rugged beauty of the Brisbane skyline. A steel bridge with its plated angles, its bold towers and broad shoulders, whether viewed nearby or afar, will express simplicity, strength and grace.

Email from:
Dermot Dorgan,
Queensland

Now Brisbane is a city that can leave a man perplexed,
It's beautiful on one day and it's perfect on the next.
But a great big bendy river runs through it like a snake
And crossing it in rush hour is enough to make your heart break.

Refrain:
Build another bridge across the river, Mr Beattie,
From Newstead to Bulimba or from West End to Toowong.
If the costs are getting scary, you can sell the Moggill Ferry
Or raffle off the Broncos to help the job along.

So they started out and built a bridge from Southbank to the city,
But it has some disadvantages, which seems like such a pity.

The arch comes from the southern shore and stands without a sway
But some twit miscalculated and it only goes half way.
Refrain
A friend of mine was driving down from Cairns to watch the cricket,
When he called me on his mobile phone, I said 'Tear up your ticket,
The Story Bridge is badly blocked, no movement either way,
And traffic coming from the north's backed up to Hervey Bay.'
Refrain
My mate's first cousin's uncle's been in hospital for days,
He was gridlocked in his Commodore at the Normanby Five Ways.
It took ten days to clear the jam and when some help came through
He'd eaten half the engine block and the windscreen wipers too.
Refrain
She was heading for the Mater with a baby on the way,
But heavy traffic held her up and would not clear away.
By the time she reached the hospital, she was pretty late, I reckon
'Cos her baby was a toddler and she was pregnant with her second.
Refrain

STORY BRIDGE (BRISBANE) URBAN MYTHS

My Auntie La lived in Queensland on Highgate Hill overlooking the university across the Brisbane River. On our rare visits to Brisbane (once by flying boat from Rose Bay!) she would entertain us with the latest uni pranks and scandals. Two stories she told were about the Story Bridge. Maybe Brisbane old-timers could tell us which is true!

Story Bridge Myth Number One

Engineering students at the uni calculated that the load on the bridge was too much and that the asphalt needed to be cut back by six inches. So, dressed as road workers, with yellow barricades and surveyors' gear, they blocked the bridge and caused traffic chaos all day. They packed up and left before anyone realised it was a prank.

Story Bridge Myth Number Two

Genuine council workers were doing maintenance work on the bridge (maybe on the 'kerlunk, kerlunk, kerlunk' span joints?). University students rang the police saying that the students dressed as council workers were obstructing traffic on the bridge. Then the students went to the council workers and told them that uni students dressed as police were going to move them on for obstructing traffic: 'Story Bridge Melee', ran the headline in the *Courier Mail*.

　　See if you can dig out the truth!

From:
Malcolm Reed,
Pennant Hills,
New South Wales

WE ARRIVED IN AUSTRALIA in August 1973 and were driven to the migrant hostel under the Story Bridge. The Brisbane International Airport then consisted of an iron hut with no facilities such as refreshments on a Sunday morning! How times have changed.

　　The Story Bridge has always been special because it was, briefly, our first Australian home. The Queensland Education Department employed Gavin, my husband, in London.

From:
Irene Shanks,
Mareeba,
Queensland

We now own a bookshop in Mareeba with thousands of second-hand books. Even second-hand copies of your books!

We did a two-month trip from Mareeba to Darwin in 1994 and saw your Darwin show and loved it—especially the water buffalo. There you were on the mike telling your audience about the water buffalo you had in the 'studio'. I scoffed until I looked around and saw it behind me. Did I jump!

We wish we could be there under the Story Bridge with you. However, our daughter, Sarah, who served ten years as an officer in the Royal Australian Navy, said she would try and make it. On her wedding day, Sarah and her husband, Chris, were stranded in all their wedding finery *on* the Story Bridge. That's another story! I look forward to listening to the show with extra special nostalgia because you'll be under the Story Bridge.

Macca talks to Australians all over at Oak Valley, South Australia

G'day . . .
ARCHIE BARTON

MACCA: One of our guests is Archie Barton. Archie, it's nice to be here with you in Oak Valley.

ARCHIE: On behalf of the community it's a pleasure having you here. When I was asked to suggest an appropriate person (to be invited to the opening of the art centre) I said, 'What about we try Macca on Sunday?' Today is something to give back to the community the pride that was more or less taken away in the 1950s when they moved from Ooldea.

MACCA: Tell people how you got your surname.

ARCHIE: When I was five years old and my sister was two we were taken away by Welfare to Port Augusta and put in a home. We were born out here in the desert and when we were taken away we didn't have a birth date or anything, and when the Welfare picked me up we were going past Barton Siding so I got the name Barton.

MACCA: That siding was named after our first prime minister, Edmund Barton. His nickname was 'Toby Tosspot' because he liked a drink. You liked a drink, too, didn't you Archie?

ARCHIE: I was a shearer and if you didn't drink you were out on your own. I had twenty-two years of it and it's been a hard road, but in 1982 I answered an ad and became a project officer, although I didn't know what a project officer did. In 1985 I became a community adviser and walked into the issue of the old men wanting to get back to their land at Maralinga. I was on the consultative committee and did a lot of negotiating during the whole seventeen years of Maralinga, including taking two delegations to London. On our second trip we took eight kilos of soil sample and I think that was the light at the end of the tunnel.

G'day . . .
SUE NATRISS

MACCA: Sue Natriss is from Melbourne and she's the artistic director of the Adelaide Festival. How's the festival been this year?

SUE: It's been really extraordinary. This festival was set up with three themes in mind—truth and reconciliation, the right to cultural diversity and environmental sustainability. It began by one of our associate directors, who's a visual artist, having conversations with the community. They were talking about Maralinga lands and what they look like. None of us have been there so we have no real understanding, and the community said they'd love to learn to paint with acrylics on canvas or wood so that they could leave for generations to come the pictures they still had in their minds of what the Maralinga lands were like. So we sent an artist up here three or four weeks ago to work with the community and they've produced these paintings, which are more than extraordinary given the length of time they've been painting.

MACCA: Are the paintings a story of the last fifty, a hundred, a thousand years, including the time when the A bombs were let off?

SUE: There are certainly images of mushroom clouds in a number of the paintings. There's a story behind each one and some of the images are extraordinary strong of mushroom clouds with kangaroos beside them, which signifies food that was destroyed through the bomb testing. But there are others with different stories. It's wonderful to be out here. I feel as if I've been on a ten-week holiday just in the few hours I've been here.

MACCA: I'm with Grant Feedler, principal of the school here, and Noeleen Cox. Grant, what's it like working in an isolated community like Oak Valley?

GRANT: I've been here since 1998 and I've always enjoyed it. It's a bit of an alternative lifestyle, and to be part of a place which has two cultures is very rewarding. I think I've got a lot to offer and the school is all about working in partnership with the community. We've got four teachers and a principal and about thirty-eight kids, but it's a transient sort of place and there are new faces every week.

MACCA: Is it hard as a white person to interact with the Aboriginal children?

GRANT: Because Pitjantjatjara is their language the children only speak English at school, so from the outset I've always had an Aboriginal Education Worker with me in the classroom to clarify what's being taught. That's the key link.

MACCA: Where are you from, Noeleen?

NOELEEN: This is my family area. I came up here in 1999 to work at the school in partnership with the community and the kids. We're trying to offer choices and to show the children that there's a wider world out there.

Macca talks to Australians all over at Lindisfarne, Tasmania

MACCA: I'm talking to David Chambers, who is president of the rowing club here. I'm told your club burnt down and you lost everything.

DAVID: Yes, we'd just had a drive to raise $30,000 to buy three new boats and they were lost as well as all our other boats. But we announced a public appeal called 'Rising from the Ashes', and with the contributions and physical help we received we rebuilt in just under twelve months.

MACCA: You're Tanya, David Chambers' wife. Have you lived here all your life?

G'day . . .
GRANT FEEDLER
and
NOELEEN COX

G'day . . .
DAVID and TANYA
CHAMBERS

TANYA: Yes, I was born in Lindisfarne. We've done a lot of travelling—I went to India and spent five weeks studying at a Tibetan university, which was a wonderful experience. But it's always great to come home to Lindisfarne. The air's fresh, the community's great, it has the best water, the best food—I can't speak too highly of it.

MACCA: Do you row?

TANYA: I wanted to row when I was about thirteen but girls weren't allowed to row years ago, so I've only just started and I enjoy it very much.

DAVID: I was in America for six months four years ago and Tanya sent tapes of your show to me and I got really homesick. When I came back to Tassie it was like God's country.

Macca talks to Australians all over at Fitzroy Crossing, Western Australia

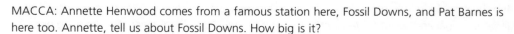

G'day . . .

ANNETTE HENWOOD

and

PAT BARNES

MACCA: Annette Henwood comes from a famous station here, Fossil Downs, and Pat Barnes is here too. Annette, tell us about Fossil Downs. How big is it?

ANNETTE: It's smaller than it used to be. In my father's day it was almost two million acres, including Lansdowne, which he later sold because it was just too big to handle. Today it's about three-quarters of a million acres, so I guess it's still big.

MACCA: I suppose you need big stations out here because the country's different.

ANNETTE: Yes, we always say that Fossil's one-third good country, one-third not so good and one-third rock. It got its name because we have a lot of fossils from the Devonian era.

MACCA: Are times good on the land at the moment?

ANNETTE: Oh, it's a pleasure to be able to say that they are at this time, but there's been a lot of tough times and we really need this.

MACCA: Tell us how Fossil Downs got started.

ANNETTE: There were glowing reports of the area in the 1870s and my great-grandfather decided he would overland his cattle here. They left in 1883 with six-hundred-and-seventy head of cattle, sixty horses, two bullock wagons with thirty-six bullocks to pull them. It took them three-and-a-quarter years to get here and, they said, a lifetime to forget it. My father used to say that it took courage to live in Kimberley but far more courage to leave it.

MACCA: Pat, you're just travelling through here, aren't you? Where are you from?

PAT: I'm from Belmont, Lake Macquarie, New South Wales. We went up the Centre to Darwin and now we're coming down the west coast and across the Nullarbor. We're travelling with four elderly chihuahuas and a nineteen-year-old cat. I've done it before but it's been much more hilarious doing it by caravan. It's been a wonderful trip, the whole area's just magic. At the Mary River there was a sign on the toilet saying 'Macca Tomorrow at Fitzroy Crossing', so here we are!

MACCA: Ron's here. Where are you from, Ron?

RON: Wilmot in Tasmania. Liz and I have been on the road for nearly a year and it's been marvellous. I was an anaesthetist at home, but I worked in New Guinea for a little while and they called me 'doctor of the long sleep'. The pidgin speakers used to say, 'doctor he kill 'im liklik no he wake up yet' which means we kill them for a little while and then they wake up!

Macca talks to Australians all over from Switzerland

PETER: This is Peter Ellis from Switzerland.

MACCA: You're in Switzerland? Tell me more.

PETER: Well, I'm a watchmaker. I build transparent watches for a company over here. My wife's in the next room listening to you on the internet.

MACCA: How long have you been there, Peter?

PETER: Since 1989. My wife's Swiss and it was easy to come over. I wasn't getting anywhere professionally in Australia and, of course, watchmaking is an easier profession here so I was able to get in.

MACCA: You mean there's no outlet now for watchmakers in Australia?

PETER: It's very hard to get in if you're not actually within the trade. When I was there it was still pretty much a closed profession, but I don't know what it's like now.

MACCA: I recently talked to a bloke in Armidale who makes clocks—the old sort, chiming clocks—and he went over to the Black Forest in Germany to see what they were doing, because that's traditionally the home of clockmaking, and he found that it's all winding down and there aren't many left at all. He was quite disappointed.

PETER: I think it's picked up a lot lately. There's a lot of interest in higher quality movements, high quality pieces. People now are willing to fork out rather a large sum of money and have a family heirloom to pass down.

MACCA: What's it like living in Switzerland? Where were you from, Peter?

PETER: I'm from a little place called Wodonga on the Murray River. And life here? Well, it's cold in winter, which is rather long, and summer's short. The nights aren't too bad in summer. It cools down so you can get some sleep rather than having the hot nights I remember in Australia.

MACCA: It must be very hard to get used to the seasons over there.

PETER: Yes. Snow's all right in photos but when you have to get out and start shovelling it ...!

G'day . . .
RON

 G'day
PETER ELLIS

When's the next shift change?

Macca talks to Australians all over from Northern Cook Island

 G'day
MIKE

MIKE: Mike calling. We're listening to you on Radio Australia here in the Northern Cook Island group on a little atoll called Penryn.

MACCA: I used to collect stamps and I think I have a stamp from Penryn. Would that be right?

MIKE: Yes, we have some nice stamps here. We're up here growing black pearls in the lagoon. We've been here since about '97. My wife was born here so it was always our dream to come back and set up a cultured pearl operation, so we've spent the last few years getting it organised and have just had our first harvest of pearls.

MACCA: And you enjoy living there, Mike?

MIKE: Oh, it's beautiful. We're on the edge of a lagoon which is about eight kilometres across and I'm looking at the palm trees on the other side. The water's crystal clear and it's about thirty-five degrees today. We have some of the local boys who've been diving for shells for us. It's an absolutely beautiful day here and I think we might even go fishing this afternoon.

MACCA: Tell us about the pearls.

MIKE: They're Tahitian black pearls, although we prefer to call them Polynesian black pearls. They come from a different oyster than the ones we have in Australia, although I believe they do have the black lip in Queensland. We have Tahitians come in to feed the pearls and it takes about eighteen months or two years to produce one. They come in quite a range of colours from very dark black and silver right through to green. There are other major pearl farming atolls in the Cooks, but it's a very new thing for Penryn so there's only a few farms here. Penryn's the biggest lagoon in the Cook Islands and it's also the most pristine, so that's why we're here. I think I'm losing you …

MACCA: He's gone. That's what happens.

Macca talks to Australians all over from Saudi Arabia

 G'day
TERRI

MACCA: You might remember this call.

TERRI: Terri here, from Saudi Arabia. I'm over here on a nursing contract. I left my family behind and decided to strike out on my own.

MACCA: Where are you from, Terri?

TERRI: I'm from Brisbane, originally from Victoria, have lived in Western Australia, love Australia, and I'm just spreading my wings a little bit further.

MACCA: So you decided to go to Saudi Arabia. What's that like?

TERRI: It's hot. It's a nice cool forty-one degrees today, which is better than the forty-five that it has been. I've been here for four weeks and I've forgotten what cool weather is like. Life is so different here. I'm working with people from fifty-two countries all over the world. There are a lot of South Africans and I met a New Zealand girl tonight. It's a bit of a case of 'spot the Aussie'.

MACCA: How long is your contract?

TERRI: Twelve months. I've booked to go home in February/March on annual leave with my return airfare paid, and I'll bring my husband back with me.

MACCA: Did you go there purely because the salary was attractive?

TERRI: No, it wasn't the salary. I'm a midwife and it was just mainly for the experience to see what birthing is like in other countries. It's very, very different. The birth rate is very high here—it's nothing for them to have ten to eighteen children and by about the sixteenth they just sort of wave the child away, they don't even want to see it. Just to give these women a little TLC is really nice.

MACCA: Yes, quite a different culture from the one you've come from, of course. You hear things about alcohol and that sort of thing so I suppose you have to mind your Ps & Qs.

TERRI: Absolutely. When I go off the compound I have to wear a black cloak and cover my hair and being a blonde I keep it covered because I really get stared at. Around the compound I don't have to wear the cloak but I do have to have my arms and ankles covered—ankles are very sexy!

MACCA: It depends whose ankles, I suppose!

That was in 2000 just before the Olympics and I've been wanting to talk to Terri again.

TERRI: G'day, Macca. I've been home for about a year. It was just the most amazing experience of my life.

MACCA: Yes, I wanted to talk to you because we had a call recently from a young girl who'd just moved to Saudi Arabia.

TERRI: Yes, I know. Someone at work told me.

MACCA: We've got a great bush telegraph. We always like to keep in touch and we were looking for you. So, what's it like being back? Did you end up enjoying it?

TERRI: I did. It was an amazing time, just so different. As I said when I first spoke to you the change is incomprehensible. I did it for the experience and what a learning curve it was.

MACCA: The experience of midwifing over there must have been unbelievable.

TERRI: Oh, my heart bleeds for some of those women. The educated ones were good and the Bedouins didn't know any different, but they were so sweet. They'd grab my hand and be so grateful when you showed them some kindness that they'd rip off their jewellery and try to give it to you. When you told them you couldn't accept it they'd think their gift wasn't good enough for you and try to give you something more expensive. The land is so full of contrasts. It's so rich and so poor. You go to the big shopping centres and it's just dripping money and then you go to the *souks*, the little market stalls in another suburb, and it's just poverty.

MACCA: So you're a changed girl, Terri.

TERRI: I grew up. I think it was about time at fifty!

MACCA: And you've settled down back in Australia. Was that one experience enough for you?

TERRI: It does instil in you a travel bug because there's so much to see and to learn. But it's nice to be home and my children were really pleased to see me in one piece.

MACCA: It's nice to catch up with you. You said so much and yet you left things unsaid.

TERRI: Oh, there's still so much unsaid that I'll have to write a book!

Macca talks to Australians all over from New York

 G'day

MARK

MARK: It's Mark from cold old New York. I've been listening to you on the internet all morning. I trade Asian equities and also broker all the Australasian stocks.

MACCA: Gee, and aren't they taking a hammering, Mark. That's a tough gig at the moment.

MARK: Macca, it's like trying to sell ice to the Eskimos. There's a big picture in today's *New York Times* of the 101st Airborne Division heading out to the Persian Gulf, so things certainly seem to be heating up here. A couple of weeks ago they raised the terror alert in New York to red and said that in the event of chemical warfare to get some duct tape and plastic sheeting and three or four days' worth of supplies. I went to the supermarket that night and I've never seen a bigger rush on duct tape and plastic, so people are paying very close attention. As far as the market's concerned, it's basically trading sideways.

MACCA: At school we used to call them shocks and scares.

MARK: Well, it's still like that!

Top: Even though she was eighty-two and suffering from dementia, my Mum Lorna was a little cutie, don't you agree? She just loved that hat.

Bottom left: Our good friend for many years, a listeners' favourite, 104 ½ and going strong, Gilbert Bennion from Tweed Heads in New South Wales. As May Jones says in her poem in the book, 'It's time to charge our glasses to wish dear Gilbert well, a really good Australian who has no parallel'.

Bottom right: Dorothy Watt's lovely poems have appeared in all of my books. This is her little companion Georgie Girl who hates having a bath but loves the electric dryer!

Above: A couple of 'thorny devils' surround Lee. That other one's David Johnson!

Left: Where did you say you were calling from?' Lee's adept at taking calls at any location on the road. Laura Bailey looks on.

Right: Harriet Nixon captivated the crowd singing the national anthem at our Sydney drought fundraiser.

Top: The weather for the Canberra broadcast was lovely. Here I talk with poet Timoshenko Aslanides, and Pam and Brian Cooke of calici virus fame.

Middle: To celebrate the 100th anniversary of Sydney's Pyrmont Bridge we broadcast from there and then enjoyed this mighty cake from Ray Kersh of Edna's Table. It tasted great.

Bottom: On Australia Day in 2003 we were in Sydney's Hyde Park where I met Louise and her kids.

Top: My Blues Brothers-style hat kept out the sun on Robert Turnbull's drought-stricken, Lightning Ridge property. It even stayed on as I helped him roll out drought fodder called 'peanut hay'.

Below: Kev and his daughter Gidgee (nicknamed after the hardy gidgee tree) found these thorny devils on the Anne Beadell Highway. They travelled from Coober Pedy in South Australia to Laverton in Western Australia, over 1650 kilometres, and 'never saw a soul'.

12

◎ *Never Smile at a Crocodile* ◎

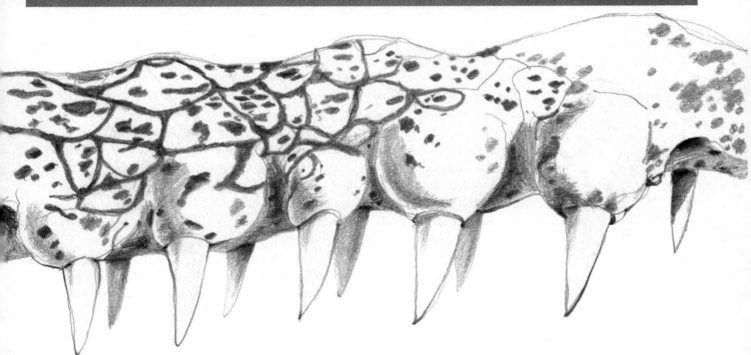

G'day Macca, it's Norm Mathiske from Swan Hill calling you from Rome.

MACCA: What are you doing in Rome, mate. Are you with the Pope?

NORM: Yes, we did a tour of the Vatican, it's on a hundred-acre paddock. I brought wheat to feed the pigeons in Trafalgar Square. My mate Shar at Bulga grew it. He gave me a matchbox full and the pigeons went 'berko' over it!

From:
Claude Marias,
Humpty Doo,
Northern Territory

WHEN I TOLD MY workmate that I was going bush for the weekend, towards the Ferguson River, he said: 'Be careful of the crocodiles.' I was a bit annoyed he was taking me for such a fool, and forgot his advice.

Off we went on a Friday morning, we being Anne, Laika our dog, and Joe, a good friend of ours. We had a good four-wheel drive fully equipped for a long trip. We also had a few beers and an old rifle, just in case. By night-time we were 300 kilometres south of Darwin.

The following day, very early, we left the track and started our long trip, compass driving towards the Ferguson River. We drove throughout the day amongst the rocky hills, the gum trees, the dust and the intense heat. Late in the afternoon we could see, at last, the Ferguson River. The air was vibrating with heat. A few paperbark trees, a lagoon with beautiful milky water, a few wild horses racing away from us. Our shirts were sticky with sweat and we were covered in red dust. Laika jumped in the warm water and so did we. It was divine after that day of dust and sweat, even though it was muddy and very, very warm.

After frolicking for a while with everybody, I suddenly thought of the warning given to me by my workmate. What about playing a good joke on Anne and Joe? I swam to shore, climbed a big rock and shouted to everyone I'd just seen a crocodile. But then I noticed about fifty metres away from the swimmers two huge bubbles drifting towards my friends. My immediate reaction was to take off my glasses and clean them. I put the glasses back on and there they were again, those big bubbles that continued to move towards the swimmers! I can still visualise the 'V' shape in the water behind the bubbles. Now that I really needed to shout 'crocodile', I couldn't. Finally, with a voice hoarse and shaky, I managed to mumble 'co-co-cro-codile'. I then grabbed the rifle that, by chance, was next to me and shot the big croc in the eye. The beast dived. Had I hit it? I will never know.

Later on my friends said I'd invented the whole story. But I noticed that evening Joe, who as a general rule, doesn't carry heavy loads, was dragging huge trunks to surround the camp-fire. Anne, who normally sleeps like a log, fed the fire all night. Crocodiles, as everyone knows, climb the banks of the rivers at night!

DURING THE 1970S I was working in the Northern Territory as a wildlife inspector chasing poachers. The Territory, like the Kimberley and the Gulf, was still wide open for people who wanted to have an adventure without too many restrictions.

I received information that a man from Cairns was catching small 'freshies' (freshwater crocodiles) in the Victoria River district on Dorisvale and Bradshaw Stations. In those years freshwater crocodiles were a protected species.

From:
Ian Watson,
Lennox Head,
New South Wales

My mate and I left Darwin and drove to Katherine, then west towards Timber Creek. At Timber Creek we crossed the Victoria River and headed north to Wumbungi Yard on Dorisvale Station.

This area is extremely isolated; no roads and uninhabited, magnificent country full of small creeks and billabongs teeming with freshwater crocodiles and wildlife. We travelled for many hours looking for the culprit. Just on dark we picked up vehicle tracks that led us to numerous waterholes. The surrounds of the waterholes had skinned crocodile carcasses, which told us that the poacher was netting small crocodiles to stuff the skins for sale to tourist shops in north Queensland. Feeling confident that we would apprehend the bloke that night, we pushed on, following the tracks that were becoming fresher all the time. Eventually, about seven o'clock we heard the motor of a truck we estimated to be a couple of kilometres in front of us.

Over-confident (a big mistake in the bush) we gunned the motor to catch up and next thing we are bogged to the axles in a swamp that appeared from nowhere. Our 'friend' had led us into the bog by going into the water and backing out, the oldest poacher's trick in the Territory! We dug and winched the vehicle for four hours until we got it free of the bog and then decided to hit the swags.

The next morning it was decided to backtrack to Katherine and attempt to catch up with the poacher in the Pine Creek area. That evening we camped on Bradshaw station. In the morning we boiled the billy, had a cuppa, packed the truck and were ready to go. But the battery was flat as a pancake! We cranked the motor and when this failed we jacked the back wheel up and tried to start it with a rope on the jacked-up wheel. But the motor was too tight.

As I was the driver who'd left the ignition on, I volunteered to walk to Bradshaw Station—approximately fifty kilometres overland. I walked without shoes for two hours, carrying a rifle and water in the heat. It was ten in the morning when I eventually came to a set of yards, a fence and a water trough. It was too good to miss and I jumped in the trough and started to cool off.

About half an hour later I heard the sound of a vehicle motor. It was my mate. 'How did you start the motor?' I asked. He had put the battery in our campfire ashes and warmed it, then pissed in the water compartment! It worked. He saved me a long walk!

P.S. We arrested the poacher two days later with 365 freshwater crocodile skins.

THIS MORNING YOU WERE talking about rabbits on an island and the fact that the Poms brought rabbits to Australia.

This is true but, of course, not quite the whole truth. A man named Austin brought them to Australia because rabbit was the fastest breeding edible animal anyone could imagine. It was either breed rabbits or starve to death in those harsh times.

He looked after his rabbits and they were secure and well fenced. But there was a severe flood, the fences were all washed away and the rabbits got out. Austin was in dire straits about this. He certainly had no intention of anyone getting his precious rabbits and tucker. The last thing he wanted was for them to escape and with it the food on his plate!

From:
J. Buck,
Penola,
South Australia

I STUMBLED OVER A press release on the Australian Academy of Science website. I was horrified and bewildered to read of the recent purposeful release of the European fox into Tasmania, the only Australian state to escape the ravages of this ruthless killer. It beggars belief that any government would allow such a thing to happen when the consequences are so well documented on the mainland. Why would they do such a thing?

I know many listeners are as concerned as I am about the effect of foxes on our small animals. You have talked about the problem many times. We need all concerned citizens to voice their outrage to the appropriate leaders so that the foxes can be eradicated before the next breeding season.

From:
David Walton,
Beerwah,
Queensland

From:
Eunice Thompson

WE HAD FOURTEEN SNAKES in and around our house when we first moved in. Over the past ten years they have returned every breeding season, so our eyes scan the ground all the time. We never let our guard down!

The carpet snakes snuff out the kittens and swallow them. The yellow-bellied black snakes come up into the walls (double brick) and make love all night behind the bed-head. Noisy creatures!

Eastern brown and taipan snakes are always outside on the ground and I have never seen them climb. We have had an eastern brown 'swim' towards us in the ponds. Shouts turned it away but it went straight for the guy with the gun. A vulnerable position for both!

G'day, this is Macca

G'day
SYLVIA

SYLVIA: This is Sylvia, in Brisbane. I rang you a few months ago about sending back to Cairns little frogs that arrived in bananas. I'm a frog carer and I've just sent back to Amiens seven whistling tree frogs that turned up in Brisbane in boxes of lettuce and celery. So frogs are getting around.

MACCA: Do they really whistle?

SYLVIA: I haven't heard them. They only occur in the border ranges.

MACCA: Gee, frogs get around, don't they!

SYLVIA: They certainly do. Heaps of them have come down in the last few weeks. But the story I want to tell you is that as a frog carer I sometimes get injured animals. Last week someone brought me a large green tree frog that had obviously had a long ride, we don't know from where, because it was found in a car park in the Treasury Casino.

MACCA: It had probably done its dough, I'd say!

SYLVIA: It had a badly lacerated eye so I took it to the vet, and I was so amazed at their care. They looked at its eye through an ophthalmoscope and decided they couldn't save it but would operate. They'd never operated on a frog before so they didn't know how much anaesthetic it would need. There were two surgeons, one looking down the ophthalmoscope peeling layers of rubbish off its eye and the other monitoring the anaesthetic. They had to be very careful that they didn't upset the muscles at the back of its eye because a frog swallows by pushing its eyes down the back of its throat to force the food down. But they did it. The frog is blind in one eye but it's fine.

MACCA: That's a nice story. Let that be a lesson to him to keep away from casinos—you do your dough and you lose your shirt and sometimes you lose your eye.

Email from:
Esme Henderson

I'VE FINALLY DECIDED TO contact you about how I do my bit to eradicate cane toads from our place. I use a special pair of long barbecue tongs and a plastic shopping bag (with no hole in the bottom!). I just grab the toad with the tongs, put it in the bag, and once I've done the rounds, I add two or three teaspoons of metho, tie the bag up, and they are dead in about two minutes—no noises, no struggling. I don't like the idea of putting them in the freezer. I usu-

ally dig a hole in the garden and empty them into it. I've been a bit worried that the animal liberationists might complain, but the native wildlife must come first.

Some frogs can look like toads too, so go to the library and see the difference, or contact a frog club for help.

IT MAY BE OF interest to you to know that the only enemy the cane toad has is the white tail water rat.

On our cane farm in Babinda, on the banks of the little creek by the farm shed, we would find dozens of dead cane toads. The water rats ripped them open and ate only their liver. This part of them can't be poisonous!

From:
Peg Robinson,
Herberton,
Queensland

◎

G'day, this is Macca

RON: Ron Standfield here, Macca. You've been talking about mousetraps. My dad, Wes Standfield, had a mousetrap business and you interviewed him years ago out at Mascot. We made our last mousetrap two years ago.

MACCA: Why did you get out of it, Ron? I suppose there comes a time.

RON: Yes, there comes a time. Dad had been at it all his life and we kept it going when he got a bit too old. He passed away on the premises at the age of nearly ninety. He made a machine that is at the Powerhouse Museum in Sydney.

MACCA: The plastic mousetraps you buy now just don't work.

RON: Well, that's modern life, Macca. It goes on right through everything.

MACCA: Exactly!

 G'day
RON STANDFIELD

◎

I KNOW THAT YOU have a soft spot for wombats. So do I. Although brought up in Western Australia where there are no wombats in the wild, I've always been fascinated by them. While in Tasmania on holiday I visited a sanctuary in the north of the state and had a close-up encounter with an orphaned wombat. What I learned that day resulted in a piece of verse I am attaching to this letter.

From:
Frances Maber,
South Perth,
Western Australia

WOMBAT

Our wombats have a bony plate where others have a tail,
They use it for protection and it really shouldn't fail,
'Cause enemies out in the bush creep up and take a bite
Then hit their teeth on bony plate which makes 'em run with fright.

Our wombats always turn their back with predators in view
(They haven't learned about our cars and don't know what they do),
So please, if wombat's on the road and you are in a car,
Don't mind if she stands still instead of running off afar,

Slow down and even shout at her then she will run away
And you can travel down that road while she goes off to play.

A car that goes too fast can't stop when mother wombat's crossing
So mother dies and leaves her baby without food or lodging.
Let's all take care upon the road to save this chunky creature
And celebrate its bony plate, which is its special feature.

From:
Barbara Handley,
North Plympton,
South Australia

I AM INSPIRED TO write to you by the achievements of my young five- and six-year-olds in their efforts to help save the bilby.

I am a junior primary school teacher at Paringa Park Primary School, North Brighton, South Australia. This year we undertook to do something for bilby conservation in South Australia. We called our project 'Operation Bilby'.

With the support of their families, each child set aside a little of their time every weekend to do something helpful around the house. For their efforts they earned small amounts of money which was then donated to our cause. All children participated with pride and enthusiasm and entered their jobs in their logbook.

Over six months our class raised $250 to pay for a tracking collar for a bilby in a conservation area on the Eyre Peninsula, South Australia.

The project culminated in a special assembly. We danced, sang and presented educational information that we learned about threatened species in Australia and around the world, with a special emphasis on the bilby.

From this experience the children not only had learned a great deal about the threatened species, they also had the opportunity to take action. They gained a sense of pride and a feeling of optimism for the future.

 G'day

JIM RESIDE

I'M JIM RESIDE FROM Bairnsdale in East Gippsland. I want to tell you about the shadows I've been chasing for the last ten years or so—the brush tail rock wallabies that live in East Gippsland's deep gorges. Sadly, only about ten or twelve of them are left in the wild. They're quite a pretty animal, very small, with attractive markings on their fur. Way back in the late 1800s hunting took a massive toll on them and several hundred thousand were exported annually for the fur trade.

We've developed a pretty exciting and innovative technique with a small captive colony we have. We're cross-fostering the tiny babies into the pouches of other wallabies, and those mothers raise them. Within a month the female cycles again and about thirty-five days later she gives birth to another one, so in one year she can have five or six young. We once brought a baby out of the bush in an improvised humidicrib made from a plastic cheese box. It took about three hours to hike out, then a four-wheel drive to the local airstrip, where it was flown to Bairnsdale, then to Adelaide where the foster mother was waiting. An eight-hour journey, but the baby survived and has grown beautifully.

◎

From:
Graeme Greening,
ex-Tamworth, NSW,
now Alabama, USA

I COULDN'T BELIEVE MY eyes. Here I was driving north on Highway 331 from Florida to Birmingham, Alabama, and just ten miles across the border into Alabama here was a paddock with three emus in it. I had to stop and take a photo of them. Gee, of all places. I wonder if the birds know that they're not in Australia. Do they wonder why there aren't any kangas or koalas?

CONCERNING 'ARCHIE' STANDING OUT in the light hail and rain, don't worry about it. Mother Nature has made sure horses and cattle were designed to withstand those conditions. When it rains the horses and cattle turn their backs to it. The rain wets the tops of their coats and hair, which in healthy animals have a certain amount of oil. The hair packs down to make a waterproof surface that sheds the water.

However, if there is wind with the rain, it drives the water up under the hair to the animal's skin, and it's then the horse or cow starts to feel cold.

If you want to see a really miserable animal, wait until you see a donkey when it is snowing. It stands with its feet as close together as possible, hunches its back, lowers its head and lays its ears right back close to its neck so the snow cannot get into them. Truly a sorrowful sight.

Sheep in full wool can be out in the heat of the sun without harm as the wool is a wonderful insulator. But if they are forced to move they quickly become very distressed owing to the extra body heat being unable to escape.

If it starts to rain with a wind blowing, horses and cattle will seek the shelter of trees or large bushes.

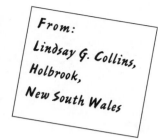

From:
Lindsay G. Collins,
Holbrook,
New South Wales

AS A PART-TIME SEASONAL worker and full-time traveller for the past eight years, I get to see a lot of interesting things.

I was relaxing at Kununurra in Western Australia in my little pup tent—the A-frame type with two poles, tent and a fly-sheet. Anyway, there I was having a rest when sugar ants started crawling over the tent. They were followed by a gecko looking for lunch. The little fellow couldn't see me but I could see it its silhouette. Now, did you know geckos are ticklish? Well, this one was! As it stopped to size up an ant I gently stroked it from chin to tail. You know when you scratch a dog in just the right spot its leg goes berserk? Well, that's exactly what this gecko did. Dead-set truth. After a couple of seconds it saw an ant and off it went, but there you have it. Geckos are ticklish!

From:
Garry,
The World

OVER THE PAST FEW months you have talked about the blue wrens. I would like to tell you about the ones that share our house. We are lucky to have about six families to share our place. Two live over in the old dairy, and as I mix up the horse feed they dance around my feet. They are so delicate I'm frightened I might stand on them. If I forget to put out their mince they tell me off! The other families live in the honeysuckle hedge around the house. One mum has just had two babies leave the nest and she brings them over to our lounge window to show them to the 'intruder bird' that lives there.

From:
Jeanette and Bruce
Elder,
Warwick,
Queensland

ONE SUNDAY I WAS hanging out the washing before we went to church and since the weather forecast was being read I had the radio with me. In one of the gum trees a young little raven was quietly stripping off the hanging bark, searching for a breakfast snack of spiders or other invertebrates.

Your programme recommenced with the 'Birds' symphonic music and the raven immediately stopped to listen. He even side-stepped along the branch to get as close as possible, and added a little chortle of his own during the musical breaks. He was obviously mystified

Email from:
Peter Hornsby,
University of
Adelaide,
South Australia

by some of the sounds which is not surprising considering most of the birds normally would not be heard in Adelaide!

Little ravens are interesting birds. I hand-reared a wedge-tailed eagle that had recovered after suffering from severe vitamin D deficiency. When it was too large to keep at home it lived at the nearby veterinary surgery, and I used to carry it home. The local little ravens used to take a dim view of this, voicing their disapproval and swooping down on us. Unlike magpies they never directly attacked, but would indulge in a curious displacement activity by aggressively snapping off twigs which they then threw aside. It was a total act of bravura because nothing else happened. But they got to recognise me and would repeat the behaviour years after the eagle had gone.

From:
Betty Grant,
Rosebud,
Victoria

I'VE JUST BEEN LISTENING to 'rooster lady' and the talk of kookaburra calls reminds me of my experience at London Zoo several years ago.

I entered an old brick complex with empty cages. Right in the middle cage I came across the dejected-looking kookaburras sitting absolutely motionless on a branch. As a child I rather fancied I could make kookaburra noises, so at over seventy I decided to give it another go, believing only the birds would hear me. Well, you'd scarcely imagine how those two kookaburras were galvanised into life. They made such a racket that people came in to see what all the noise was about!

Of course, I immediately stopped my performance, but it gave me some satisfaction to 'fool' those bored and lonely kookaburras into such a lively rendition of their laughing powers for the Londoners!

SIGHTS AND SOUNDS

From:
Jenny Harris,
Port Fairy,
Victoria

Currawongs call with piercing shrills.
First light bathes the distant hills.
The cattle stir as a fox lopes by.
Parrots chirp in the air in the new day's sky.
Bronze-wings fly in their own bush haven.
Small birds hide from the old black raven.
White cockatoos and pink galahs
Fly past to flee from passing cars
Whistlers, swamp and brown hawks sway
Down on rabbits, mice and prey.
As brolgas dance the swans swim on.
Kookaburras and magpies burst with song.
Blue wrens, firetails and other finches
Dart back and forth within inches.
These are some of the sights and sounds
That live and die on God's own ground.

WE WERE STAYING WITH a friend on a farm west of Gympie. At about 2.30 a.m. my husband, Don, heard a noise and reached to the bedside table for his torch. Although round, it didn't feel like a torch so he dropped it. Turning on the light, he discovered it was a snake! We woke our friend to remove the offender and he had to go up to the shed to get the required equipment for the job. On the way back he found another snake just outside the front door. Meanwhile, Don saw a tail disappear over the bed-head. There were two snakes in the bedroom! We searched the house and, would you believe, we found another one, five or six feet long, coming into the kitchen through a hole in the wall. I thought it was a bit of pipe but our friend assured me otherwise. The next night another snake was found in the pantry!

They were all brown tree snakes, which are nocturnal, but five snakes in such a short time is unbelievable. Although they are venomous, their fangs are set back so they have difficulty in biting.

Later whilst on Fraser Island we related the story to the rangers. The next day when they opened the money drawer in their office, they discovered a brown tree snake in it!

From:
Judy Wilkie,
Bargara,
Queensland

I THOUGHT YOU MIGHT like to share a letter from our daughter, Lara, sent to us from Coconut Beach, Cape Tribulation, where she is a tour guide:

Due to cyclone and continual flooding, I've been cut off from the outside world for a few weeks now—no phones, no mail services, etc. So, I'm writing an update letter to tell some of the details of my adventures over the last few weeks, beginning with cyclone 'Rona'.

Rona, a category three cyclone, hit with winds up to 180 kilometres per hour and there was widespread flooding. Cape Tribulation copped the worst of it and the rainforest was flattened. The other small resorts had to close due to flooding and tree damage, but ours was fine. The amount of dead wildlife from the cyclone is evident along the roadsides and clearings. Being a registered Queensland Wildlife Rescuer I have collected an assortment of injured wildlife over the weeks. It's devastating to find some animals that have survived a catastrophic event get run over by thoughtless tourists. Bandicoots, melomys, snakes, goannas and frogs are the main casualties.

I was on my way home from work, crossing the flooded causeway and dirt roads in my poor little Mazda, when I came across the largest python I've ever seen, an amethystine, Australia's largest and one of my favourites.

I've handled plenty of them around three or four feet on night walks and it's my job to remove them from around buildings and roads. But never one of this size. It was as thick as my arm and long as my car! It was sprawled full length across the road, with a bump in the middle where I assumed it had been hit by a car. I stopped to see if it was okay. I prodded it a few times but it hardly responded so out came the rescue kit. I could see it wasn't going to fit in my usual wildlife box, but luckily I had my washing basket in the car to use instead.

I hesitated at the sheer size of it but convinced myself that an injured snake, no matter how big, deserved a chance and would probably be fairly docile. Anyway, I gingerly reached for its head to get the usual grip behind the neck so it couldn't bite, but as soon as I latched on tightly so did it! The unsuspecting python was apparently not injured at all, and in shock at being viciously attacked while sound asleep, was doing everything it could to kill its attacker. That meant I now had the biggest python I'd ever seen wrapped three or four times

From:
Dawn Emerson,
Illawong,
New South Wales

around my neck, under my arm and down to my elbow, squeezing me so hard I was choking.

I realised I was now in a life-threatening situation. I pictured the snake winning the battle and me lying dead on the road in front of my car next to the washing basket. I wondered what the next passing tourist would make of that—let alone what they would think if they saw me now, staggering in the middle of the road with a massive snake coiled around me! I think that's when the adrenaline started to kick in and I gained a new release of strength. I uncoiled it from my neck and furiously threw the snake down the embankment. It must have wondered what had happened and later I felt bad that maybe I'd hurt it. I got back into my car and shook like a leaf all the way home, furious with myself for being so stupid.

G'day, this is Macca

G'day
NOEL SCURRY

NOEL: It's Noel Scurry calling from the top of Mount Kosciuszko. I'm one of a group of scientists from CSIRO's Division of Entomology. We're up here trapping and collecting flies. Because of the fires we've decided to see how they affected the insects.

MACCA: How many varieties of flies are there in Australia?

NOEL: We don't exactly know, but there are well over twenty thousand. The ones you see are a very tiny part of them. The particular interest of this group is in a fly called the stiletto because it's got a body like a stiletto heel. They're pretty ancient flies and a group of Americans who are working on a theory of continental drift are looking at parts of Africa and so on to try to find out if this fly has come from the Australian continent with the drift.

MACCA: Did they survive the bushfires?

NOEL: It's amazing, there's heaps of them around. There's always been lots of flies here. The first settlers and the explorers complained bitterly about them.

13

Pasta Joke and Other Fair Dinkum Poems

What would we do without the cathedral of nature
And what little there is left of her creatures and their habitat?
Things like tree, song, bush, park, leaf, moth, bird, or even worm and frog.
To dictatorial, dollar-greedy bureaucracy and developers
They are all just four-letter words!

FROM: *Jean Goadby*

From:
Judi Cox,
Kenmore,
Queensland

PASTA JOKE?

So we have Gough Whitlam's face selling pasta sauce.
It seems a brilliant use of a natural resource
But why stop there, let's use PMs pasta their use-by date
To do TV commercials and give it to us straight.
Maybe Keating selling antique clocks and his Placido Domingo CD
Or Bob Hawke hawking No More Tears and blanched hazelnuts on TV.
Fraser could do a trousers ad and a book to enrich the mind
Called 'A hundred and one excuses why I left my pants behind'.
We look forward to commercials which raise us from our stupor
And rejoice that these will supplement ex-PM's meagre super.
And prime ministers that have pasta way to that big Lodge in the skies
Will no doubt be applauding Gough Whitlam's enterprise.
And so, prime ministers past their use-by date can still be controversial
By trying to speak Italian to do a sauce commercial!

From:
Robyn Mitchell,
Yungaburra,
Queensland

THIS FAIR DINKUM SHEILA
© Robyn Mitchell

She arrived out here in the heat and the dust,
To rewrite her life as a woman must
When her man succumbs to the demon drink,
And it no longer matters what others think
About how a woman can leave her sons
to work out here 'midst the cattle runs.

For a woman will do whatever it takes
To clean off the slate and erase her mistakes.
She'll survive and provide for herself and her child,
And spit in the face of gossip run wild.

Though her old man's gone sober, the damage is done,
So she's looking to build a new place in the sun.
She can no longer walk beside him with pride
For the grog has destroyed any love left inside,
And while piecing together her raw shattered pride
the stale dregs of her marriage she brushes aside.

Her three little sons she's left far behind,
'Til she's back on her feet and she's sure in her mind
That she can afford to buy them new shoes
And fill their boy bellies with good wholesome foods.

It's red, and it's bare, and it's starkly obscene,
And compares not at all with the childhood green
Of her forests and beaches and beloved coast,
But the thing that she really misses the most

Is the soft snuggling bodies as they ready for bed,
Jostling for places around her head;
Wriggling and squirming and eager to hear
Her loving renditions of stories held dear.

The taxing demands of her teaching conspire
To make each day's toil a baptism of fire.
Her patience tried sorely they put her to test,
But she'll not buckle under, she'll not give 'em best.
They're a tough bloody mob, but she's bringing 'em round.
With stubborn compassion, she's wearing 'em down.
It's funny to watch, they can't understand
How a woman, no less, can bring 'em to hand.

But she gives 'em respect and shows that she cares.
She reins 'em in hard, but she's always fair,
And that befuddles them every time,
For her punishment always fits the crime,
And they know in their hearts it's their own bloody fault
If she loses her cool and fair gives them a jolt
With a bloody great bellow that'd stop a team
of recalcitrant bullocks from a Drover's Dream.

Now her own little brood has been flown in today.
Appreciative bosses it appears would say,
'You've done the job that was asked of you,
You've stuck to your guns and you've seen it through,
And the day-to-day dramas of teaching Out Back
Have stiffened your spine, you'll never look back.'

And we never knew she had a grin quite as wide
As the grin that she grew, when, beaming with pride,
She showed off her sons, in obvious bliss
To the friends she had made and the friends she would miss.
And she marvels to find that her heart will be torn
'Twixt our fiery red dusks, and her moist verdant dawns.

And I'm glad to have known her for she's taught me this much,
Not to judge city folk by their clothing and such.
So I raise up my glass and propose a toast
To this fair dinkum sheila come in from the coast.

In the sunlit outback country where the Cooper's running free
There was news for one old drover of the tax called GST
The mailman brought the package with the explanation sent.
The drover scratched his head and said, 'Now what's this ten per cent?'

There were no accountants handy for they charge a hefty fee
So he boiled his blackened billy and sipped his milkless tea

From:
Max Fatchen,
Smithfield,
South Australia

And he read the information to his dog, a canine wise
While the dog's hair fairly bristled, which should come as no surprise.

So they sent a tax consultant to that Never-Never land,
A fellow quite impatient. There was so much to understand
And he lectured the old drover though his words were quite well meant
For the crux of all his story was that flaming ten per cent.

But the dog growled as he listened and he let his jaws relax
For he loved his mate, the drover and he hated words like 'tax'
And he took some action in trying circumstance
He bit the tax consultant on the back part of his pants.
We must praise the dog's perception for he bit with skilled intent
Though the trouser seat was missing … he still left ten per cent.

Macca talks to Australians all over, Max Fatchen

G'day . . .
MAX FATCHEN

MAX FATCHEN: I came from a farm at Angle Vale. I was an only child and very fond of animals. We had Clydesdale horses and I drove a team of seven when I was twelve—very badly, I might say—and this got me off the farm very quickly in case the plains blew away. But I was a reflective child and I loved the countryside. I'd take about an hour to walk home from school because I liked to watch the hares and sparrowhawks. I think a country life teaches you to live, to a degree, within yourself. If you're an only child you find yourself befriending the things around you, the chooks, the cows, the birds and the horses, and dreaming when you should be turning the separator for the milk or going over to feed the horses. But at the same time it gives you the love of the countryside, which I know you've got, and which deepens as you grow older.
MACCA: Were your parents farming folk?
MAX: My father was a farmer. It was a small farm but we grew wonderful hay. He was a quiet man who absolutely loved the countryside and to see him out in a good crop was to see a man at prayer, you might say. My mother was a lively, forceful lady who did a great deal for charity for which she got an MBE. She believed that women should be liberated and my parents were unusual in that sense. They gave me a wonderful upbringing.
MACCA: When did you realise you wanted to be a journalist?
MAX: Well, I always wanted to be a writer. That was the ultimate thing. I wrote poetry from the time I could put words together and I spent my time writing and reading. My father tried to make a farmer out of me and that was a dismal failure, but the will to write and to compose and to rhyme was with me as soon as I could do it. Of course, I loved reading and poetry and I remember my first great poetical triumph was at ten, when I composed a poem at a meeting at Angle Vale, which said, 'Though nations may tremble, though kingdoms may quail, though empires may totter, there's still Angle Vale.' It brought the house down and a poet was launched.
MACCA: Read us one of your little poems.
MAX: Well, this, of course, comes from the farm.

When wind is dancing through the wheat
To shake each ripened head,
I seem to see, not golden crops,
But loaves of crusty bread.
And when I have a piece of bread
I think it's rather nice
The wind, the sun, the dancing grain,
Are there in every slice.

Australians all let us rejoice,
We'll have the GST
We've unchained ads to make us mad,
All paid by you and me,
Our lounge abounds
With Cocker sounds,
It's more than we can bear
In unchained strains then let us sing,
Advance Australia, where?

DO IT NOW

If with pleasure you are viewing
Any work a man is doing
If you like him or you love him, tell him now;
Don't withhold your approbation
Till the Pastor makes oration
And he lies with snowy lilies on his brow.

For no matter how you shout it
He won't really care about it
He won't know how many teardrops you have shed;
If you think some praise is due him
Now's the time to slip it to him
For he cannot read his tombstone when he's dead.

More than fame and more than money
Is the comment kind and sunny
And the hearty, warm approval of a friend;
For it gives to life a savour
And makes you stronger, braver
And it gives you heart and spirit to the end.

If he earns your praise, bestow it
If you like him let him know it
Let the words of true encouragement be said;
Do not wait till life is over
And he's underneath the clover
For he cannot read his tombstone when he's dead.

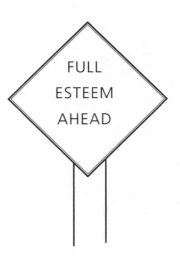

A LOVE SONG TO A YABBY

From:
Grahame
'Skew Wiff' Watt,
Kyabram,
Victoria

We were sitting by the waterhole,
My girl and I one night.
When we heard a yabby singing,
A love song clear and bright …

'If I could only hold your claw,
And gently touch your feeler.
I'd be yours for evermore,
And you would be my sheila.

'I'd get down on my sixteen knees,
For me, it's just frustration.
I feel for you, my shell goes weak,
You are my own crustacean.

'You're the yabby that I love,
I've gone and flipped my flippers.
We could settle in the mud,
And raise lots of little nippers.'

◎

SILENCE

From:
Ron Bone,
The Gap,
Queensland

We are driven from our home
By the mower's dreadful drone,
At the shop the loud PA assaults our ears.
It seems that ceaseless noise
Intrudes on all our joys,
And the decibels bring us close to tears.

The smart sidewalk cafe
Beside the main highway,
And traffic roaring by with horns full blast.
No quiet lane to walk,
No quiet place to talk,
No time to pause and watch the world race past.

If we picnic in the park,
Even when it's growing dark,
There's no respite from the endless roar of mowers.
And when the grass is cut
They don't stop to pick it up,
But scatter it around with howling blowers.

If we go down to the beach
We are still within the reach
Of cleaners banging bins, our ears to stun.
And the shade trees are no more,
Victims of the wild chainsaw,
Now we have to sit and roast, out in the sun.

There is no rest in bed,
We lie awake in dread
Of police sirens wailing through the night.
With revellers from the bars
Closing up their ten-door cars,
We're glad at last to see the morning light.

I think we must escape
To the north of this great state,
Where the silent stars cruise the deep night sky.
Where the softly whispering breeze,
Murmurs quietly through the trees,
And secret creatures of the bush go padding by.

There in that peaceful scene,
Our rested souls can dream,
Away from all the noisome city strife.
Where the rivers softly flow,
In the moonlight's gentle glow,
Where we can contemplate the values of this life.

A SPRAY OF WATTLE BLOSSOM

Out in the trenches
Out across the foam
Someone is thinking
There, tonight of home.
But whether in the trenches
Or watching o'er the foam
There are shouts of hearty welcome
When the mail comes in from home!

So send along a letter
With a spray of wattle bloom
It will cheer him up and help him
Through the lonely hours of gloom.
As he gazes on our emblem
That very tiny bloom
He'll forget he's in the trenches
Where the cannons roar and boom.

From the boy away in Flanders
Far across the leagues of foam
Comes a letter to a mother
Waiting in the dear old home.

From:
L.E. Galpin,
Bolgallah,
Victoria
(September 1918)

'You don't know how it cheers me,'
The welcome letter said,
'To see that bit of wattle
However dry and dead.'

So send along a letter
With a spray of wattle bloom;
It will cheer him up and help him
Through the lonely hours of gloom.

◎

A MEMORY OF POETS

From:
Alan Gourley

Oh poets … where art thou now
Did thee desert us, or we thee
In past ages thee were mighty
We honoured, admired thee, loved thee
Yea, perhaps even worshipped thee
Thee brought us pleasing thoughts when there were few pleasures
Thee brought us heroic example when there were many fears
Where art thou now?

Today 'tis the athlete we honour
The discipline of muscles mighty
Endurance, precision, timing; our golden heroes
Steel-tempered flesh to graceful poems form
Are these our poets now?
Do word athletics now bore thee
Will thee no more make sacrifice for disciplines of thought
Precise poetic craft, is it no more worthy its agony?

Recall past pleasures in rhymes and rhythms charming
Romance beautified in graceful stanza
Uplifted virtues in neat verse gave us reminder
Our tears we dried in thy rhythmic humour
Thy fantasies set us dreaming
Why deserted are we in this hour of need
Why now find we only scarecrows in poetic cloth
Scarecrows guarding weeds where once bright gardens bloomed
Did affluence dry thy crystal waters
Poison thy roots?
Oh poets … we miss thee.

◎

From:
Dorothy Watt,
Briagolong,
Victoria

FIFTY YEARS OF THE ABC

When first we came to this great land in nineteen-fifty-one
The ABC was oh so prim, some things were just not done!
For bush types must be civilised, colonial traits erased,

Good English diction was the thing—bush standards must be raised.
So Auntie's programmes aimed to teach the outback to reform
Their roughneck ways and tame their speech, of 'nicer' things inform.
Then, swear words on the air were banned, correct speech was the thing,
The Oxford accent was the norm, no rough bush ways should cling.
For years it talked at listeners, who never answered back,
Who'd want to hear on radio the bush bred Jill or Jack?
At last these ways began to change, we heard each day on air
Russ Tyson's voice inviting us to suggest songs to share,
To play for those both young and old, for those confined to bed
In hospitals and those at home, some happiness to shed.
From then on 'talkback' sessions grew, all subjects came to air,
And now on Sundays Macca reigns with true blue Aussie fare.
Bush poetry is heard once more with yarns about the past,
With rhyme and rhythm tales are told—we've come of age at last.
We're proud of what this land's become, a mix of old and new
With folk from lands across the sea and each may state his view.
The ABC provides for all, broadcasts a varied fare,
Encourages all types to speak, their thoughts and hopes to share.
'Cos Auntie now is one of us, no longer so highbrow,
All have the chance to air their views, a real Australian show.
Now snobbery no longer reigns, this land's a better place,
It's one for all and all for one, the great Australian race.

everyone's

◎

E-MAIL
© Helen Brumby

E-mail's very handy
For sending funny jokes,
Or sharing clever sayings
From extra witty folks.
You can send the minutes
From a recent meeting,
And it's an almost cost-free way
To send a cheery greeting.
It's good to use for business
For swift communication,
Sending data round the world,
And also round the nation.
But when it comes to friendship
Then I know something better:
If you really like me,
Then please—send me a letter!

From:
Helen Brumby,
Rose Bay,
Tasmania

 ◎

From:
Ellis Campbell,
Dubbo,
New South Wales

ECSTASY IN PLASTIC
© Ellis Campbell

She loved her window-shopping, all that finery ablaze,
a poignant longing lingered only purchase might erase.
She wandered past the jewellers' shops and paused at every one
such wondrous joys to light her life, they gleamed like morning sun.
Exquisite furniture galore, all patiently arrayed;
electrical appliances so cleverly displayed.
The coloured television sets, and videos as well,
all twinkled gaily from their shelf and cast a magic spell.
A hopeless 'shopoholic' with decisions often rash,
and Nancy felt embarrassed when she ran right out of cash!

Then she discovered credit cards, the secret to success,
Grace Brothers, Visa, National, American Express.
No more she'd wilt in envy she could have the very best;
a frenzied shopping spree she planned with unrelenting zest.
She bought the highest quality in underwear and shoes;
renewed the lounge room carpet and she booked a summer cruise.
A cocktail dress and pants-suit for occasions she'd attend;
brand names of fashions long renowned—no more she need pretend!
A sparkling bracelet soon adorned her slender sun-tanned arm;
she even bought a beauty aid from someone's emu farm.

A statement on her credit cards arrived without delay
a minimum of eighty bucks was all she had to pay!
She shopped around for furniture and bought a motorbike;
a dozen CD playing discs she thought that Jack would like.
She signed up for gymnastics class and ballet at the school;
she modernised the garden and enlarged the swimming pool.
But then disaster came her way, poor Nancy lost her purse
with all her personal effects—her credit card—much worse!
Her husband was reluctant to report the theft, she knew.
He said, 'Perhaps the bloody thief won't spend as much as you!'

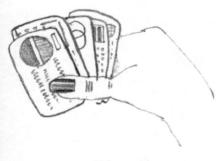

Pick a card . . .

SHARKOPHOBIA

From:
Ross Henry,
New Norfolk,
Tasmania

When in the surf
I sometimes pause
And think about
That movie *Jaws*.

Glassy eyes
With teeth like razors
Finely honed
For stray lifesavers.

I've mixed with Danes
I've known some Swedes
I'll go where
Multiculture leads.

But when the sea
I find I'm in
I never want
To meet a Fin.

Lethal missile
Heading for me
Bondi bull
About to gore me.

I know he's part
Of Nature's plan
And he must eat
Where'er he can.

But come my end
I have no wish
To meet it from
A monster fish.

For swift and silent
comes the crunch
At dinner, brekkie
Or his lunch.

Take my word
I could not hack it
R-I-P
In a sharkskin jacket.

And my preference leans
To a jet-black hearse
Not a watery ride
In a pale grey nurse.

So, deadly denizen
Of the deep
From me your distance
Kindly keep.

For come too close
And threaten harm
And they will sound
The shark alarm.

And you'll be hunted
No mistake
You could be eaten
… labelled 'flake'.

From:
Margaret Gibbons,
The Gap,
Queensland

VISIT THE MUSEUM
© Margaret Gibbons

Nestled low beneath the mountain
Chimneys reaching to the sky
Coal dust, clanking noise and limestone
Here men worked and just got by.
Many laboured all their lifetime
Burning eyes and aching backs
Listening for the knock-off whistle
Home they'd walk on dusty tracks.

Cement was king in 1930
and it built the Harbour Bridge.
Kandos town was always busy
Nestled just across the ridge.
Trains came up and shunted slowly
Turned around, and pointed south
Mudgee Mail went past each evening
News was spread by word-of-mouth,
Little shaggy coalmine ponies
Dusty tails and dusty manes.
Football on the flat on Sunday.
Cricket—picnics on the trains.

Now times have changed—the work is done
The Sydney tunnel's all complete
No dusty men walk home at midnight
No ponies stamp their aching feet.
But you still can see old Kandos
Catch a glimpse of days gone by.
And you still can see the chimneys
Reaching high into the sky.

◎

MACCA IN NARRANDERA

From:
Robin Tiffen,
Leeton,
New South Wales

There was excitement in Narrandera, for the word had quickly spread,
That Ian McNamara would be here.
For a morning with great Aussies like Father Hartigan and Macca,
The people streamed to town from far and near.

'H' was in the audience, and Mick Batchelor was too
And it seems that all of Grong Grong came along,
They came in from Echuca, from Griffith and Galore
To hear the talk and poetry and song.

The gentle wit of John O'Brien and his altar boy, Frank Bell
Kept us entertained and quite enthralled,
While the expert on the poetry, and St Mel and Hanrahan
Informed us of the background when he called.

'H' recited poetry by Paterson and Lawson
And forgot some vital lines along the way,
He gamely carried on with his feathers in his hat
And became the laughing legend of the day.

It could not have been more Aussie with the expo about flies,
Whose twenty thousand species came to hear.
Galahs flew overhead, truckies tooted, children played
And groups of happy magpies clustered near.

We were inspired about Barellan community recordings
Of the ordinary happenings of the day,
And the lady in Alaska and winemakers and some travellers
Took the opportunity to have their say.

Bill Oliver from *Sugar in the Blood* recited poems,
And recounted lovely tales about the trees,
And the history of Narrandera and the district came to life
As the autumn sunshine warmed us in the breeze.

So two thousand folks or more sat around the Boree log,
And listened to the songs and information
And relaxed with Macca's magic and the programme which we feel
Keeps us all together as a nation.

◎

ABSOLUTELY NOT!

Absolutely is an adverb was what I learned at school,
Now absolutely's anything, a conversational tool,
It seems absa(bloody)lutely,
Is trapped in every human throat,
And it's absolutely getting on my absolutely goat.

I've deleted absolutely from what I write and say,
And in one week's communication I've recovered half a day,
Maybe Willy Shakespeare, the acknowledged English bard,
Created medieval buzzwords that oldies found quite hard.

In an ever-changing vocabulary it's a price that we must pay,
'No worries', I'll 'chill out', and to you all
'Have a nice day'.

From:
David Bearup,
Guyra,
New South Wales

◎

THE SOUND OF RAIN

I never thought the sound of rain could be so good to my ears
until the drought of 2002 and with it all the tears
the dust, the heat, the dying cattle
the courageous look upon the faces of the bush folk
coping with their battle

From:
J. Birkett,
Crystal Creek,
New South Wales

no green grass, no not a blade but hard rock and dirt
the bush folk have nothing to show for all their hard work
the frogs all buried in the waterholes
with skeletons of cattle
no water falling from the sky, no rushing gutters to rattle
oh, how I missed the sound of rain, the wet wind upon my face
the dripping leaves, the waterfalls running from every place
and then the storm, the lightning flashed
the darkness split with thunder
and heavy drops of water fell, washing leaves asunder
my spirits rose, my spirits soared, I felt like I was floating
and all the grass and all the trees, the wonderful rain was coating
there's nothing like the sound of rain, an army of feet are drumming
with it grows the green, green grass and soon, it must be coming.

WOOD FOR THE FIRE

Come join me while I'm 'cracking'
On a chill, still winter's day,
Fathering those small branches
That the gums drop when they sway.
Look, there's a long one, grasp one end
And brace it with your boot,
A quick jerk, then the sharp, crisp 'crack',
Just like a rifle shot,
Goes speeding across the valley
'Til it reaches Razorback,
Plays tag against the mountainside
And then comes racing back.
The echo has a softer sound,
Perhaps a distant bell
Peals up there on the ridges
Where majestic eagles dwell.
The sun slips downwards, colours change,
A gold hue lights the west.
Pick up our load, head down the hill
As birds fly to their nest.
Oh, how I love these afternoons
On sunny winter days!
Come into my warm kitchen now,
The tea time table's laid.

From:
Pat Binskin,
Menangle Park,
New South Wales

THE 2000 BUG

They say that a bug called millennium bug
Can consume what you have on computer,
And if you should meet with this horrible beast
You must zap it or use bug-shooter.
This problem the programmers should have foreseen
Before it could eat up their data.
It's the 2000 which is coming our way,
The millennium's due a year later.

The bug that bugs me is the way they persist
In naming this creature so wrongly.
It's millennium this and millennium that
On this matter I feel very strongly.
For we all know Australia was born at the start
Of this century nineteen-O-one,
Which means that just ninety-nine years have gone
When 1999 is done.

And 2000 must end to make one hundred years
Since Australian Federation.
In 2001 we will all celebrate
The Centenary of our Nation.
In 2001 the new century starts
And the third millennium as well.
Whether better or worse than the second one,
Only time will tell!

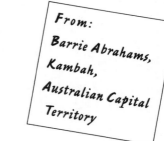

From:
Joy Suto,
Donvale,
Victoria

MY POND

Most welcome guests
They land upon my grey reflecting pond
Like flying boats from some exotic isle
Or maybe from our dried up inland sea,
The water bows beneath their creamy breasts
Then slowly fades away
As my pelicans drift
On still and cloudy waters
Holding carp and perch
And slimy shopping trolleys.

Passively they sit, contented,
Without a hint of call or song.
Gazing ahead like some myopic judge
Peering over long pink nose and wrinkled jowls,
Waiting to pass sentence on me and my surrounds,
And as I watch and wait

From:
Barrie Abrahams,
Kambah,
Australian Capital
Territory

They scoop their beaks and flip their catch
Then slowly glide away
Until their whim will take them from me,
Amid the traffic and the noise.

THE LITTLE CORMORANT
© Stephen Whiteside

From:
Stephen Whiteside,
Glen Iris,
Victoria

I saw a little cormorant
Upon a rock, and grinned.
Her outstretched wings were soaking wet,
And drying in the wind.

I called to her, 'You live
A very inefficient way.
Why, I reckon you'll be standing
On that rock for half the day.'

The cormorant replied, saying,
'Stop a while, and think.
I never need to take them off,
And wash them in the sink.

'I never have to spin them dry,
Or hang them on the line,
So tell me which procedure
Is the simpler, yours or mine?'

Some rain had started falling.
Though I knew I'd beat her yet,
I had to run for shelter.
I was scared of getting wet.

BLOODY TRACTOR

From:
Trevor Sweeney,
Hamilton,
Victoria

I remember my old Granddad, who's departed from this earth
He was an inspiration and a constant source of mirth
Like the time he spent one August out there in the shed
He went to start the tractor but the bloody thing was dead

He turned the key like normal, the engine groaned and popped
A cloud of thick white smoke came out and the bloody thing just stopped
When he turned the key again there was not a sign of life
Granddad got his toolbox and that always lead to strife

First off came the bonnet, which wasn't really hard
He took out the radiator and put it in the yard
Then the words I dreaded most, 'Son you watch and learn'
And like everything that Granddad did, things took a nasty turn

'I know what I am doing, I've been doing this for years'
What Granddad did to farm machines reduced grown men to tears
He went and got a shifter, and he undid all the bolts
He got his biggest hammer and gave the head a jolt

He should have been more gentle, used a bit more care
That would have stopped the chunk of head flying through the air
'Bloody alloy castings! They make these things from crap'
Well anyway the tractor's head was now a lump of scrap

Granddad not defeated drained the oil from the sump
Well he kind of sort of drained it; it came out lump by lump
He took out all the pistons, laid them in a row
They looked to be in real good nick, 'Why won't this thing go?'

Granddad's on the blower, 'I need to order parts
I've pulled down all the motor, I hope the damn thing starts
I will need all new gaskets,' and he asked about the head
When told the price I can't repeat the things that Granddad said

Granddad asked the parts man if he had one second-hand
Of course the tractor Granddad bought was some obscure brand
'I don't think you will get one,' the parts man had a gloat
The parts man said, 'I'll order one, it'll take a month by boat'

The day arrived the parts turned up, all the bits were right
Granddad said, 'I'll make it run if it takes all bloody night'
He came out in the morning with this enormous grin
He turned the key and as you've guessed not a bloody thing

Granddad wasn't happy you should have heard the din
We had to bite the bullet and call a mechanic in
Granddad didn't like it, he didn't like to lose
The cause of all this trouble, a lousy two-cent fuse.

A KNITTER'S LAMENT
© Jean Gillespie

The wool shops are going, all over the town
Signs all say the same, 'Clearing Sale', 'Closing Down'.
Once there were so many, big, busy and bright,
Well-stocked with wool, now it seems there's a blight.
I loved to go in to browse for a while
Through patterns in cable, lace, Aran, Fair Isle.
There was wool on the shelves in all different shades,
A rainbow of colour was for us displayed.
Baby wool in pastels and various plies,
Silk, mohair aglow, a feast for the eyes.
Cotton for summer and homespun in brown,

From:
Jean Gillespie

Alpaca, angora, soft as thistledown.
All fluffy and pretty, light as a soufflé
Or tweed, bobbled, speckled or curly bouclé.
Knitting needles, buttons and tapestry wool,
Garments on display to make us all drool.
At least we've got woollen mills and the chain stores,
But hand knitters equate with the dinosaurs.
The outlook is bleak, of that there's no doubt,
We're oddballs whose dye lot number's run out!
Our children no longer learn plain stitch and purl,
They internet into a different world
Wearing designer labels, handknits are uncool,
Whilst farmers ask, 'What will we do with our wool?'
With no wool shops around we'll all feel the draught,
And wonder what will become of our craft?
Superseded, outmoded, we'll just fray and dye,
Till we meet at the Great Wool Shop in the sky!

AUTUMN'S GUEST
© Felix N. Jenkins

From:
Felix N. Jenkins,
Kingscliff,
New South Wales

I come from the Antarctic, born in the cold dark seas
Cruise over the shining waves, bypassing many lees
I reach the rocky shores of our sunny forested land
I dither here and there, making ripples in the sand.

I reach the Snowy Mountains, pass them with ease
The chill of my breath says, migrate to wild geese
Out over the grassy plains I swiftly flow
To bring to the Blue Hills a promise of snow.

Over a threshold of trees, I spy the coastal plain
Basking in autumn's sunshine, it will be in vain
For I'll rustle the trees' leaves with winter's first chill
I'm the harbinger of frosts and a heavy power bill
I am autumn's first chilly wind.

FOOD: FAST, FADS AND FANCIES

Some doggerel written in memory of the twentieth century

From:
Jean Maclean (90),
Regents Park,
New South Wales

Once father carved with poise and flair
while family sat with in-drawn breath
and mother doled two vegies out
and kids kept quiet on pain of death

The family table is no more
instead Mac's golden arches call
the kids to hurry down the mall
to buy Big Macs and chips galore.

When I was young I always thought
Gran's dinner roast was famous
now I'm told that pasta's better
and I'm just an ignoramus.

Mum's cooking now is out of fashion
finger food is all the craze
get delivery of a pizza
turn on TV—get out the trays.

Bread is the staff of life they say
once damper raked from ashes hot
now loaves in shops served straight away
today it's sliced and wrapped—so what!

Tea was Australia's favourite drink
from countryside to city square
'til Repin's opened coffee shops
and sales of tea went down the sink.

There is no substitute for tea
stirred with a dry and gummy stick
served underneath a wattle tree
there's nothing like it for a kick.

When only winos drank the red
beer was the order of the day
now all the nation loves its wine
from good old plonk to chardonnay.

What will the new millennium face
apart from terror, war and strife?
What food and drink will it embrace
to give its people zest for life?

What takeaway will be the craze?
Will sausage sizzles still hold sway?
Will cappuccino be no more?
And the jargon of the day?

Alas I won't be there to say.

From:
Greg Dillon

ALL FINGERS AND THUMBS

G'day Macca,
How you doing, mate?
I thought I'd write this little poem
and tell you how your show should rate.

Now I'll only use my fingers to score
though I'd like to use me toes,
but I've been working hard all day
and my feet are on the nose,

The show's content is a problem
and it makes me quite irate,
I can never get enough,
the best I'll give is eight.

Aussie songs, and I live where I live,
Bird song and frogs now what will I give.
Mixed with music nature sounds great
you've got me again, I'll give you an eight.

The switchboard's a worry I can never get through
I can ring up the moon but can never get you.
You're always too busy or I'm running late
but don't worry Macca, I'll give you an eight.

All the poems and the letters
from Aussies abroad
for the way you recite them
another eight scored.

Now the name of your show I have to agree
is real patriotic to a man like me.
Australia All Over, well strike me dumb
I'll give you eight fingers, and a couple of thumbs.

14
◎ *Why I live Where I Live* ◎

'Where do you live, Arnold?' asked Macca.
'Bondi, where else.' he replied. 'If you're not living
at Bondi, believe me you're camping out.'

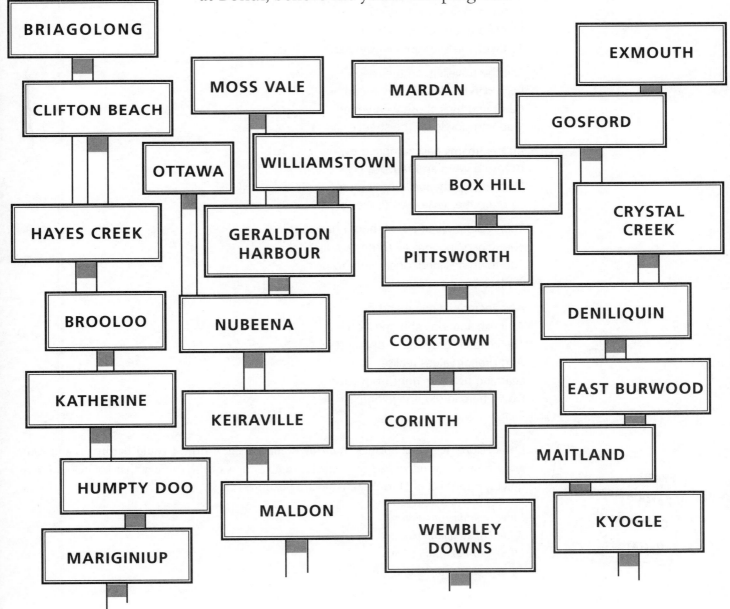

From:
Dorothy Watt,
Briagolong,
Victoria

BRIAGOLONG

Briagolong, Briagolong,
It's here we feel that we belong.
Just listen while I sing a song,
The story of Briagolong.

When roads were mud or choking dust
And horse and bullock teams a must,
Then tales of wealth made sane men bold
And tempted them to search for gold.

They saw as they passed through the town
A hostelry of wide renown,
A blacksmith, stores, a butcher's shop,
The last before the final stop.

Clip-clopping horses passing through,
Cattlemen, and packers too
Loading goods of every kind
To take whatever gold was mined.

See the travellers on the road,
Each one burdened with a load;
Can't you hear those weary feet
Trudging slowly up the street?

Bullock teams pass rumbling by,
Cracking whip and raucous cry,
Plodding up the well-known track
To bring the new-sawn timber back.

Then gold ran out … the boom had bust,
The miners' dreams all turned to dust.
The town declined, once more to be
A place of sweet serenity.

As generations come and go,
And expectations ebb and flow,
The children grow up strong and wise,
And proper values realise,
Learning to know right from wrong,
Down here in old Briagolong.

ON A FLIGHT TO ALICE Springs from my hometown in Cairns, I could hardly draw myself away from the window as I marvelled at the vastness of the country that lay below. I was quickly reminded of Dorothea McKellar's poem:

From:
Karen Ambrose,
Clifton Beach,
Queensland

I love a sunburnt country
A land of sweeping plains
Of ragged mountain ranges
Of droughts and flooding rains …

The landscape I saw revealed the strange beauty so simply captured in her verse. It was a mixture of oddly shaped, craggy hills, vast, barren expanses and a network of dry river beds that one day would bring the soil to this eerie yet fascinating part of Australia.

Alice Springs itself is a welcome oasis in the middle of nowhere. A drive just a few kilometres out of the town is testimony to the isolation of the place, and makes one reflect upon the hardships faced by the pioneers who toiled and settled this unforgiving part of our great continent. The redness of the soil and the stunted growth would have provided little shelter to wildlife and stock, let alone to people.

The glint of a homestead roof from the air had me admiring the families who still experience the hardships that come with outback life, with only the love of the land to hold them there.

My nice Queensland home, with its lush tropical garden and views of rainforest, is much removed from the dryness of the Alice. Yet I am privileged to have now experienced both.

Dorothea was right. This is truly a land of beauty and terror!

SURROUNDED BY A STREET BREED

The street where I live resembles a pound,
After a while you get used to the sound.
They bark at the kids, they bark at the bus,
Each house has at least one dog except us.
The two dogs next door are Prince and Rover,
They've chewed every football we've kicked over.
The faithful friend behind us on a chain,
Howls at the moon and every passing train.
The dog with no tail is very well strayed,
Garbage night is when the poor dog is fed.
Then there's the two guard dogs at the side fence,
I wish people would show some common sense.
Two huge dogs in a small backyard don't fit
They get paranoia,
We pay for it.
A dog's life round here means being restrained,
I think some dog owners need to be trained.
I saw the back of the ute-dog today,
It wasn't even click-clacked to the tray.
The ute-dog yelped out as the car stopped quick,
The dog tried to give its sore paws a lick.
In our street all the dogs are left alone,
I wish someone could give them a good home.

HAVING DISCOVERED YOUR PROGRAM, greetings from Canada seem in order. 'Australia All Over' comes to me over the internet and the sound of 'home' is most cheering in the midst of a Canadian winter struggling to be spring.

From:
Paul McCann,
Moss Vale,
New South Wales

Email from:
Stephen Haines,
('The Big Bunyip'),
Ottawa,
Canada

Regrettably, I'm not a dinkum Aussie. Born and raised in California, the aroma of gum ('eucalyptus' there) trees and the sound and feel of Pacific surf are familiar. Canada lured me away during the soul-besmirching Nixon years, but I've never quite identified with it.

In 1991, a five-dollar investment in a lottery was rewarded with two tickets to Sydney. Stepping off the aircraft my soul was swept by the feeling that 'I'd come home!' Six weeks around the south-east coast and a second, year-long journey in 1995–96 (including, to be perfectly honest, some illegal time in the bush) only intensified the feeling that Oz is where I belong. I spend money I don't have on Australian writers, pushing their books whenever I can. Accessing the internet each morning I open *The Sydney Morning Herald* before all else. I long to be back in The Alice or Torrens Creek. Applications for immigration have been rejected because, wait for it, I'm too old at sixty-three!

So there you are, the desire to return burns hot within me. Your programme brings some solace, but to smell the gums, feel the desert wind and hear the thunder of Pacific rollers would bring a fulfilment equal only to a religious experience (whatever that is).

From:
Casey,
Hayes Creek,
Northern Territory

MY NAME IS CASEY. I live sixteen kilometres from Hayes Creek, a goldmining area located midway between Katherine and Darwin. It has a local population of thirty-six and was first settled in the early 1870s, when engineers installing the Overland Telegraph Line accidentally struck gold. At one point 1,300 Chinese and eighty Europeans worked the mines here. Today, they've all gone and the area has more or less returned to its original state. I'm caretaker for a gold lease. I've never found any gold and have little in the way of other income. But I consider myself richer than any millionaire.

My camp lies in a valley at the bottom of a dirt road that leads off to the Grove Hill siding. It's a simple place, built of tin and corrugated iron. It has no windows and only two walls. It has no fridge, no running water, no electricity. I cook over an open fire. I have no locks and need no key. And the long-drop's out in the open air. Yet I have a swimming pool (the back of a dump-truck filled with water from a nearby creek), and a golf course. (The first hole, a tuna can sunk into the ground and surrounded by meat-ant nests makes for a very quick putt.)

I have a luxury bathtub, an old rainwater tank I heat with water boiled in a big copper pot. Crouched inside, with my knees pulled up to my chest and the piping water lapping round my neck, I tilt my head back and gaze at the magical stars. I even have a driveway. It's an unobtrusive circle cut into the bush, where the ghosts of our predecessors make their presence felt in the deserted mineshafts, dilapidated railway tracks and rusty old machines embedded in the landscape. I wake to the sound of blue-wing kookaburras, bower birds dancing in their nest and the light flicking of the willy-wagtail as it hovers under the roof, cleaning up the spiders.

From:
Ian Pollock,
Brooloo,
Queensland

FOR MANY YEARS MY wife and I have owned a succession of Volkswagen Kombis. These vehicles have enabled us to see much of Europe and Australia, one even taking us from England to Nepal.

A camaraderie exists between Kombi owners and it is common for the occupants of passing vehicles to acknowledge each other. The latest model Kombi we owned proved to be the least reliable and we have now changed to a campervan. But I still feel a touch of nostalgia when passing a Kombi and sometimes find myself involuntarily starting to raise a hand!

In the main we travel minor roads and like to stop at small rural towns. We find most inland towns clean and well appointed. Some of the inland roads seem to be mainly occupied by grey nomads turning the routes into superhighways—'super' as in 'superannuated'. The large caravan park at Cobar in central New South Wales seemed to have a clientele composed entirely of retirees. This must provide a financial input to rural areas.

A VIEW OF DARWIN BY A KATHERINITE
© Keith Maynard

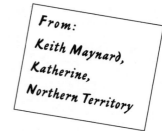

From:
Keith Maynard,
Katherine,
Northern Territory

Darwin was a shattered town
With harbour full of wrecks
And creeping vines bedecked the ruins
Of walls and broken bricks.

The streets were wide and dusty
The houses rude and bare
People came and gardened them
To live and flourish there.

Migrants came from overseas
Chinese, Greeks, Malays
The children knew no colour bar
In those past halcyon days.

There was no law of loitering
We could gather in the street
And watch the great procession
Of dragon and drumbeat.

Clouds like mountains in the sky
Piled up day by day
Will it rain and give relief?
No! Again they pass away.

The wet would come and wash it clean
Oh, how we loved the rain
Lightning flashed and thunder roared
And cooled the air again.

Darwin was a shattered town
And oh, we loved it well
Now speeding cars infest the streets
They've turned it into hell.

◎

WHY DO I LIVE IN Humpty Doo?

Well, we have the great bluish eucalyptus trees with their dry fragrance, the magnetic anthills—cathedrals made of dry mud—kookaburras that laugh half an hour before sunrise and at sunset, the white cockatoos (two of them even speak French), and the black cockatoos with magnificent red feathers. Of course, we have the green frogs that eat plenty of mosquitoes.

We have the great vibrating silence of the bush with its slightly smoky fragrance (there is always a fire somewhere), and an occasional jet roaring overhead with its passengers downing the last beer before landing in Darwin.

We have a bush pub, very rough, and we have the name Humpty Doo. Where does it come from? The accepted version is that in 1910 two locals, the Herbert brothers, named their shack on Koolpinya, 'Umpity Doo' (Koolpinya covered most of what is now Humpty Doo). Why Umpity Doo, you ask? Good question.

Umpity Doo, now Humpty Doo, is forever and I love it!

I'M AN ELEVEN YEAR OLD. I live in Williamstown, Victoria, and I'm going to tell you why I live where I live. I have recently travelled around Australia in our four-wheel drive. I enjoyed it but I really missed home.

I missed living over the road from the bay, the park and the football ground. I missed the familiar smell of the flowers on the gardenia bush in my backyard. I missed living around the corner from my friends. I missed the sound of the ships sounding their horns early in the morning. I missed being close to a deli where I can buy fresh bread and milk. I missed the feel of the cool ocean breeze on my face. I missed taking my dogs for a walk and getting an ice-cream. I missed seeing pelicans flying. I missed the view of the city from over the bay. I missed watching the *Spirit of Tasmania* set off on its long voyage. I missed collecting the pine cones that had fallen off the trees. But I will always miss the millions of desert stars that shone in the night sky on our trip!

'AI YA! COME ALL THIS way from Malaysia only to go and live in such an ulu place!'

This was my mother's response when I moved to the Tasman Peninsula. My son Callum is four-and-a-half and has mastered the spelling of a fifth of his name. He can manage 'c-a-l-l-u-m'. I hope he'll not regard us too harshly when filling in forms. Full name? 'Winwood Callum Ming Jiang Howard'.

Callum and his sister Heather provided the impetus for Mark and I to move to White Beach. It seems like ages ago that we lived squashed next to five other families in a concrete box in Sydney. Their quarrels, daily activities and routines as familiar to us as ours to them. Each night, car alarms and roaring motorbikes invaded our unit as surely as the cigarette smoke wafting up from the unit below.

Now the swoosh, swoosh of waves crashing on the rocks complements the view of Wedge Bay from our window. At night, we spotlight our gum trees for possums and wonder at the excited grunts of our resident wombat. The echidna ambles by some afternoons, interrupting Callum and Heather's play in the straw-bale castle or pirate ship. The children watch for tadpoles in our tyre pond and vie to spot the flame robin first, reminding each other of the lapwing's nest last summer. (They didn't see the kookaburra making a meal of a blackbird chick.)

We stare out of the window a lot. Dolphins and seals always cause excitement, but I'm still waiting to glimpse the displacing swell only a whale could make. Whilst contemplating my next batch of vegetable seedlings and what I'll harvest from the garden, I often forget the smog, noise and aloneness that was Sydney living.

Our home is simple, warm and comfortable. Cosmetically, it's woefully incomplete. However, the vegetable plot is finally starting to hint at possible self-sufficiency. My worm farm is encouraging even if our excuse for an orchard is seldom discussed. Duck eggs taste great and crabs and fish come free when caught at Wedge Bay. My children have a healthy curiosity and appreciation of the plant and animal life down in the rockpools in our 'front yard' and on our land. In this 'ulu' place—'ulu' is Malay for 'Whoop Whoop' or something similar—I've come to appreciate the richness that life can offer.

I CHOOSE TO WRITE on where I like to spend my weekends and not on where I live. It is Saturday and I am sitting on the verandah of our weekender at Lake Conjola. The weekender is situated in the second row of a small enclave of similar buildings, most built in the early '50s. The house is on a cliff top and looks north over the lake.

The effort of carving this place from the virgin bush seems long ago. The blackbutt gum growing on the lower block, which had been a telegraph-pole size when we were building, is now a mill log. The twisted branches of an apple gum which almost died now provide perches for a range of parrots, including the beautiful king parrot, threatened gang-gang parrots, and other birds. The more elusive male bower bird is only seen as a passing flash of vivid blue in the ferns of the gully beside the house. My nieces and nephew call the noisy friar birds the 'clickety clack' birds because of the loud sound they make with their beaks as they swoop past them when warding them off during the nesting season. Black cockatoos frequently come to chomp on the cones of she-oaks growing in the gully.

In the foreground is a geebung tree, carefully saved with wet bags from the clearing fires, the creamy white of lichen standing out stark on its almost black bark. A bangalow palm that once grew in a pot on my table now grows as a mature tree some thirty feet high. By its side a cabbage tree palm grows, also a graduate from an inside pot plant originally grown from seed collected in the Myall Lakes National Park. As I sit, the last light of day catches on a melaleuca tree in the gully by the house, highlighting areas of delicate sunset pink bark in stark contrast to the dark colour of burnt and mould-marred areas.

As night falls the sound of frogs is returning after the recent prolonged drought. During the drought several of the frogs had taken up residence in the toilet bowl, a precarious existence as they were continually being flushed down the drain. On occasions when they escaped into the bathroom they had the remarkable ability to match their colour to the tangerine walls or yellow and brown floor tiles. I remember that my grandmother referred to this place as 'frog hollow'.

One often hears in the night a swish followed by a thud against a tree as a honey glider possum lands on a tree trunk, or the sound of a wallaby as it forces its way through the underbrush, or sees the burning eyes of an owl as it comes to sit on one of the fence posts by the house. Sometimes a ringtail possum, with a young possum on its back, will come and sit on the end of the flagpole and taunt the dog, or a marsupial bush rat will run cheekily

From:
Barry Johnston,
Keiraville,
New South Wales

Quick, throw the lifepaper

through the open door to be followed by an explosion of activity by a much-too-slow dog.

These are the pleasures that can be had sitting on the verandah. This is why I choose to spend my weekends here.

Email from:
Kevin Beecroft,
Mardan,
Victoria

JUST A SHORT NOTE to paint the picture of our corner of Oz. We live in Mardan, in South Gippsland. We moved down this way three years ago from Sydney. Both my wife and I were brought up city kids. I always loved the idea of farming and when I was a kid I hoped one day I would fulfil the dream, and I have. So, if anyone in one of those small backyards in suburbia has the same crazy thoughts, give it a go.

My wife, Leisa and I and our two young kids live on a 350-acre dairy farm. It is fairly hilly but the views are spectacular. We milk 150 cows and are making a good living. The grind of dairying sometime gets to you but the freedom this type of lifestyle gives you is rewarding.

Our farm has bluegums and the koalas love them. It is amazing being out in the garden or the paddock and having them stroll by. I was going down the paddock one day and saw a fully grown koala dozing in a three-foot high tree! I was amazed it didn't bring it down.

Eagle hawks, possums, blue wrens and any other number of birds live here. It's great to have all these beautiful things around you and call it home. We are very lucky—the beach, the snow within an hour give or take, and Melbourne only two hours. Well, I'd beter go to bed, I have a five o'clock wake up call. Thanks for all the listening hours in the shed!

From:
Helen Reid

YOU READ OUT A letter from a man in Queensland who lives in a shack with no television. For eight years I had no electricity or generator. People were horrified, could not understand how I could live without a refrigerator. But it was no television that caused remarks such as, 'What on earth do you do?' I do think it is probably a bit harder for a woman on her own, but I cope very well and certainly have no regrets.

I now have power but would still never watch television. I would much rather be outside, as I just love all the birds and animals. I put out seed, bread and water for the wild birds, and have about thirty different species. I have kangaroos, wallabies, echidnas, snakes and lizards, and in spring my block is a kaleidoscope of wildflowers, bees, butterflies and insects. I have put nest boxes up trees for the possums, and many more on the fence posts which are then home to parrots during the breeding season.

I really love it here, as it is so peaceful. I am far enough out of town to be isolated but close enough to travel to work. I only have twenty acres but it is my little bit of paradise.

From:
Kathleen Silver,
Box Hill,
Victoria

A FEW YEARS AGO I was privileged to have a letter read out by you where I extolled the delights of my delightful Melbourne suburb. How everything changes—and not always for the better. The little shopping strip that was so wonderful for the many elderly residents like myself still living in the area has now been stripped of its facilities. The two banks have gone, the self-service has closed, as it could no longer compete with the large supermarkets, and likewise the greengrocer, the delicatessen and the chemist.

It was all so convenient and friendly and I hate being forced to shop elsewhere, to stand in queues and be asked, 'How are you?' by folks who really don't care.

P.S. Your programme is a tonic.

PITTSWORTH

I like a town where I know
The way to the dump
Where the electricians say 'Don't panic'
When I can't hear the pump.

I like a town where the staff at
Australia Post recognise my name
Where the librarian sends for dusty books
By authors of long ago fame.

I like a town where we talk of life
As I pick up the milk
Where the vet gives pause for grief
Twin calves, eyes liquid silk.

I like a town where the neighbours tell
Tales of the land
Sharing their knowledge
Lending a hand.

From:
Jan Collier,
Pittsworth,
Queensland

I MOVED TO QUEENSLAND for work purposes after living in the New England area, Sydney, Tasmania, London and travelling overseas, and since being in Queensland have lived in Brisbane, Toowoomba, Longreach and now Cooktown. I reckon I've found the best spot in Queensland—a little tin shack overlooking the ocean and with bush around. I've got my dog, MacDonnell, a bitsa with Aboriginal camp dog blood and named after the magnificent ranges in the outback, for company, and a small beach with palm trees below the shack. I've got paw paws and passionfruit and if I cast a line from the wharf or beach, catch barramundi and mangrove jack. Sounds okay, doesn't it? Of course, such idyllic living has its drawbacks, with crocodiles, stingers, cyclones and isolation. But it all weighs up.

I rang last week to tell you that each time you play the bird songs, two little sunbirds sit on my paw paw tree and whistle back at the radio.

From:
Lindsay Winter,
Cooktown,
Queensland

JUST A NOTE TO chat about why I live where I live. I live in a bus—in fact a thirty-six foot Denning coach. My husband and I are travelling—very slowly I might add—around Australia. Over two years ago we set off from Perth, travelling north, and have made it only 1,200 kilometres to Exmouth on the North West Cape.

I guess you could say that us 'baby boomers' are freeing ourselves from traditional shackles and creating a new lifestyle. But for whatever reason, we are having a great time. We are entirely self-sufficient in the bus, and our beautiful German shepherd, Sasha, travels with us. Both of us can work so we feel we contribute to a community before moving on. I'm a foot reflexologist, and offer other natural therapies as well as we travel. We stayed ten months in Kalbarri, where the Murchison River meets the Indian Ocean, as caretakers of the three-acre Police and Citizens Youth Camp. Kalbarri is a stunning part of Western Australia as it has surf beaches, the calm river as well as spectacular inland and coastal gorges.

From:
Linda and Stuart
Wilmot,
Exmouth,
Western Australia

We are currently living thirty kilometres south of Exmouth, right on the Gulf where the bus is about one hundred metres from the water's edge. A few months ago the migrating whales passed right by us. Dolphins are regular visitors to our beach, and we have the most amazing wildlife and marine creatures to delight us each day.

It is very hot here at the moment, and up to now we have been most fortunate that no cyclones have come this way. Cyclone Vance devastated Exmouth and the marine life in the Gulf in March 1999. We're glad we weren't here during that frightening time.

We intend slowly continuing northwards, then meandering into the Northern Territory. I have internet facilities in the bus that keep me in contact with all our friends, as well as allowing me a community web page with our travel photos uploaded so that everyone can have a peek. Now, two years down the track, we wouldn't swap this lifestyle for quids.

From:
Val and Lionel
 Daniels,
 Gosford,
 New South Wales

ABOUT SEVENTEEN YEARS ago I wrote to tell you that I was a 'fishwife' on a mackerel boat and lived at sea. We were fishing out of Weipa in the Gulf of Carpentaria and the highlight of that particular week was being chased out of my creek bathtub by a wild pig.

Things are now different. After twenty-eight years of living at sea we decided it was time for a change. Port Douglas was home base for all that time and while it is still a lovely spot we had seen lots of changes. Sometimes it is a pity about 'change'.

Not having lived in a house in those years we had some decisions to make. *Where* do we live and *what* do we do? Having lived a fairly mobile life on a boat, to us a house or a unit would be a jail.

The answer was a four-wheel drive ute with an off-road caravan. Australia, here we come! Our address may say Gosford but it's just a mail forwarding service. This letter comes to you from a hundred square mile paddock on a cattle property near Georgetown in far North Queensland. With solar panels on our roof we are self-sufficient and happily sit out in the bush for weeks at a time with an occasional foray in the ute to town to collect mail, stores and fill the water tank. Our main interest is gold detecting, and in our first three months we have found eight pieces ranging from a gram, about the size of half my little fingernail, up to fifteen grams, the size of a marble, but an out-of-shape marble. It is an interest, good exercise and finding gold is a bonus.

We must have a miner's permit and, more importantly, the property owner's permission to go on their land. We have stayed on a few different properties in the area. The view from the van window today is red dirt and lots of anthills, a variety of bush trees and the distant mountains a typical blue haze. Curious cattle, galahs and other birds complete the picture. Heaven on earth and natural noises.

When we married, Lionel told me that since childhood his dream was to live in a log cabin in the bush just like the one on the Log Cabin tobacco tin. He has now achieved his dream, only his log cabin is made out of aluminium and has wheels!

From:
June Birkett,
 Crystal Creek,
 New South Wales

MY ADDRESS HAS CHANGED, not because I choose, but because the RTA acquired our dairy farm for the Coopernook bypass. Such a pity to take good, productive dairy farmland that can feed so many people, and put it under cement! Such a pity to rip people away from their roots, from loved family, grandchildren and old friends. Such a pity!

We relocated to Crystal Creek, Murwillumbah, a very beautiful area with mountains and rivers. Crystal Creek lives up to its name by the crystal clear water we drink. The birds are so many, varied and beautiful it is an everlasting delight. These last weeks, hundreds of painted finches, yellow, blue and red, have dropped onto our lawn. The river flats and hills have all varieties of trees, including a beautiful bunya pine of some age. Flowers are everywhere and my home is filled with them. Most things planted grow easily, including a vast variety of weeds!

When I walk out the door I face a beautiful mountain range that has an 'amphitheatre' near the top covered in trees. In the mists of morn, it is beautiful.

We again have a dairy farm and have found the settling in strange and different. I do hate the toads, such fat, ugly, horrible creatures, worse than frogs, which seem rather kindly compared to toads. I must mention the cockroaches. They are six to ten feet long (or so it seems) and are always racing around in the dark. Heaven help you if you tripped over one going to the toilet at night, for you would end up in hospital!

I left my heart at Coopernook, with so many loved ones and Crowdy Head with its white lighthouse on the hill. Well, cockies and toads, looks like I'm here to stay. Get used to it!

HOME

This is the place
I show my face
Every weekend and holiday.
I do what I do
And I do it how I want to do it
Because here I cannot be criticised.
I do things my way
With no fear
Because here
There isn't a peer
In sight
Who isn't my family.
To work the
Sheep and cattle,
To hear Dad's bird* rattle
At us through the window
Reminds me of who I am.
I am the daughter of a farming father
And a well-educated mother.
This is the place
That knows my face
This is the place
Where I belong.
Home.

*Dad's paranoid pet parrot!

From:
Daisy Huntly (12),
Deniliquin,
New South Wales

◎

From:
Glen and David
Mitchell,
Maitland,
New South Wales

WE LIVE ON AN ISLAND that is surrounded by several mighty oceans and seas. Out backyard is about seven and a half million square kilometres and there are some nineteen million people scattered about, most of whom are friends we are yet to meet. We are part of the army of 'grey nomads', 'runaway grandparents', 'geriatric gypsies', itinerants or whatever label you wish to attach to we sensible seniors who have escaped Urbania and discovered the great outdoors. For six years now we have spurned lawns, gutters, garden, vacuum cleaners, rates, etc. We support towns all over by buying food, fuel and paying for campsites, and if we free camp we pay our dues by picking up rubbish and leaving nothing but footprints. Our lifestyle is healthy; we get plenty of exercise discovering unexpected beauty almost everywhere. If we disagree with our neighbours we simply move on, but this has rarely happened.

We'll never 'rust out' as each day there is something new to learn, see or do to keep our little grey cells active. The folk we meet are always interesting and some of the stories we hear around the campfire are inspirational, awesome and challenging. We'll never have enough time to see everything this great land has to offer.

Give me a home among the gum trees, with lots of honey trees, a sheep or two and a kangaroo, clothes line out the back, awning out the front and peace everywhere.

Keep up the good shows Macca, we love having breakfast in bed with you!

◎

From:
Max Strong,
Kyogle,
New South Wales

THESE DAYS I LIVE a semi-nomadic life based around a town you know well, Kyogle on the northern rivers.

On Monday mornings you are likely to find me mustering cattle among the flooded gums of the 350-acre property hidden away on Cambridge Plateau. In the twenty years that I've owned the place I've probably made the smell of an oily rag from cattle and splitting posts, but the farm has kept me fit and out of the pub! More to the point, I could never hope to put a dollar value on the pleasure I get from each regent bower bird or pademelon or platypus that I spot on the place.

On Wednesday mornings you will find me walking to work at Kyogle High School. Rainbow lorikeets and king parrots along the way are far more raucous than my students.

Maybe I'm naïve but I still have my house and car unlocked in Kyogle. One day my neighbour brought in my washing when I was away at work and a storm threatened. She left me a note saying, 'Max, your washing is folded up on your bed. Don't forget to lock your house you silly bugger!'

On Saturdays at sunset you will probably find me fishing for tailor at Wategos Beach, an hour to the east of Kyogle. Whether the fish are on the boil or not, the view up the coast to Julian Rocks and Mount Warning is always worth the drive and the hike around the rocks. A surf in clean, uncrowded waves and a feed of fresh, grilled tailor often caps off another week in my personal paradise.

◎

From:
Dot,
Wembley Downs,
Western Australia

I LIVED ALL MY life in the wheatbelt of Western Australia until retirement, when we bought a suburban home on a hill about four kilometres from the sea. Just far enough to pop down for an early morning swim.

From our back verandah we overlook a golf course and can watch the players trundling their buggies or driving their carts around the fairways. There are many trees in the suburb and the street trees vary in species—rubber trees, gum trees, and many species of bottle-brush, which this year have made a splendid show of reds through to bright pink. On Australia Day we have a good view of the fireworks over the Swan River, as we are only six kilometres from the Perth CBD.

I miss the sunrises and sunsets of the wheatbelt, and the quietness. However, I don't regret leaving the dust storms, power blackouts, blowflies, and driving miles to get essentials.

We had many birds on our farm, pink and grey galahs, green twenty-eight parrots, white cockatoos, miners and small birds, as well as black and white magpies, one of which had a particular dislike for me. It would dive on me every time I took a walk. This went on for twelve months of the year.

There are a great many birds here too, magpies, honeyeaters, white-tailed black cockatoos, white cockatoos, pink and grey galahs, pigeons, doves and often one hears the raucous laugh of the kookaburras on the golf course. We have a big jacaranda tree and the birds gather in that. One night I heard a night owl outside. I never thought I would hear that in the city. Who knows, perhaps one day I might even catch a glimpse of a curlew.

The weather is so much more moderate near the coast than inland. No more white crisp frosts to burn off the lawns, and in the summer the Fremantle doctor blows in every afternoon, making air-conditioning unnecessary.

I love to live here so I can indulge in such happy pastimes as reading stacks of library books, visiting the theatre, writing, and especially trying to educate city folk what country life is like.

I live where I live because I've found peace and contentment like I have never known.

ABOUT FIVE YEARS AGO I was made redundant from my job and at the same time my marriage was breaking up. My life was in chaos. I decided that the time was right to make major changes and move back to the country and bring my girls up where they could have the lovely childhood that I'd had. I had grown up all over country Victoria, my Dad being a teacher. I came up to Maldon, looked at three houses, bought one on the spot, moved up a couple of months later and have never looked back.

Maldon is the place where my grandmother had lived most of her life and it holds sweet memories for me. I had only been here a short time when a local girl died of meningitis. Three organisations in town all held fundraising events to assist her family to pay for the funeral. I knew then that I had come to the right place.

Since then we've settled in. We have chooks, a couple of dogs and cats, and a fat woolly pony. We've had rabbits (including a baby one the cat brought in and let loose in the kitchen), guinea pigs, geese, and a sheep for a short while. We've planted twelve fruit trees, and then replaced the ones the pony ringbarked. The children play footy in the paddock next door, climb trees, dig holes, make cubbies, play and play …

We gave up central heating for an open fire, a burglar alarm for good neighbours and a woofily dog. We have an outside loo with no light, and on frosty mornings we crunch our way there across the frozen grass. When someone offered to put a light in the dunny we decided against it—we love looking at the stars. We know half the town and join in everything. I've landed a local part-time job as a community worker.

We sometimes visit Melbourne as Granddad still lives there. What I notice most is that it's so noisy. In shopping centres I want to cover my ears. Up here (in the best little town in the world) you can hear the wind in the trees and the beating of a bird's wings—and on weekends we hear church bells and the whistle of the steam train.

From:
Tanya Waterson,
Maldon,
Victoria

Extended family

From:
Michael Brimmer,
Corinth,
Greece

'YASSOO' FROM XYLOCASTRO, A small town thirty kilometres west of Corinth in the Peloponnese, Greece. My wife Niki, son Nicholas and I abandoned Sydney almost two years ago and have since lived in this beautiful little pocket of the Mediterranean on an extended working holiday. I just thought I'd drop you a line to give you some idea about what life is like here in Greece.

In many ways our address is like a dream come true. Just off our front verandah is the deep blue Gulf of Corinth. Across this stretch of water sits Mount Parnassos, one of Greece's highest mountains, in whose foothills rests ancient Delphi. The mountain is blanketed in snow at the moment and it is a magnificent sight, literally rising up out of the water. Behind us, hills covered in citrus and olive groves lead into the rugged mountains of the Peloponnese. You can swim for about eight months of the year and in the cooler months the hills provide wonderful opportunities for long walks, and even longer lunches in village tavernas! Even though it gets very quiet here in winter, there's still plenty to do.

We work in a local language school, teaching English to Greek schoolkids of various ages. Most English here is heard in American films so my Australian accent can really throw them. One of the nicer aspects of life here is the friendly, easygoing nature of the locals. You can't walk down the road without saying 'Yassoo' to an acquaintance or shopkeeper. On one occasion a friend of mine was visiting and arrived in town clueless as to where our house was. He asked at a local café and it soon erupted into a conference: 'Poo ine spitee sto Afstralos?' ('Where is the Australians' house?'). Adonyi, the owner, borrowed a couple of bikes from the patrons and led our friend on a town tour to locate our house!

When Greeks discover that I come from Australia, they always respond warmly and may remark about a relative they have there or about Australian soldiers they had met during World War Two here on the mainland, or on Crete. For the most part I can sense a feeling of admiration for Australians here and there is a bond between the two countries.

Sometimes I get a little homesick. Little things about life in Australia are often missed. Lazy Sunday mornings reading the papers and listening to your programme, beaches with surf, family get-togethers, the banter with mates over a cold beer, Aussie hamburgers with the lot—ironic really when you consider they are usually cooked by Greeks—magpies cawing in the garden, the smell of a freshly mown lawn, swimming laps at the local pool—I could go on but I'm sure listeners who have spent time away from home will know the feeling.

I'd better stop now as it's time to go and teach gerunds and irregular verbs.

From:
Brenda Cantwell,
SV Bacchus,
Geraldton Harbour,
Western Australia

WE HAVE JUST LISTENED TO your story about the *Batavia*. As you were talking we were sailing past Beacon Island which is where the *Batavia* was wrecked. Talk about being in the right place at the right time! We have just spent a week sheltering from strong winds in Turtle Bay on East Wallaby Island. The Houtman Abrolhos Islands are fascinating as they are full of contrast—low, uninhabited islands surrounded by reef, then small islands crammed full of lobster fishermen's huts. From a distance it looks like Aberdeen in Hong Kong. The fishermen are in residence from November to June.

We bought *Bacchus*, our forty-four foot sloop, seven years ago. Living on board was a major lifestyle change for me, though not so much for my husband as he has always had a love of boats. Neither of us had sailed before, so that in itself was a challenge and one which we have enjoyed, although there have been times when I would have sold my soul for a kitchen rather a galley on a twenty-degree heel!

We have been 'on the dolphin', or maybe 'on the turtle' this time since leaving Cairns for Perth to spend about six months with my elderly mother. We will have covered a distance of over 3,000 nautical miles. It has been a wonderful journey with only a few spots of bad weather. We've always managed to find a safe anchorage to hole up while waiting for the weather to improve. We've seen dolphins, humpback whales (heard them talking through the hull while sailing—magical!), crocodiles, turtles and lots of birds. One night, just off Port Hedland, we had about twenty terns hitch a ride. It was very noisy and rather messy as the first light at dawn revealed! Our cat, Isaac, nearly went mad and we had to keep him below. We were more concerned that he would fall over the side in excitement than actually catch a bird. We counted twenty-five turtles waiting to go ashore at Serrurier Island to lay their eggs. Two sea eagles shared Turtle Bay with us, we saw their huge nest and watched them every-day as they glided over the bay looking for food. While walking along the beach we came upon a lone seal sunning itself and it was not at all perturbed by our presence.

WE LIVE IN MARIGINIUP (marr-i-jin-i-up) about sixteen miles north of Perth and feel we have the best of both worlds as we're close enough to town amenities for comfort but far enough for peace.

When we built our home here we kept as many native trees as possible—mostly big, old jarrahs and several varieties of banksias. There are beautiful wildflowers, which I spend a lot of my time drawing and painting.

The birds are plentiful and wonderful. There's a 'home troop' of about a dozen magpies which arrive every morning and afternoon to sing to us, often accompanied by butcher birds and pee wees (pied mudlarks) plus heaps of galahs, twenty-eight parrots and other parrots, lorikeets, willy-wagtails, crowned and bronze-wing pigeons, black-eyed cuckoo shrikes and various 'part-time' visitors. Flocks of black cockies land in our paddock trees announcing their comings and goings with raucous cries. We have a lake close by and this attracts many water birds so we often have ibis, herons and ducks wandering around the place.

Beside all of these feathered friends we have many frogs. Most nights we have half a dozen sitting on our kitchen windowsill. We have to check our gumboots and watering can for frogs before use. Other tiny frogs occasionally sit spreadeagled on our windows watching us with solemn, owl-eyed faces. Our dogs don't seem to mind sharing their drinking bowls with frogs, or their bones or dog biscuits with magpies—in fact, all of our animals (horses, cows, etc.) manage to get along just fine. People could learn a lot from their tolerance.

From:
Gloria Paxman,
Mariginiup,
Western Australia

WHY I DON'T LIVE where I want to live!

Nestled into the hills of the Otway National Park rainforest sits 'Lizard House'. Situated 220 metres above sea level, the view to the east is one of the most picture-postcard vistas the Great Ocean Road can offer. From the kitchen window, where I presently sit, the rolling hills above the West Barham River recede to the township of Apollo Bay. Beyond lies the blue mass of Bass Strait; the distant horizon often imperceptible, blending into an ever-changing sky.

Sunrise, moonrise, sunsets through the mountain ash and tree ferns, clear crisp days, Milky-Way midnights, Otway showers raging down the valley, sea mists whirling and rising, forest clouds like a rooftop descending ... any time or season is magic in the hills above Apollo Bay.

From:
John Dean,
East Burwood,
Victoria

Such was our luck to acquire this humble little cottage. 'Lizard House' is where one day we will come to live permanently.

For the present, I live in 'Smelbourne', the big smoke, where I work to pay off the bank loan that enabled me to secure this Otway paradise. I drive a bus. I see life on the streets, the battlers of the suburbs. I feel the road rage, smell the smog, hear the aggression of selfish ignorance yet at the same time marvel at the friendship between total strangers. So many people who never see the flashing wings of the king parrots, or the wedge-tailed eagle soar and bank into a howling westerly, harnessing the full force of nature and disappearing without a single wing beat as if entering a fourth dimension.

'Lizard House' is a time warp. Life and its frantic pursuits come into the context of *real* time—a far slower and more gentle pace than many city people can ever comprehend.

15

◎ *McNamara's Bump* ◎

About three weeks ago we were pounding through the acacia scrub on the eastern side of the Tanami Desert looking for a landmark. Out of the bush loomed a granite hill which we raced up—the view was absolutely superb. I said to Andrew, 'We should name this Mount McNamara.' He looked at it thoughtfully, then replied, 'No, it's too small for a mountain, let's call it McNamara's Lump.' I responded, 'You can't call it that, it sounds like a disease!' So, he thought again before suggesting McNamara's Dome, but I said, 'No, he's not bald.' So, after much deliberation, out came McNamara's Bump!

FROM: *Kieran Kelly*, Seaforth, New South Wales and *Andrew Harper*, Deniliquin, New South Wales

G'day, this is Macca

(G'day
ANDREW and
KIERAN

MACCA: We're going to cross to Andrew and Kieran and find out where they are.

ANDREW: G'day, Ian, it's Andrew here. How are you?

MACCA: I'm great, mate. Tell us all about it. Where are you?

ANDREW: We're about 395 kilometres north-west of Alice Springs or 300 kilometres south-west of Tennant Creek. Since we spoke to you last we've crossed the Lander River and left all kinds of roads and fences behind. We're well and truly in the Tanami Desert.

MACCA: I've been thinking about you both and how you're getting on. The first thing I thought of was shoes. Now, you obviously don't wear joggers; you wear proper boots out there. Is there spinifex, Andrew?

ANDREW: Oh, there's spinifex all right, Macca, but I'm just wearing my work boots which I wear every day. I just poke along in shorts and an open shirt and a pair of leggings. You couldn't go through this country with sandals or anything like that. The country here is, in a word, flat. There's a tremendous amount of vegetation, a lot of white gum, various types of acacia, quite a lot for the camels to eat, which is important. The predominant plant, of course, is spinifex. Kieran and I have what we call a Category 2 and a Category 1 spinifex. Category 2 at the moment is knee deep and you've just got to lift your legs up and plough through it as best you can. The camels don't like it all that much. Like us, they don't like having the hair ripped off their legs, so they try to walk around it and it does slow us down a bit. Nevertheless, we're still doing about twenty kilometres a day so we're poking along pretty well.

MACCA: Do you mean the camels don't go through it so you're not travelling as fast as you'd like?

ANDREW: We're still making good time, Ian. I meant that the spinifex here, rather than growing in clumps like in the Simpson Desert, where you can walk around it, grows in one great big mass and there's very little open ground, so you've just got to plough through it. With five camels it's like driving a road train in traffic.

ANDREW: Have you seen any feral cats or rabbits? What's the wildlife story out there?

ANDREW: We've seen a couple of camels and plenty of signs of feral cats just by looking at their scats, which are quite distinctive. We've certainly seen their tracks but I think they see us before we see them. We did see signs of rabbits for the first time about three days ago, but not now. Yesterday where the grevillea was flowering there were finches, budgerigars, willy wagtails, a lot of birdlife around. Right through, of course, there are signs of wild camels.

MACCA: You're used to this, aren't you, Andrew, because you did that big walk across Australia, but I don't think Kieran's used to it. How's everybody holding up?

ANDREW: Pretty well, Ian. Kieran's going well, but he did kick the billy over the other night so he lost a few marks for that. We've covered about 250 kilometres now and we've got the routine, so now it's just a matter of adapting each day to what we come across.

MACCA: Each day I keep imagining where you are. Is it flat country you're going through?

ANDREW: Yes, it is, Ian. There are no sand dunes in this part of the Tanami. We probably won't see any of those until we get closer to the WA border. Apart from a couple of isolated rocky rises it's mostly pretty flat, which suits the camels down to the ground. They're used to walking over

ere's Andrew Harper (left) and Kieran Kelly at the start of their journey across the Tanami Desert. Their phoned reports ● the programme lead to hundreds of letters and calls.

he Little Sandy Desert in Western Australia provided a beautiful backdrop to Pauline and Richard Ayton's wedding.

A magic radio moment at Uranquinty in New South Wales; the sun's just up as we broadcast under the silos beside the railway track.

Ron and Gladys Bone from The Gap in Queensland are a picture of contentment after travelling over half a million miles 'on the road'.

Millennium blues? Les Oxenbridge called from Chatham Island in New Zealand (those are his grand kids in the phone box) reckoning it was the first place to welcome the new millennium. Les, you were a year out!

Top: It's just amazing who you bump into miles from anywhere. Paul Scharenberg and Steve Walters keep the trains running 'across the paddock' —— the Nullarbor Plain!

Left: On the side of the road with Alf Garrard from Ingham in Queensland. He's telling me why he lives where he lives, Australia all over.

Right: 'G'day mate, how's the drought going?' I asked Toby Bunion just outside Gulargambone in New South Wales.

Top left: A frog mural! These green tree frogs love posing at Penny Murphy's home at Meandarra in Queensland.

Top right: Read all about it, read all about it. News travels to the remotest of areas.

Bottom left: Great Aussie humour or a bad joke? A few days after a 'shoot out' on the Oodnadatta Track in South Australia this tree was decorated with feral cats and named a 'pussy willow'. You decide!

Bottom right: Just in case you don't get the message!!

sand dunes in the Simpson Desert so they're probably finding this trip fairly easy going.

MACCA: Andrew, nice to talk to you. I'm sure you're enjoying life out there.

ANDREW: Well, it's a pretty good lifestyle, Ian. It keeps you fit and there's not a hell of a lot to worry about out here, just seeing what the desert serves up to you each day. I'll pass you over to Kieran.

KIERAN: Good morning, Ian.

MACCA: How are you, mate? Do you want to hear any news, like what's happening with the Stock Exchange?

KIERAN: Can I read you something?

At 3.50 camped, some of my horses being nearly done up for want of water and having nothing to eat but spinifex. We are expecting every moment to come upon a gum creek but have been disappointed. I have not so much as seen a water course since I left the Lander and how far this country may continue is impossible to tell. I intended to have turned back sooner but I was expecting every moment to meet with a creek. I wish I had turned back earlier, for I am almost afraid that I have allowed myself to come too far. I am doubtful if all my horses will be able to get back to water. Tomorrow morning I must unwillingly retreat to water for my horses. There is no chance of getting to the north-west in this direction unless this plain soon terminates.

That was written on Thursday, 3 May, 1860, by John McDouall Stuart. He'd pushed out into the Tanami and he'd reached a ridge and looked out over this hell of a country, this flat frying pan of a desert, and said, 'I can't go on any more.' He'd run out of food and water and decided to turn back.

    It was quite something for Andrew and I to reach there the night before last and camp exactly where he did, to look back to where he'd come from and to contemplate what he contemplated, then the following morning to get up and cross that ridge and lead the camels out onto that flat, red plain and see what he'd have experienced. Now we know for sure that he'd have been a dead man if he kept going. We've come about twenty kilometres further on and we can see the country that was in front of him. He was quite right, the plain doesn't terminate. It's a dense, red hell of spinifex and aridity. The thing that's amazing me about the Tanami is the lack of water. Since we left central Mt Stuart the naturally occurring water we've seen wouldn't fill half a bucket, and that's about 230 kilometres. This is the dryest place I've ever seen; it's almost impossible to describe. We've been following Stuart's track exactly. Each time his compass course changed I changed ours and yesterday morning we came out here onto the plain and he was no longer with us. I've packed his journal away and I almost felt like he'd waved us goodbye and was heading back and we were going on. It was a very strange feeling.

MACCA: Kieran, you've painted an amazing picture, mate. Why didn't Stuart take camels?

KIERAN: As you know, he was competing with Burke and Wills to try to cross the continent and the only camels in Australia then had been imported by Sir Thomas Elder and given to the Burke and Wills expedition. There just were no camels in Australia to use. I was walking along behind the camels yesterday because it's very hard for us to walk through this country together, and every camel was carrying water, some of them are carrying nothing but water, and my attitude to water has changed completely on this trip. When you plough through that spinifex and the sun's beating into you all day, you're dirty and sweaty, and at the end of the day your only reward is half a quart pot of water, about three cupfuls, to have a bath in. It makes me realise what a dry place this continent of Australia is. The only difference between us and Stuart is that we can carry a lot of water.

MACCA: Kieran, I understand you kicked the billy over the other night! You said to me once, 'Ian, a cup of tea will fix anything.' Is that still your philosophy?

KIERAN: Yes, a cup of tea will fix most things, and when you've only got enough water to wash your hands and face at night, it's amazing what it can do for you. It's just a lovely feeling and, yes, a cup of tea is a good thing. Before we go, Ian, I'd like to read you a couple of scratchings from 'Banjo' Paterson.

The narrow ways of English folk
Are not for such as we.
They bear the long-accustomed yoke
Of staid conservancy.
Yet all our roads are new and strange
And through our blood there runs
The vagabonding love of change
That drove us westward of the range
And westward of the sun.

I think that describes what we're trying to do.

MACCA: Keiran, keep in touch. We're all with you but we're not sure about the spinifex!

Kieran a week later.

KIERAN: Good morning, Ian.

MACCA: G'day, mate. How are you? You sounded a bit weary last week.

KIERAN: Well, yes, I'm tired in places that no human being's ever been tired before, but we got here and for that I'm greatly relieved. We've answered all the questions that I was uncertain of, such as can two people walk across the Tanami—nobody's done it before. Can we link Gregory's expedition with Stuart's—the answer's yes. Can you take a city office worker fifty years old away from the toasted focaccias and the caffe latte in the corner coffee shop and send him across 700 kilometres of saltpan and acacia scrub? I suppose the answer to that also is, yes. But it wouldn't want to have been 701 kilometres or I'd have been face down out in the mulga with the dingoes arguing over the choice bits. The reason we're here is because this is the furthest point east that Augustus Gregory got to before he turned back. On 5 March 1856 he climbed Mt Wilson and he wrote:

From the summit of the hill nothing was visible but one unbounded waste of sandy ridges and low rocky hillocks which lay to the south-east of the hill. All was one impenetrable desert, as the flat and sandy surface which could absorb the waters of the creek was not likely to originate watercourses. Ascending the hill I named it Mt Wilson.

It's quite something to stand up there where the myth of the inland sea was finally exploded. He stood on that hill and said, 'There's no water out here,' a bit like Stuart, I suppose, on the other side of the desert. This desert extends down to the south-west, past where Alice Springs is today, to where Stuart got to. So this is a very historic part of Australia and it's a tremendous thrill to stand up there, if for nothing else than the superb views. I asked Andrew, 'Was it worth walking 700 kilometres for?' and he looked at the view and said, 'Absolutely!'

From:
Carol Black,
Arana Hills,
Queensland

I WANT TO TELL YOU how much I have been enjoying the segment on 'Australia All Over' with Kieran and Andrew on their trek in Central Australia.

These men are really showing the true Aussie spirit of adventure—with hardships. My heroes are the early explorers and pioneers of Australia (not highly paid sportsmen and women). I always feel in awe of those people and what they did: William Landsborough; Nat Buchanan; A.C. Gregory and his brothers; the Jardine brothers; Burke and Wills; Leichhardt; the Durack family, to name a few. So, to listen to modern adventurers is a privilege.

So three cheers to these two. Kieran told you that he was a city softy. His physical body may have been a bit under-conditioned, but his heart and spirit certainly aren't. There is hope for Australia yet when people like Kieran and Andrew show us such 'get up and go'.

I MUST SAY THAT I really enjoyed the Tanami travels of Kieran and Andrew. Having been fortunate enough to have travelled in air-conditioned coaches across the Tanami Track on two Society for Growing Australian Plants safaris. I have a little appreciation of both the rigours and the delights of the journey. Memories of the sun rising and lighting spinifex clumps one-by-one; of semi-circles in the sand, 'drawn' by the grass as it moved to and fro in the wind; of the wondrous sculptures, both big and small, of the termite mounds; of two sets of tracks joining and only one set moving on; and of one of my friends telling me that plants were furry so they wouldn't get cold in the wintertime. These are part of my recollections of those wonderful trips. But to be as close to everything as Kieran and Andrew were with their camels, so apart from everything else, would have been an almost mind-blowing experience. I enjoyed listening to their calls to you, and know others did too. One Sunday I was sitting in the car park at church hoping the conversation would end before I had to go into the service, and in the car next to me, two other parishioners were doing the same.

From: Beth McRobert, Jamboree Heights, Queensland

I WORKED FOR FOUR years in the Tanami as an exploration geologist. I do not want to take away anything away from the guys who are walking from Central Mount Stuart to Lake Gregory, but they are in error claiming to be the first whites to walk across the Tanami with camels. They are covering the area travelled by hundreds of men in 1931–32 during the Granites Gold Rush, some in cars and trucks, some on camels, some walking and nearly dying in the process.

There is surface water in that stretch of the country. It is in the form of granite rock holes, laterite namma holes, and soaks. The traditional owners lived out there while the water lasted, and when the modern-day walker sees a soak filled in, they naturally think it needs maintenance. This is a mistake. The Aborigines knew if they opened it up the water would evaporate, so they only excavated when they needed to. The rock holes and namma holes are often tiny in area but deep—up to three metres or more. I have seen zebra finches disappear into a hole and come out chirping and wet. This probably explains the presence of those eternally chirping little beggars in the middle of nowhere!

Those who have gone before include Allan Davidson, who crossed from Barrow Creek to west of Tanami in 1900 then back to Barrow again on camels and took about six months. He had the advantage of Aboriginals still living out there and was able to follow their smoke and tracks to water. Davidson discovered gold at Tanami and the Granites, until recently the only operating mines in the district.

The Tanami Gold Rush of 1909–10 saw several hundred men descend on Tanami by any means available, one chap even cycling to and from Darwin. When eleven-and-a-half inches

Email from: Paul Hynch

of rain fell in four days they all went crazy to get into the desert, prospecting while the surface water lasted.

Charles Chewings in the early years of last century carried out an expedition into the desert north and west of Central Mount Stuart, searching for a potential stock route and undertaking anthropological study.

Alec Ross, when an old man in his 70s, crossed from Tanami to the Lander River on camels in about 1910. (He had been a cameleer with Giles and Tietkens when they crossed from Port Augusta to Perth in 1875.)

Joe Brown, a famous central Australian bushman, did the crossing between the Lander River and Halls Creek and vice versa in the 1920s and '30s so often that there was a route between the various rockholes known as the JB Track.

Ben Nicker, another famous bushman of the Centre, crossed on horseback and with camels on several occasions. Jimmy Wickham, another famous (or infamous) prospector and cattle duffer, crossed a few times. Billy Braitling of Mount Doreen Station also got around quite a bit in the '20s and '30s.

Thomson's Rockhole was discovered in 1928 by Thomson, who walked with camels from Alice Springs to Tanami and back.

I am glad these modern cameleers, Kieran and Andrew, are bringing attention to a fascinating part of our country and wish them all the best. I just thought I'd add to that interest a bit of history.

Incidentally, Tanami was originally pronounced 'Chan-ah-mee', which meant 'never die' in the local dialect. It refers to the more than 35,000 gallons of water in the 'camel rockholes' in the face of the range at Tanami.

◎

Email from:
Peter Hornsby,
University of Adelaide
South Australia

I WAS INTERESTED TO hear the remarks of your caller from Cook, on the Nullarbor Plain, about trains hitting camels. The current severe drought is causing the camels (like kangaroos and emus in other parts of South Australia) to move south in search of feed. The slightly elevated railway track creates an albeit small additional rainfall run-off, leading to a few bits of green pickings alongside the line, and this is what the animals are going for. (This also is why they feed at the edge of the roads as well.) Unfortunately, on the railway, they often stand on the track, invariably leading to their demise.

While working out from Tarcoola some years ago we found kangaroos being killed in the same way. We were working about three kilometres from the line, and you could hear the trains approaching for anything up to half and hour before they arrived, so how was it these animals got killed?

Looking into the question supplied some unexpected answers. Firstly, sound from trains is dispersed laterally so you can hear them quite easily from the side. And secondly, very little sound travels directly forward in the direction in which the train is travelling. Assuming the animal is looking at the approaching train, it hears virtually nothing, and because the train is being viewed straight on, there are no visual clues as to how fast it is moving. By the time the animal realises the danger, it often is too late for it to get out of the way, with the inevitable consequences.

The situation is even worse if the animal has its back to the train, and they can be killed without ever being aware of the danger. The train driver knows what is about to happen, but other than sounding the horn, there is little he can do about it.

AT PRESENT MY WIFE and I are relieving at Wingellina Community near Surveyor-General's Corner where the borders of Western Australia, South Australia and the Northern Territory join. We did a trip south into the Great Victoria Desert and 250 kilometres south of Wingellina we visited what should have been a fine rockhole with beautiful fresh water. Instead we found a dead camel in the water, drowned while trying to get a drink. These days everywhere we travel out here there are signs that camels, desperate for something to eat, are tearing small bushes and trees apart. Experts say feral camel numbers are doubling every seven years. Live camels are being exported from the Northern Territory but it is not possible this far out because the distance and condition of tracks makes the cost of trapping and transport prohibitive. The only solution is shooting. While some people who see the camel as some kind of outback icon may oppose this, it is the only way our desert areas are going to be protected from a steadily increasing problem.

From:
David Hewitt,
Alice Springs,
Northern Territory

RECENTLY YOU ASKED THE men crossing the Tanami Desert about camels. In the 1850s my great-grandfather took up land at Oomberatna in the northern Flinders Ranges and his two sons followed. My grandfather, S.J. Stuckey, realised camels would be the best animals for carrying wool from the outback. He and his brother were in partnership with Thomas Elder, who financed the camel project. S.J. Stuckey sailed to Melbourne to interview Mr Landels, who had brought camels to Victoria for the Burke and Wills Expedition. S.J. sailed to Bombay on the P&O steamer *Salsette*. Then he proceeded to Karachi and after much trouble eventually sailed to Port Augusta with thirty-one Afghans, 124 camels and thirty-one donkeys, arriving there on 31st December, 1865.

From:
G. M. McArthur,
North Adelaide,
South Australia

HEARING YOUR INTERVIEW WITH those intrepid travellers crossing the Tanami reminded me of an experience I had in this area some sixty years ago.

During the war I was one of many convoy drivers carting goods between the two railheads of Alice Springs and Larrima. On one trip, approaching Central Mount Stuart I was privileged to see an Aboriginal family on walkabout. The father, carrying two or three spears and a woomera, was stalking several hundred yards ahead of his group. The mother was loaded down with all their goods, spare spears and boomerangs and a bundle of furs balanced on her head and a young child on her hip. The rest of the children filed obediently behind, the elders brought up the rear. They were headed into the Tanami Desert.

The next trip a week later was a disaster. It had rained all night and the track was under water. As we neared the place where I had seen the Aboriginal family, a minor creek had become a raging river as water poured out of the adjacent Central Mount Stuart Range and we could go no further. That night we witnessed the awesome power of nature as the storm surged up and down the range, lightning continuously striking the ridges. It was five days before we could continue.

From:
Ron Threlfall,
Glenelg North,
South Australia

YOU WERE TALKING ONCE about Giles and his exploration in the 1870s. I've been reading Giles' account of his journeys in facsimile editions of books first published at the time of his explo-

From:
Desley McDonagh,
Stanthorpe,
Queensland

ration. I found *Australia Twice Traversed* very interesting because he was writing about places in the centre that I'd visited years ago.

One thing that stands out for me in these books is his use of the English language. We are now poles away from the language Giles used. I was fascinated with his use of two words in particular. When we go camping we go camping, we may even set up camp, but when Giles put up camp for the night he encamped and when he broke camp to move on he decamped.

I found the language rather hard to read but as I am very interested in the English language, I enjoyed reading it as it used to be written.

And now I'll decamp!

◎

I HEARD YOU STRUGGLING manfully to describe the joys of the wide open spaces. I know the problem. This is the closest I've come to finding it adequately described. It's from a Russian book, *A Hero of Our Own Times*, by Michael Lermontov, a nineteenth-century writer. He is describing a remote region of the Caucus Mountains in central Russia. But I reckon it applies equally to central Australia, in spirit, if not description:

The road appeared to be leading up into the sky, for it continued to mount as far as the eye could see, and at length vanished into the cloud which had stayed since overnight upon the summit of Gut-Gora like a kite hovering over its prey. The snow crunched beneath our feet. The air was so rarefied that breathing was painful, and the blood continually went to my head; but, for all that, a delightful feeling of exhilaration spread through my veins, and I was full of joy at being, as it were, on the roof of the world—a childish sentiment, no doubt, but when we get right away from the conventions of society and close to nature we involuntarily become children once more. The soul sheds all that it has artificially acquired, to be what it was in its prime and probably will be again some day. Anyone who, like myself, has wandered among the wild mountains, has feasted his eyes on their fantastic shapes, and has eagerly inhaled the vivifying atmosphere of lofty passes—will readily understand why I long to reproduce these magical impressions.

From:
Russell,
Canberra,
Australian Capital
Territory

G'day, this is Macca

G'day
GLENDA

GLENDA: Glenda here. I'm ringing from a phone booth just south of Broome and I thought you might like to hear about a really wonderful experience we had on the Tanami Track.

MACCA: Yes, I would.

GLENDA: We camped for the night and, just on dusk, suddenly there was movement from the spinifex and all of these beautiful little spinifex-hopping mice came out. My husband set up a light and I put out some bait of Weetbix and peanut butter and syrup and we just sat there and watched them for about an hour, coming out and eating the bait and running all around our feet.

MACCA: Well, that's lovely. That's food for the soul, as a lady said to me one day.

GLENDA: Oh, absolutely. Then we camped near an old mining dam and it was quite a different experience. I'm a very keen birdwatcher and I was out looking at the birds and, looking down into the dam, I saw this large goanna come out and walk around the edge of the dam. I was panning around and I thought, that looked like a crocodile ... What? I panned back and there was a two-and-a-half-metre freshwater croc, as fat as mud, sunning himself on the bank. That just blew me away.

MACCA: Where was this?

GLENDA: South-west of Hall's Creek would you believe, out in an old mining dam, and here's this big fat crocodile, so don't ask me where it came from. We thought that was rather interesting, and when we went into Hall's Creek we were talking to a chappie and he said, 'Oh, there's a great big salty in the Mary River and a lot of people don't know that when they jump in to have a swim!' So I said that was the last time I'll put my feet in any water up here.

BALLAD OF A FOUR-WHEEL DRIVE

From:
Max Fatchen,
Smithfield,
South Australia

We zoom to Broome to enjoy the view
Or the wonderful world of Kakadu.
And how the landscape comes alive
As we travel along in our four-wheel drive.

It carries us there and it carries us back
From the tropical north or some outside track.
To the Birdsville pub or a township store
Or the bubbling brink of an inland bore.

The ranges are wearing an ochre tint
And the whirlwinds dance where the gibbers glint.
The brumbies race and the camels stare
And the Cooper's flood has reached Lake Eyre.

The parrots will touch the trees with fire
The wind's conducting its coolibah choir.
The motor purrs and the waterbag swings
As we set a course for Alice Springs.

We've fossicked for gold with a hopeful pan
We had a hoot from the passing Ghan.
We've drunk a toast from a billycan brew
When the stars come out at Uluru.

There are campfire yarns of a day well spent
In our sleeping bags where the sky's our tent.
We're far from critics that fret and strive
And we have sweet dreams by our four-wheel drive.

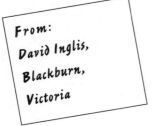

From:
David Inglis,
Blackburn,
Victoria

I THOUGHT YOU JUST might be interested in this story which illustrates the increase in tourism in recent years. In October 1958 a friend and I went on a camping trip to Ayers Rock (as it was then), the Olgas and Alice Springs. To get to the Rock we turned off the Port Augusta/Alice Springs road and from that moment until we returned several days later we didn't see another living human soul. The track to Ayers Rock was red sand and earth (as was the Port Augusta/Alice Springs road itself) but easily driveable in our ordinary Holden sedan. There had been good rain a few weeks previously so we were fortunate to be surrounded by masses of everlasting flowers and Sturt's Desert Pea.

At the Rock itself there were few signs of previous visitors except for the scattered remains of a few camp fires. The surrounds of the Rock were tidy so obviously the few visitors adhered to the old dictum 'Clear up before you clear out'. There were waterholes around the base of the Rock which we used for both swimming and drinking.

We were young, fit and energetic and had arrived determined to climb the Rock. We drove right around the base several times but could not with any certainty identify a spot where we might safely start to climb. Bearing in mind the complete isolation we decided that it would be foolhardy to attempt it.

The sense of peace and loneliness at the Rock and at the Olgas a mere forty-four years ago remains with me to this day and must provide an enormous contrast with the present.

16

Macca's on the Airwaves, Merry Christmas All

All the bells are gaily ringing
Birds in every tree are singing
Let us in the golden weather
Gather Christmas bush together.
FROM: *John Wheeler*

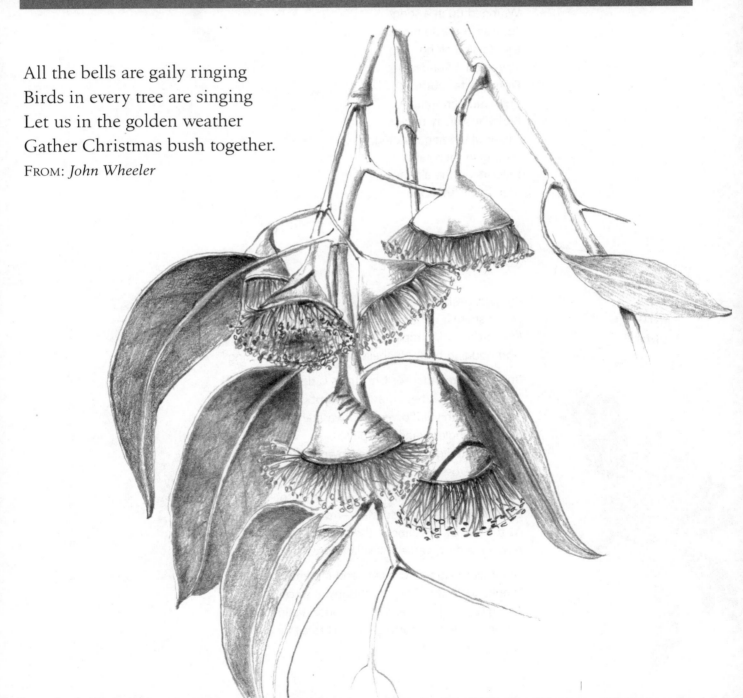

From:
Max Fatchen,
Smithfield,
South Australia

Macca's on the radio
Crocodiles and 'roos,
Blokes along the Nullarbor
Tune in for the news.
Someone in the Kimberleys,
Someone down at Hay,
Someone with a yarn or two
Phone from Byron Bay.
All at Ulladulla
Wish the listeners well,
Tales of droughts and drenchings,
There's so much to tell.
Here's a bit of folklore
Wrapped up in a song
Tourists in the Territory
Like to sing along.
Voices on a Sunday
From the far outback
Bulls and barramundi,
Birdsville's dusty track.
Cheerful women chatting,
Putting in their call
Macca's on the airwaves,
Merry Christmas all.

◎

CHRISTMAS WISHES

From:
Eve Cumming,
Mortlake,
Victoria

Bring us a Christmas that dawns bright and clear.
Let us share it with family and friends, loved and dear.
May a choir of magpies carol a hymn,
And nodding bush-bluebells peal praise to the King.

Bring us a tree that for Christmas is decked.
Not a pine, let it be a grand eucalypt
Trimmed with wildflowers, red waratah,
Banksia candles, kangaroo-paw;
Haloed with light from these Down Under skies,
And the Cross of the South, star-spangled with five.

Bring fragrance of Summer, heady, intense,
Like the lifts of the Wise Men—myrrh, frankincense.
As the tale of the Babe in the stable is told,
A mountain of wattle will shimmer with gold.

Grant us the grace to reflect and remember,
Thanks be to the Child for this joy in December.
And give us all faith as we pray once again
For peace here on earth. Goodwill to all men.

BUSH CHRISTMAS

'Twas the night before Christmas and all through the bush
Not a whisper was heard in the gum-scented hush.
All the bush creatures, feathered and furred,
Waited for morning, not one of them stirred.
No lone Christmas star, but a bevy of five,
Silver filigree cross in the dark Southern skies.
Far down in a clearing where the river runs free,
There'd been some preparing of a bush Christmas tree;
Never before was such a tree dressed,
Atop cockatoo candles flamed bright sulphur crests.
No gaudy, glass baubles adorned the tree's limbs,
There were crimson rosellas and blue fairy wrens;
Garlands of wildflowers that in the bush grow,
And swags of clematis, like fresh-fallen snow.
Now was it my dreaming, or did I see true,
With a pouch filled with presents, a red kangaroo?

'Twas the morning of Christmas, through the still, saffron dawn
Came carols of birdsong, the day was now born.
Then the beasts of the earth and the birds of the air
Wished the world joy at Christmas, and peace for New Year.

From:
Eve Cumming,
Buchan,
Victoria

MY NAME IS HEATH PAWLEY and I'm eleven. I live in a town called The Basin. It's right at the bottom of the Dandenongs. A bit of a scare when the fires started but they didn't get as far as us. Just thought I'd give you a poem I wrote at Christmas. Hope you like it.

From:
Heath Pawley,
The Basin,
Victoria

WHAT HAPPENED LAST CHRISTMAS

It was on Christmas day
And I've come to say
That Christmas was one to remember.

It was scorching hot
And we'd all lost the plot
And the spirit of the 25th of December.

We all brought food
And I yelled 'yo dude'
When Aunt Sharon pulled out a pavlova.

Aunt Gery made a cake
I said 'How long did it take
To make it in the shape of a clover?'

Nan had some chicken
Which Milly was flickin'
All over the table and floor.

When Pa got mad
I was awfully glad
I hadn't given him a chainsaw.

Grandma and grandpa
Had made some damper
And had presents for us all.

We had a game of cricket
Got a footy and kicked it
It happened to be Josh's new football.

The oldies had tea
But didn't notice me
When I nicked a bottle of wine.

And later Mum found
Me slumped on the ground
And Uncle Dick, Liz and Alan said I was fine.

Filled with pavlova
And a slight hangover
I went to bed to sleep

But before I slept fast
I completed the task
Of counting two million sheep.

◎

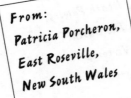

CHRISTMAS

From:
Patricia Porcheron,
East Roseville,
New South Wales

Christmas comes once a year
Full of stress, turkey and good cheer.
Perhaps that's why in every way
We're so relieved on Boxing Day
We eat cold and read our books,
Watch the cricket, mind our looks,
And when we need, have a nap,
Resolve next year to avoid the trap:
This I-give-you, you-give-me
That hangs about the Christmas tree;
Concentrate on deeper meanings,
Be not concerned with shopper's gleanings;
Remember how it all began
Because one bright star
Shining form afar
Led Three Wise Men to Bethlehem.

REMEMBER

So tell us of the Christmas theme
That comes from times both old and far.
The shepherds: did they have some dream
Or voices and a steady star?

Was Bethlehem a fable then
As centuries went rolling by?
Can we believe in three wise kings
With wise men in short supply?

Computers, programmed for today,
What can they make of stables mean,
And where our lighted candles sway
Can we recall a manger mean?

Amid our twentieth century din,
With prophets crying woe and doom,
Don't let your air-conditioned inn
Put out a sign that says 'No room'.

From:
Max Fatchen,
Smithfield,
South Australia

I SAW SANTA (I DID!)

Last year I waited for Santa,
I waited for sounds of 'Ho! Ho!',
Is he real this fellow called Santa?
For nobody sees him I know.

I waited and waited last Christmas,
For 'Me' was then only four,
I tried to keep open my tired little eyes
But I couldn't stay awake any more.

He left lots of presents (a football and games),
So he must have called in all right,
He ate up the cake and the lollies I left
He must have been there Christmas night.

But this year I was bigger and brighter,
I was ready to see Santa call,
I pretended to sleep when Mummy looked in
And waited for darkness to fall.

Next thing I heard the door creaking,
And in the half light I could see,
I opened my eyes a tiny wee bit
It must have been Santa by gee!

From:
Grahame
'Skew Wiff' Watt,
Kyabram,
Victoria

But he wasn't in a red suit, no big white beard,
No reindeer and no jingle bell,
Santa was dressed in singlet and shorts
And his face needed shaving as well.

He didn't look 'jolly' like you see on the cards,
No shiny black boots like they say,
He wore a big frown and thongs on his feet
And he staggered a bit on his way.

Then Santa said 'words' that I've never heard,
Such words I've never heard said,
He swore and he called out terrible names
When he stubbed his toe on my bed.

I shut my eyes tight, I tried not to hear,
As Santa blessed everyone's soul,
His language must be the way that they talk
When he's home at the frozen North Pole.

Then he tipped out a boxful of presents,
Filled up my sock and all,
Stumbled around in the darkness
Trying so hard not to fall.

Oh! Then Santa moved up to my bedside,
I stopped breathing—my heart gave a 'miss',
He said, 'Merry Christmas young feller!'
And he leant down and gave me a kiss.

I must have been dreaming I reckon,
For Santa's not really that bad,
He reminded me 'sort-of' like someone
In the morning I must tell Dad.

◎

◎ Bonnie from Halls Creek in Western Australia phoned us. ◎
As she signed off she said,
'Walilu', an Aboriginal farewell, and a fitting way to end this book.